5 KINDS OF SELF-CARE

USING YOUR COMMON SENSES BOOK 1

CW DURAND

1
INTRODUCTIONS, PLEASE...

I moved 23 times in my first 22 years. Much of my childhood was spent in the back of a station wagon that carried six kids, our parents, a German grandmother and a carsick dog.

It was never boring.

Being a military kid taught me that people were pretty much the same wherever we went. Everyone got up and went to bed about the same time. Everyone needed to brush their teeth and wash their hands. Every neighbor had funny stories about dogs and family. We always had something in common with our new neighbors.

I really liked moving around as a kid. It was a new adventure every time we set off for a brand new place to explore. We were always excited and curious about new things awaiting us on the way to our new home.

Six kids, three grown-ups and our dog in the station wagon for eight hours at a time was more fun than it sounds. After running out of car games or conversation, the car would be quiet as we watched the country roll by the big back windows.

The houses, gardens, toys, and backyards changed as the kinds of trees did. I watched culture and nature change from region to region...until we arrived at the nightly campsite.

An ongoing conversation during quiet times in the car, and around the campfire every night, was much fun it would be to camp all year round. How much food would you need? What kind of food would you grow? What kind of shelter would be cool in the summer and warm in the winter?

Just when I was certain that I had an answer for almost everything, Dad would stump me with one question. What if you get sick? That conversation-stopping point stayed in the back of my mind for the rest of my life...this book is my answer to that question.

Every place we moved into was unique in its own way. Their jokes were new. Our jokes were new to them. Their games were a little different than we were used to. New foods were *usually* fun to try.

The most important thing to about a new place was how the locals dealt with the weather. I learned pretty early that everyone alive needs to adapt their food, clothes, games and schedules to the weather. Nature bats first, and last.

Since we usually arrived just before school started, we always asked the neighborhood how long Summer lasted here...and when Spring typically arrived. Once we knew that, we knew what clothes we would need and what kind of food Mom would be learning how to cook this year.

In places that were hot most of the year, people were really good at cooling off. They drank mint tea (a natural refrigerant), iced coffee, they automatically put ice into cold soda and water. They ate cold or spicy hot meals in the heat more often.

Southerners used spicy hot food more in the summer to make them sweat. Perspiration makes even a little breeze feel cooler. Northerners used spicy hot food more in the winter to increase their body heat.

We learned to play in the shade or have water balloon battles, and wear hats in the hot sun. We wore loose, light clothes, and either moved very slowly or didn't go out at all on the hottest of summer days. We ate whatever the neighborhood kids ate to stay cooled off.

Southerners had kitchen gardens designed for more day-to-day eating than northerners. They only needed a pantry cupboard to last a couple of months before they could replant.

The entire day was about staying out of the heat, and keeping the house cool enough for sleeping at night. It's what they were used to. We learned how to do it from our neighbors.

People that lived with heat most of the year had a hard time staying warm in the bitter cold than we did. Both of my parents were from New England. We ate, and dressed, like northerners during the cold. We showed our neighbors ways of staying warm.

In a places that are cold most of the year, people are very good at staying warm. They wear layers of insulating clothing, move very quickly or don't go out at all on the coldest of days.

The kitchen gardens of the north are designed for filling a winter pantry. They have to. It will be six months before replanting, eight before you harvest anything fresh. There is a lot less space in the garden for using in day-to-day meals. Filling the pantry is the priority, not dinner that night.

Northern people use more warming foods like dairy, bread, hot coffee, hot cocoa, warmed milk, and eat more hot meals all year round. Pantries are filled with ingredients for winter food to keep you warm. It's what they eat most of the year.

Winter food is designed to keep you warm, not really helpful in the heat. Heat waves melt people of colder weather...they don't cool down enough to enjoy the warmest seasons because they simply don't know how easy it can be.

Moving around as a kid taught me how to adapt to the heat, or the cold. Just a couple of lifestyle tweaks is all it takes to be comfortable in any weather extreme.

When I moved into my own home an adult, we ate like Northerners in the winter and Southerners in the summer. My pantry garden included herbs and foods that kept us healthy and well fed in any weather. I knew how to keep us cool in the summer and warm in the winter without difficulty.

Blending my childhood experiences made sense, and it worked.

We were almost never sick. When we were, I could use over the counter medicines and a doctor just as my parents had.

All was well, until my father's question of "what to do if you get sick," changed my life.

Our son was ten, it had been a fun, but busy snow day home from school. Sledding and snow fort building in the front yard with hot chocolate and cookies afterward.

After dinner, it began to snow again. This sudden squall hadn't been called for in the forecast that morning and it was getting heavier. It became a whiteout blizzard. Couldn't see enough to drive, or even walk on familiar paths. It wasn't letting up. Uh oh.

The TV broadcast a winter warning just before cable went out, it was going to last all night. We started getting ready with extra wood and got candles out. This was not unusual for Vermont.

Then the power and phone went out at the same time. The snow must have weighed down the lines somewhere. Maybe an accident had taken down a pole.

Being snowed in with no power was okay because we heated with wood, I had water set aside in the pantry, and dinner was finished. So we lit the candles and started playing some games. No choice but to pass the time until the storm stopped.

While playing cards in the dark, I noticed my sons eyes were shinier than usual. He had a fever. I went to the medicine cabinet and remembered why I was supposed to go to the drug store today on the way to sledding. I was out of fever medicine.

No safe access to the road, the swirling heavy snow was too dangerous and town too far away. No power. No phone. This was a time before cell phones. We were cut off.

Danny quickly developed a high fever. I was out of medicine. Helpless. My father was being proven right. People did this all the time in the olden days. My mother, and grandmother, would have known what to do. But, how?

I racked my brain for what they had done when we were kids. I used cooling towels, soothing words, and kept him hydrated...but that was all I knew to do.

His fever broke before dawn. Power and phone were restored. We were plowed out by ten. I was in the library when it opened at eleven. I was determined to never feel that helpless again.

I checked out every herbalism and self-care book available in our library. As soon as the snow melted, I dug my first medicinal herb bed.

Every herb I learned to grow, store, and use, felt like one more illness that I wasn't helpless about. Each remedy I learned was empowering. I didn't need doctors as often as I had been taught. You could prevent, or heal, a lot of symptoms by yourself...people used to do it all the time.

The longest night of my life began a life long passion.

I traveled from Maine to Mongolia looking for answers to my father's question, "what if you get sick?" I had four years worth of asking, and hearing answers for that question.

Many, many, many teachers told me exactly what to do if you get sick. I learned answers from Indian Ayurveda, Traditional Chinese Medicine (TCM) and Traditional Tibetan–Mongolian Medicine (TTMM).

The enormous amount of information was challenging to understand at first. Each of the traditions used their own resources and descriptions of illnesses in their native tongue. Like many, I speak no Sanskrit, Chinese, Tibetan, or Mongolian.

Instead of trying to memorize and describe the simply unpronounceable for me, I started listening beneath their words as I had as a child.

I went to 13 schools before graduating from high school. Many times school was a building full of a heavy accent that I had to decipher as quickly as possible. It took at least a week to completely understand what the teacher was saying.

My father taught me to listen beneath the words for meanings. Hear something that sounded like a familiar pattern, then ask a question. I decided to do the same thing with the Asian Medicine language barrier. I started listening to what sounded familiar, and asked questions.

I saw more and more of a pattern form with each question. This book is an explanation of what I learned, without the language/resource barrier.

These three traditional Asian medicines used very different techniques for diagnosing an illness, but treatment for the symptoms were very similar. The reasons why someone got sick were very similar.

They all agreed there are five kinds of illnesses, five kinds of reasons why people get sick, five kinds of remedies, five kinds of ways to stay healthy. Most importantly, there are five kinds of people.

There were only five categories of information to learn.

Once I understood these five categories, the intricate information and techniques were much easier to learn. There was a distinct pattern to what was agreed to be part of each category. I learned them all at the same time. I blended the traditions and their techniques in my practice for fifteen years.

I used what they had in common in my practice. The five categories were enhanced with techniques or resources from any or all of the three traditions.

Instead of choosing which one of the traditional medicines I wanted to use for a particular client, I normally used all three. People got well faster. A lot faster.

Experience showed me that each of the three ancient medicines has a specialty.

Classical Indian Ayurveda is an excellent source for using foods and spices as remedies. Their diet/resources are more similar to ours than farther eastern Asia. Their use of the chakra system empowers the mind and spirit for assisting with self-healing.

Traditional Chinese Medicine is extraordinary for pinpointing a culprit symptom in body, mind, or spirit. Their use of the meridian system is precise and can give astonishingly fast results for physical symptoms when used wisely.

Traditional Tibetan–Mongolian Medicine is the most effective of the three for using your lifestyle as a remedy an illness…and for figuring out why someone is sick. Knowing the reason for an illness can eliminate the illness. Very effective for self-care homework. Changing your lifestyle and/or perspective, even a little bit, greatly improves your health.

After many years of study, I finally knew the answer to my father's question. I knew what to do if I got sick. I'm also humbly aware of when to call someone with a symptom beyond my abilities.

Western medicine is necessary, when traditional methods can't completely heal an illness, or if it gets worse. Western medicine is absolutely the best for emergency care and lab tests for diagnosing serious illness.

Asian medicines stress the importance of making wise lifestyle choices to be healthy. Lifestyle choices include everything you eat, drink, wear, listen to, and what you do for fun.

There are five kinds of people. Each with a dominant amount of traits in one of the five categories. You're born that way. Your lifestyle needs to **BE** the self-care needed for the body you were born with.

What does lifestyle have to do with self-care?

Imagine being on a hot beach. You instinctively choose to eat and drink anything that cools you off, and wear loose, cooling clothing. Those are lifestyle choices. Self–care is the art of making wise lifestyle choices. Every day.

Everyone that came into my practice began their treatment with learning what kind of body they had and self–care needed for maintaining it.

Clients were responsible for their own self–care between visits. After a week of mandatory "lifestyle homework," they either got completely better, or the real problem began revealing itself.

It was easy to explain the five categories to the CEOs, psychologists, psychiatrists, farmers, teachers, students, artists, dancers, grandmothers, mechanics, nurses, doctors, children, hair dressers, truck drivers, bus drivers and snow plow drivers that came to my practice.

I taught people how to take care of themselves a little better and their symptoms went away. When they stopped using this kind of self–care, symptoms came back. Every time.

No surprise.

If you don't take care of your car in certain ways, the same mechanical symptoms come back...every time. The same is true of your body. Maintenance counts.

Recuperation time was reduced, and prescription needs were decreased by their doctors as they became healthier. They got better and knew how to keep it that way.

Clients, and their doctors, asked me to write my methods down when I retired. So, I did.

Five Kinds of People

From one side of Asia to the other, traditional medicines describe five kinds of people. Their descriptions of the five categories of people are practically the same.

Everybody has some of each of the five categories. Each of the categories is responsible for 20% of your bodily functions, mental activities, and sense of self.

If you have a majority of personality traits from a category, you are vulnerable to the symptoms found there. If you only have a symptom from that category, you are vulnerable to all other symptoms in that category.

There are five kinds of self-care, one for each category. If you have a majority of traits, or just a symptom, from a category...you need to use the self-care from that category to feel well.

When the symptom is gone, return to the self-care your kind of body usually needs. It usually only takes very minor tweaks here and there to get back on track. Self-care choices are as easy as choosing to walk instead of run...or playing more. No kidding.

What kind of body do you have?

Think of the five kinds of people as five different kinds of vehicles. Vehicles all have their strengths, weaknesses, and unique flair that makes them a little different than other models. Each kind requires slightly different maintenance. Just like people.

When you rent a car you have to choose a vehicle based on what kind of trip you are taking. There are usually five kinds of vehicle choices. You can choose a little race car, a sporty sedan, an SUV, a truck, or a van.

Your choice depends on what your trip is going to be like. Once you have the vehicle, you have to take care of it for the length of your trip.

Your body is like that rental...but you're born with it, you can't get another one if this one breaks. It's your job to take care of it. Knowing what you can or can't do improves your trip.

1. Some like to go fast…

A little race car likes to go fast all the time. It needs high performance fuel, and needs to be fueled often. A sports car is streamlined and focused on getting to a destination as fast as possible. Straight roads are better for fast speeds. A to B as fast as you can. Anything in their way is a challenging obstacle to be overcome.

The fastest moving people are called Type A in this country. They are focused, often athletically built, competitive even with themselves, adrenaline junkies, they can be the tireless life of the party when they want to be, they get things done...and don't like to waste time.

This first category of people have an **Active Body**.

Ayurveda calls this dosha Pitta. It's the element of Fire in China. Mongolians call this nyepa Blood/Circulation.

I call it your **Common Sense of TOUCH**. The most motivating of senses. This kind of person reminds me of people that lived in the really hot places of my childhood. To stay healthy, they need to get good at cooling off.

2. Some like to have fun with their car...

A sporty sedan can go really fast if it wants to...but prefers to play with a winding road at a slightly slower, more playful speed. Having fun with every swooping corner or hill to climb. It burns through high performance fuel quickly and efficiently. It deals with sudden surprises in the road as a pleasure, not obstacles.

People with a majority of traits in the second category are curious, playful, flirtatious, intelligent, inventive, and team players that like to volunteer in their spare time. They are never bored. They look at multi-tasking as puzzles to be solved simultaneously and have fun while doing it.

This is the part of you responsible for enjoying life with all of your physical senses. Not being able to enjoy yourself is a symptom.

This second category of people have an **Active Body & Flexible Mind = Active Mind**

Ayurveda calls this dosha Pitta–Vata. It's the Element of Wood in China. Mongolians call this nyepa Bile.

I call this your **Common Sense of SIGHT.** The most enthusiastic of your senses. This is the category where enjoying your physical senses takes place. This is the part of you that creates happy hormones, your natural painkillers and stress busters. This category is responsible for turning your food into fuel to burn.

This kind of person needs a clear mind to focus, and maintain their sense of humor about life. Both of those things are easily done with the right food and enough play.

3. Some need their car many different tasks...

An SUV isn't as fast as the first two categories. Changing direction and making a lot of stops requires a slower speed. These drivers need self-care to complete a constantly changing, complicated travel plan. They usually need to use their brakes more.

This third kind of people are compassionate, resilient, talkative, nurturing, adaptable and extremely creative. They can talk to anyone.

They can change their minds, emotions or schedules quickly and easily. Multi-tasking is a way of life for them.

This third category of people have a **Flexible Mind**.

Ayurveda calls this dosha Vata. It's the Element of Earth in China. Mongolians call this nyepa Wind.

I call this your **Common Sense of TASTE**. This category is about being able to change. This is the most emotional, creative, nurturing and adaptable of your senses. Seamlessly adapting from one busy part of their day to the next. Adapting their communications skills to whoever they are talking to is a skill they were born with.

Adapting too much becomes too distracting. People like this need to finish what they start, a common symptom in this category. Staying focused becomes difficult when tired.

Finishing one thing before starting another is necessary whenever possible. Their nurturing trait makes them vulnerable to losing track of their own needs. They usually need to practice saying no as a part of self-care.

4. Some have a specific purpose in mind…

A truck is not going to win a road race. Seating is only adjustable with effort. Trucks are not as flexible as an SUV, some roads are too narrow or fast for their comfort zone. Their strength is in reliability, strength, and safety.

It will get you from A to B the same way as the other cars, but needs more time to change direction. It doesn't like surprises in either the road or the agenda.

People with a majority of traits in the fourth category are methodical, quiet, and loyal. Love of nature is in this category. They don't like change or surprises. Structured timetables, touring quiet seasonal beauty, and known culture comfort them. They prefer small groups to crowds.

The rhythm of your day, week, or year, matters to your health. Its your lifestyle pattern. This category is where pattern recognition and rhythms of your life are formed. Changing a pattern/rhythm, and letting go of old habits or ideas can be difficult for them.

This fourth category of people have a blend of an **Structured Mind** and **Calming Spirit = Structured Spirit**.

Ayurveda calls this dosha Vata–Kapha. It's the Element of Metal in China. Mongolians call this nyepa Phlegm.

I call this your **Common Sense of SMELL.** It is your most watchful category. It makes you alert, and wary, of any changes in the air.

Traditions are respected, and nature revered in this part of you. Rhythms, routines and loyalty are found here. People in this category need to remember to let go of old rhythms and beliefs when necessary.

5. Some prefer a slower, inspired route…

A van goes very slowly in comparison to all the other categories of vehicles. It holds the most cargo as it goes quietly about its day. Full of things that are needed, but only the driver decides where the things will be delivered.

It requires a steady, predictable, quiet ride so the driver won't be distracted from delivering his much needed cargo.

The fifth category of people is the calmest. This is the part of you that needs quiet to hear yourself think. Your innermost thoughts and dreams begin here and grow into ideas.

The cargo in the delivery van are all of your dreams, inspirations and new ways of looking at things. Your spirit, inner voice, is the driver. Spirit delivers inspiration cargo to your mind…your mind decides what to do with the idea.

This is where your inner voice, physical structure and stamina all come from.

This fifth category of people have a **Calming Spirit**.

Ayurveda calls this dosha Kapha. It's the Element of Water in China. Mongolians call it Lymph (Yellow Water).

I call it your **Common Sense of HEARING.** The most calming of your senses. People with a majority of traits in this category remind me of people that lived in the really cold places of my childhood.

To stay healthy, they need to get good at staying warm...from the inside out. Laugh. Dance. Learn new things with friends. Keep moving in body, mind, and spirit.

EACH OF THESE categories require eating well, playing well and getting enough sleep...just like we did as children. Be your own parent and give yourself plenty of good food, fun, and sleep. Honestly, would you treat a child the way you treat your own body? Why not?

All five Common Senses have a physical, mental and spiritual purpose. Everyone has at least a bit of all five. Consider them as five essential tools in a tool box.

If you have a symptom, it means that at least one of your Common Senses needs either increasing or decreasing, your natural balance is off.

You can increase or decrease the influence of your Common Senses on your life with simple choices. Foods, activities, aromas, music, or any other lifestyle choices you make in your day will change your chemistry. This book is about how to make those choices...wisely.

Timing is everything.

> *A string too tight breaks, and the music dies.*
> *A string to slack has no sound, and the music dies.*
> *There is a middle way.*
> *– Buddha*

2

FOUR STEPS OF HEALTHCARE

I have worked with healthcare professionals from all over the world. They all use some form of these FOUR logical steps. You can use these same steps for healing yourself.

1. **Determine what is normal for you**...and what's really a symptom.

2. **Determine what kind of symptom you have.** A symptom happens when your body, mind and/or spirit have become either too stimulated, or too calmed.

3. **Clean up your act with self care** (water, sleep, good food, and play) before using a more invasive remedy. If your body, mind and/or spirit are too stimulated, use self-care choices to calm down. If your body, mind and/or spirit are too calmed, use self-care choices to warm up.

4. **Choose a way to bring you back to normal.** After general self-care has eliminated minor symptoms, whatever discomforts that remain are the ones that need special attention.

Then do it.

All your body usually needs to heal itself are the simple necessities of life: enough water, good food, lots of rest, and some playtime. Making sure you have these every day is self-care.

If you begin to feel a symptom is beyond basic self-care balancing, trust your intuition.

When you need a professional, tell them exactly what life is like when you're well. Tell him or her what your life was like just before you got sick. List everything you've tried so far and what the outcomes were. Even herbal teas and supplements you've been trying count. Being more irritable, restless, or withdrawn than normal are also symptoms. Each detail is a clue. Think of it as explaining car trouble to your mechanic.

Symptoms are like jigsaw puzzle pieces. The more pieces you identify, the easier it is to solve the puzzle. Each health care provider will solve the puzzle differently, just like the different styles people have for solving jigsaw puzzles.

Some sort all of the colors into piles. Some only sort for certain shapes. Some put the puzzle together in order...across the top and then down. None are right or wrong, just different techniques. It's the same with different kinds of medicine. Professionals may have different ways of solving the puzzle of your wellness, but they all need as many pieces as possible.

Whether it is you doing the solving, or a pro, the steps towards wellness are the same in any form of self-care or medicine.

No kidding.

Step 1: What is normal for you?

Identifying a symptom in your body is easy, but not all symptoms are physical. Symptoms are more than a problem your body is having. Your mind and spirit also develop symptoms.

Some of your personality/emotional traits are just you being you, some aren't. You know when you feel angrier than usual, or quieter. Even if nobody else has noticed. If it's unusual for you, it's a symptom.

Normal for you is when you are in your comfort zone. All is right with your world and everyone in it. Being happy and full of energy are signs that your body, mind, and spirit are all in their comfort zones. Life is good.

Stress based symptoms happen whenever your life has drifted out of your comfort zone in some way. Symptoms are warning flags that something in life is causing a problem. Every symptom can help pinpoint the origin of a problem.

Symptoms goes away when your comfort zone is restored.

How hot do you like your bathwater or shower? Do you prefer swimming in cold river water or a heated pool? It isn't learned. Babies know what is too hot or too cold for them, it's **normal** for them. It's their comfort zone.

Stimulating traits and situations are like the hot water in a bath. Some thrive in fast-paced, multi-tasking, emergency situations. Sailing through challenging situations like a game to be enjoyed and won. Some like it hot.

Comforting, calming traits and situations are like the cold water in a bath. Some people enjoy life at a low and slow pace. They thrive in a steadily paced, quiet life with as much serenity and simple fun as possible. They enjoy knowing that their lives are in order and will be tomorrow. They are cool.

Everyone is a mix of the two. Nobody takes a pure hot shower without being burned. Nobody takes a pure cold shower without being chilled. Your life needs to be a blend of excitement and calm. You need a bit of both to be healthy. You are born with a lifestyle/pace comfort zone. If you go beyond your comfort zone for too long... symptoms begin.

Your comfort zone is the blend of excitement and calm that your body, mind, and spirit were born to thrive in.

The five comfort zones are Hot, Warm, Neutral, Cool, and Cold. Your immune system, metabolism, and lymph system are built to handle a certain amount of excitement/calm in your life. Your life-long comfort zone is your normal, not your recent history of symptoms or lifestyle choices.

Step 2: What kind of symptom do you have?

Asian medicine categorizes all illness into either hot disease (too stimulated) or cold (too calm) disease.

Excitement creates adrenaline. It stimulates your body, mind, and spirit into action. Everything moves a little faster. If your body, mind, or spirit get too much excitement/stimulation, symptoms happen.

Hot diseases happen when you are working your body, mind and/or spirit too hard. Everyone has a limit. Someone that dances on the edge of stress all the time will develop many of the same symptoms as someone undergoing chemotherapy and radiation.

Stress really does kill. Symptoms of hot disease are heart issues of any kind, migraines, rash, fever, burning eyes, and insomnia. Hot disease needs to be calmed.

Self-care choices would be to make sure you rest and play every day. Slow yourself down whenever possible. *Walk* to the same place every day, outdoors, for at least fifteen minutes.

Calmness quiets your body, mind, and spirit. If your body, mind, or spirit get too quiet...symptoms happen. Asian medicine puts this kind of symptom into the cold disease category.

Cold diseases happen when you aren't working your body, mind, and/or spirit enough. When your life feels like it's in a rut or you are sad...your body, mind, and spirit all feel cold. You have the blues. Your whole self begins slowing down.

No momentum in your body, mind, or spirit to go any farther than you have to. No enthusiasm or desire for anything new in your life are symptoms of cold disease of your mind. Your spirit exhibits cold disease by not wanting to be around anyone, ever.

The physical symptoms of cold disease are feeling world weary, chronic fatigue, sighing, depression, wanting to sleep more than normal, frequent colds and flu, bronchitis, pneumonia, diabetes, chronic illness and fungal infections.

Cold diseases slow you down gradually. You slow until you are sleepy all the time. Just like being out in a blizzard. You go slower and slower until you just want to curl up in that snowbank and go to sleep, and happily freeze to death.

All cold disease needs to be slowly motivated back into normal movement of your body, mind and/or spirit. Self-care choices would be keeping yourself motivated and moving a bit more every day. Add new things slowly. Feeling easily overwhelmed is a common part of cold disease. Start slowly and keep the momentum going until you can dance again.

Step 3: Clean up your act (water, sleep, good food, and play)

Imagine being on the beach in the summer. Hot, really hot! You sweat, your mouth gets dry, your heart beats faster and you get a headache. Hot disease symptoms.

Instinct makes you change into lighter clothing, choose cold drinks and food when it's hot because you don't want to overheat/stress your body. Don't make a symptom worse if you don't have to.

If you add a hot day and a stress together you are adding more heat to hot disease. Self-care needs to be extra cooling and calming during the summer and/or very busy days.

Calm your body, mind, and spirit with lots of water, a fistful of nuts, juicy fruits and veggies that will fuel your busy day every few hours. Water first. Don't forget quiet play. Walk, don't run.

If you are in the cold too long, your nose gets clogged, you slow down until you have no motivation to move, your circulation slows down, and you start feeling a little more introspective and emotionally quieter than normal.

The same cold disease symptoms happen to your body, mind and/or spirit during a day that is too cold, boring, isolated , or too emotional. If you add a cold day and the blues together you are adding coolness to cold disease.

You instinctively grab a sweater and a hot beverage when you know its going to be really cold outside to keep your body warm.

Self-care for your mind and spirit on cold days needs to be warming, too.

Surround yourself with warm colors, cheerful company, and laughter. No sad lyrics in the music you listen to. No news if you can help it. Dance if possible.

A happy child has an adult around to make sure they drink enough water, eat well, play a little every day, and get plenty of sleep every night. This is how children feel nurtured, safe, and well cared for.

As adults, shouldn't we feel that way, too?

We hear a lot about our inner child needing to play. What about feeding that inner child well and making sure that inner child gets enough sleep?

If you aren't feeling well, be your own parent for a week or so. Then treat yourself to something special when you are feeling better.

Step 4: Bringing you back to normal...fixing what ails you

Your immune system will feel better after cleaning up your act for a week. The symptoms you still have are the ones that you need help with from any kind of practitioner...or a more focused effort by yourself.

If you have been trying to remedy your symptoms with self-care, but your intuition says the remaining symptoms are beyond your scope, get some help.

Eastern or Western, practitioners will use their skills, techniques, and training to cool off a hot disease symptom...or warm up a cold disease symptom. Choose a practitioner that you feel comfortable talking to.

Writing down all of your symptoms is important whether you are hiring someone or trying to do it yourself. Everything that isn't normal for you should be on that list, including personality changes like being angrier, more restless, or quieter than normal.

What is your life like when you're happy and full of energy?

Feeling that way again is the goal. Imagining every detail is the first step to getting back into your comfort zone.

Tell a practitioner about your self-care routine in as much detail as you can. Don't worry if it seems to silly to mention. Better to give too much information than too little. All of these minute details are clues that help to either warm you up or cool you off.

Continue taking care of yourself through the treatment with enough food, water, sleep and play. You are not just part of your healthcare team, you are in charge of the maintenance committee.

If a lingering symptom (or side-effect) is bothering your body, mind or spirit with being too hot...continue cooling off until it is gone. This usually takes about a week after your prescriptions are done.

Cool your body with calming foods and lots of water. Flush the residual chemicals from your lymph system with at least two *extra* glasses of water a day. Cool your mind with less news, more comedies, and reading or doing crafts instead of TV before bed. Cool your spirit by spending time in nature, community volunteering, and making time to play with friends and family.

If the symptom (or side effect) is from a cold disease symptom... warm yourself up. Drink the same amount of water to flush out the chemicals from your lymphs, but use warming decaffeinated tea instead of glasses of water.

Warm your body with stimulating, flavorful foods that are colorful to look at. Go for a walk every day for a week, then make it a little longer for the next week. Warm your mind with learning something new or brushing up on an old passion. Warm your spirit by celebrating an occasion with friends. Make one up if you have to.

Laugh, play, dance.

3

WHAT KIND OF BODY DO YOU HAVE?

There are five kinds of bodies. All of us are born with five Common Senses: Touch, Sight, Taste, Smell, and Hearing… but not with the same amounts of each.

Some have a keener sense of touch, some can hear better than others. Like your eye color or being left-handed, you are born with it. It's just who you are.

Everyone is dominant in one of the five physical senses. Just having good eyesight doesn't make Sight your dominant sense.

There are hundreds of traits and symptoms found in each category. Personality traits count. Preferences for different kinds of hobbies count. What you are passionate about counts. What makes you sad or angry counts. Frequent or life-long vulnerability to certain symptoms count. So do all your lifestyle choices. Everything counts.

So how do you determine what kind of body you have? Answering lots questions about yourself. Questionnaires in the traditional side of the hospital in Ulan Bator, Mongolia were ten pages long. The more information, the better. A pattern begins to emerge about half way through.

The questions I am asking of you are the same that I would ask in my practice. Not nearly as detailed in physical traits as it would be in

Asia, but this is enough to determine what kind of basic self-care someone needs.

Read the following descriptions and see which one is most like you. Check off all familiar traits, symptoms, and things you like to do, as you go. Duplicates count.

1. **Your Common Sense of TOUCH:**

Personality traits: Passionate, communicative, charismatic, natural leadership, not a follower, athletic, competitive in all things... even with themselves for being faster than last time they did something, physically active, goal-oriented, mind always working, strong digestion, fast metabolism

Symptoms: Heart disease, irregular heartbeat, migraine, rash, fever, burning eyes, insomnia, controlling others, anger, nosebleeds, infections

Hot action Activities: Running sprints, downhill skiing, racing of any kind, all competitive sport, carpentry, playing cards for money, dance

_____ **Total** of traits, symptoms and activities found in your common sense of **Touch.**

2. **Your Common Sense of SIGHT:**

Personality Traits: Creative, can talk to anyone...of any age, physically active...but not aggressively, team player, flirtatious, sensual, enjoys life, inventive, impulsive, community involvement likely, multi-tasking, athletic...but not competitive, loves puzzles and playing most games

Symptoms: Jaundice, hot flashes, distractible, obsessiveness, substance abuse, migraine, infrequent rashes, fever, burning eyes, insomnia, controlling

Warm action Activities: Running X country, skiing slaloms, obstacle courses, dancing, swimming laps, emergency services like first response or firefighting, crafts, birdwatching, playing cards in a group, photography, puzzles,

_____ Total of traits, symptoms and activities found in your common sense of **Sight**.

3. **Your Common Sense of TASTE:**
   Personality Traits: Energetic, intuitive, talkative, team player, compassionate, creative, enjoy helping others, nurturing, adaptable, enchanted by music and/or dance
   Symptoms: Digestion problems, Sleep problems, Unhappy...but not depressed, Sudden fatigue, Cravings, Twitching, Joint pain, Weight management, Anxiety, Unable to finish anything
   Neutral/Nourishing action Activities: Running distance, Skiing, downhill, Swimming for fun, Teaching, Artwork, Cooking, Creating new games using cards, Playing a musical instrument
   _____ Total of traits, symptoms and activities found in your common sense of **Taste**.

4. **Your Common Sense of SMELL:**
   Personality Traits: Methodical, disciplined, gentle, reserved, wry sense of humor, logical to a fault, self-controlled, deep love of nature, appreciates routines, strong
   Symptoms: Spacey, sighing, judgmental, compulsive, respiratory illness, coughs, dehydration, skin problems but not a rash, pins & needles feeling, constipation, general unhappiness...but not depressed
   Cool action Activities: Hiking, skiing, slow cross country, playing in water, doing puzzles, flower arranging, playing a card game built for two, writing
   _____ Total of traits, symptoms and activities found in your common sense of **Smell**.

5. **Your Common Sense of HEARING:**
   Personality Traits: Peaceful, tolerant, traditional, introspective,

research, watchful, thrifty, philosophical, curious, long memories, slow metabolism

Symptoms: Depression, sluggishness, lots of colds /flu, sinus congestion, bronchitis/pneumonia, water retention, eye problems, eating disorders, skin outbreaks, isolationism, judgmental

Cold action Activities: Walking, snow shoeing, wading in shallow water, reading, listening to music, playing solitaire, surfing the web

_____ **Total** of traits, symptoms and activities found in your common sense of **Hearing** that are currently part of your life.

TOTALS:
    1._____
    2._____
    3._____
    4._____
    5._____

1. Touch — Active Body
    aka Pitta in Ayurveda
    aka Circulation/Blood in Traditional Tibetan-Mongolian Medicine
    aka Element of Fire in Traditional Chinese Medicine

2. Sight — Active Mind
    aka Pitta-Vata in Ayurveda
    aka Bile in Traditional Tibetan-Mongolian Medicine
    aka Element of Wood in Traditional Chinese Medicine

3. Taste — Flexible Mind
    aka Vata in Ayurveda

aka Wind in Traditional Tibetan-Mongolian Medicine
aka Element of Earth in Traditional Chinese Medicine

4. Smell — Structured Spirit
aka Vata-Kapha in Ayurveda
aka Phlegm in Traditional Tibetan-Mongolian Medicine
aka Element of Metal in Traditional Chinese Medicine

5. Hearing — Calm Spirit
aka Kapha in Ayurveda
aka Lymph (Yellow Water) in Traditional Tibetan-Mongolian Medicine
aka Element of Water in Traditional Chinese Medicine

THE BIGGEST TOTAL determines your dominant Common Sense. If your numbers are even across the board, your dominant Common Sense is Taste. If it's a tie between two, use your instinct to tell you which one is more correct.

There are five kinds of people, each with different self-care requirements to be happy in body, mind, and spirit. You are a bit of all five categories. Chances are pretty good you have had symptoms from each of the categories.

Read about all five of the senses, not just your dominant one. Everyone needs all five to stay healthy. All five play a part in your immune system and peace of mind.

4

FIVE KINDS OF PEOPLE

Every new car comes with an Owners Manual. It gives you a general idea of how the car works. A necessary, and very handy, little book full of answers about how to take care of your new car. If something goes wrong...there's always a troubleshooting guide for fixing minor issues.

A car owner's manual tells you what kind of fuel and oil your engine needs to stay running smoothly. It tells you how fast this kind of car should go. If you follow the manuals advice, your car will last longer than a poorly maintained car like yours.

If your car is making a funny noise, you fix it as soon as possible because you know it could get worse if ignored. You need your car. You make the time because you have to.

If your mechanic says your car would run smoothly again if you used a different fuel or oil, you would do it. Immediately.

Most people take better care of their car than they do their bodies. If you choose to neglect your car, you can get another one. You cannot get another body. It's illogical to treat your car better than you treat your body.

There are many kinds of cars. Each car model has its own style and flair. Each comes with a different Owner's Manual.

People come in just five models. Each of the five models has a particular style and flair. This book is an owners manual for each of the five kinds of people.

The last three chapters are easy to understand descriptions of the three traditional medicines I used in my practice: Classical Ayurveda, Traditional Tibetan-Mongolian Medicine, and Traditional Chinese Medicine.

Each of these chapters includes an overview of their teaching on the five kinds of people. The Classical Ayurvedic chapter explains the aura and chakra system. The Traditional Chinese Medicine explains the meridian system. The Traditional Tibetan-Mongolian Medicine chapter includes what the root of the illness might be, and lifestyle advice to alleviate symptoms in each category.

I included them for context. Some people need more context than others. I am not an instructor of these modalities, nor do I want to be. I am merely trying to explain how I used these incredibly wise traditions in easy to understand terms.

From one side of Asia to the other, traditional medicines describe five kinds of people. Their descriptions of the five categories of people are practically the same.

The very different medicines group symptoms, diseases, remedies, activities and personality traits in the same five ways. What worked for the ancients, works for us. Our bodies haven't changed much in five thousand years. Resources have.

The five categories include personality, physical traits, symptoms and activities that have exactly the same effect on your body, mind and/or spirit. Some of the categories are stimulating, some are calming. Everything in each category either gets you moving OR calms you in the same way.

Remember the questions about you in chapter three? Which category has the highest number? You are most vulnerable to symptoms in that category. Leaving your comfort zone within a Common Sense will cause the same symptoms every time.

It's who you are, learn to be happy with yourself. Live within your preset boundaries and your life will change for the better. Doing otherwise is choosing to be ill.

Some categories are motivating. The *most* motivating traits are found in your Common Sense of **Touch**. Also motivating, but in a more creative way, are traits related to your Common Sense of **Sight**. Touch, Sight and Taste are all motivating senses.

Symptoms from these categories mean your life has become too fast or stressful. Your body, mind, and/or spirit are asking you to slow down. Like overheating the engine in your car, you need to stop and let it cool.

The third category of stimulating traits is your Common Sense of **Taste**. This category is about dealing with, or creating change on many levels. It's not too hot, it's not too cold…it's the ability to slide between the two seamlessly. Change takes effort, too much change causes hot disease.

Symptoms from this categories usually mean your life has been changing too much, or too suddenly. Your body, mind, or spirit are having a hard time keeping up. Slow down until the symptoms are gone. Say no more often.

The final two categories are calming. Your Common Senses of **Smell** and **Hearing** are about the flexibility, structure, and stability of your mind and spirit. If your mind and spirit are calm, so is your body.

Symptoms from these two categories mean your life isn't changing enough. Something has slowed your body, mind and/or spirit down too much. Why is easily discovered. These cold disease symptoms need warming remedies.

Body, mind, and spirit all have to get moving. Then moved a bit more. Stay physically warm, surround yourself with color, grow something, create something, have fun conversations with friends and family, move your body a bit more every day.

My mother had a great piece of advice when I was little. If you're feeling sorry for yourself, go help someone or make them smile. She was right.

Everybody has traits from all five categories. Each is responsible for 20% of your immune system, digestion, peace of mind, and production of happy hormones.

As tempting as it is to just read about your dominant sense, do yourself a favor and read about all five parts of yourself. Think of each category as a team member. Reading about all of them give you a better understanding of how all your parts work together as a team.

Being happy and healthy means your whole team is doing its job.

5

YOUR COMMON SENSE OF TOUCH

Your first Common Sense of Touch is your most motivating of senses. Asian Medicines call this category different names, and use different techniques to remedy symptoms found here…but the category itself is nearly identical in all three traditions. It's the source of all movement in your body, inside or out.

It rules the heart, blood circulation, physical movement and spiritual motivation.

Ayurveda: In India, this category is the hottest Dosha, called Pitta

Traditional Tibetan-Mongolian Medicine: In Mongolia, this category is called the Nyepa of Blood (Circulation)

Traditional Chinese Medicine: In China, this is The Element of Fire, always listed first.

WHAT YOUR COMMON Sense of Touch does...

- **Body:** Responsible for turning food into energy, metabolism, circulation and moving your body.
- **Mind:** Focus, motivated about achieving goals
- **Spirit:** Feeling safe, survival

Common Sense of Touch Traits: Passionate, Focused, Dedicated, Communicative, Charismatic, Natural leadership, Athletic, Competitive, Physically active, Mind always working towards a goal, Strong digestion, Fast metabolism

Symptoms of too much movement: Heart disease, Irregular heartbeat, Migraine, Panic Attacks, Rash, Fever, Burning eyes, Insomnia, Controlling others, Anger, Nosebleeds, Infections

Activities of hot action movement: Running sprints, Skiing – racing of any kind, All competitive sport, Carpentry, Landscaping, Cards for money, Dance

Meridians involved: Governing, Heart, Small Intestine, Pericardium and Triple Warmer

Season of maximum movement: Summer

Touch is the most motivating sense.

Imagine an athlete running as fast as they possibly can in an important race. Pushing their bodies hard to cross the finish line first. The motivation to win releases stress hormones to make muscles move.

Blood is pumping as quickly as it can. Their mind is focused but calm. Being calm makes it possible to use all of your lungs for extra air. Their spirit is excited about accomplishing a goal. Body, mind, and spirit working as a team towards a common goal.

After the race, athletes let their muscles calm down slowly, drink some water, then eat something light and nutritious to get ready for the next race. They know the importance of taking care of their bodies between races. Their minds remain calmly focused on what they have to do next. Their spirits are excited about doing even better next time. They call it training. I call it practical self-care.

Now imagine another kind of running. Imagine being chased. You push your body as far as you possibly can to find safety. Your body, mind, and spirit are on the same full alert for a different reason. This time it isn't motivation, it's fear. Your mind and spirit don't feel safe. Your brain responds by releasing stress hormones to make your muscles move as fast as they can.

Your body is on auto pilot when survival instincts are present. Fear makes you breathe too fast. Your body can't get enough air. Pain from your legs and lungs wants your body to slow down, but you can't. Your mind is flooded with worst-case scenarios that motivate you to keep moving through the pain. Your spirit is only focused on feeling safe.

When you are finally safe, your spirit calms but your body and mind need some time to recover. Making sense of the situation, and beginning to let go of the fear, relaxes your mind. Your mind is no longer on full alert.

That's when your body finally stops producing stress hormones and you can breathe again. Your mind begins to clear, you can think. Then your heart rate and breathing slow back to normal. Deep breath. The emergency is over.

The stress hormones involved with being chased are exactly the same ones that are on full alert during a stressful day at work, with the kids, or if you are on chemotherapy.

When you are being pushed as hard as you can be pushed...that's when symptoms from your Common Sense of Touch happen.

You should recover from those symptoms in the same way the sprinting athlete did...let your muscles calm down slowly, rest, drink some water, then eat something light and nutritious.

Emphasis on resting between stressful situations.

The Common Sense of Touch is responsible for maximum physical effort. **Motivation** to move your body, mind, and/or spirit. If that physical effort is supported by a calm mind and spirit, your body gets rid of the stress hormones quickly.

If you aren't stressed, your mind is clear. A calm, clear mind is more productive, enthusiastic, and makes fewer mistakes. All it takes is the same tiny effort as the runner made. Calm down between races.

Your body is only built to handle four emergencies a day. Its takes a long time to get all systems back on track after a full alert.

Your metabolism automatically slows during a crisis. Vitamins and minerals aren't absorbed. Food isn't digested and turned into energy until you calm down.

Calories will be stored until the emergency is over. Your immune system is also off–line while stressed. That makes you more vulnerable to colds, flu, virus and infections.

Being calm and cheerful alleviates stress...and prevents symptoms. It doesn't really matter why your body is stressed. Being calm helps. A lot. Your body won't relax until your mind does. There are a lot of ways to calm down and even become cheerful after stress.

Be more like the runner between races. Acknowledge that yes, it's been stressful. Find something good about the experience while you rest your body, calmly focus on what you have to do next, and be excited about doing even better next time.

Your sense of Touch is a tool used used for movement and motivation in your life. If you have been moving as fast as you can lately, you need to put this tool away for a while and let it cool off.

Very few tools are meant to be used all the time. Think of the competitive, highly motivated part of yourself as a tool used only when necessary. When you are finished with your task, calm down for a while. Let your body, mind, and spirit rest between stressful situations.

TRADITIONAL TIBETAN-MONGOLIAN MEDICINE *calls this category Blood (Circulation).*

They teach that the symptoms that are caused by an unhealthy amount of Aggression/competition with yourself or against others.

Definition of **Aggression,** noun

1. Hostile or violent behavior or attitudes toward another; readiness to attack or confront.

2. The action of attacking without provocation, especially in beginning a quarrel or war

3. Forceful and sometimes overly assertive pursuit of one's aims and interests

Mongolian Om

AGGRESSION CAN BE TRANSFORMED into joyous, cautious attentiveness followed by well thought-out action.

Traditional Tibetan–Mongolian Medicine calls this the Circulation/Blood nyepa. Their tradition teaches that too much aggression is the poison root of all symptoms in this category, causing too much movement for your comfort zone in body, mind, or spirit.

When used wisely being aggressive can get a project going, inspire people around you to finish the job done quickly and efficiently. When defense is necessary, the tool of aggression protects you. This is what aggression is really for. A tool to motivate yourself and others to faster physical action when necessary.

Physical action can be for competition, protecting yourself against something harmful, organizing projects, or accomplishing any goal. Every journey starts with a single step. A single step begins with an aggressive motivation to move. How much aggression you use determines whether it's being used wisely as a personal tool to reach your goals...or as a weapon to control others, for any reason.

If motivation/aggression turns into anger, you are causing harm to yourself and others. Anger is the toxic side of aggression.

Being angry at yourself for failure, frustration, is not motivation. Would you allow a boss, friend or family to push you that hard? Probably not. Why do it to yourself?

The remedy for too much aggression is compassion.

Whenever you feel yourself becoming angry or overly aggressive about getting something you want, step away and breathe. You are making a task much harder than it has to be. An angered, stressed mind makes mistakes.

Rest. Calm your mind. Have a bit of compassion for all involved, including yourself...then get back to the job at hand with a clearer head.

Aggression makes your body age faster than it should. Cortisol, a stress hormone (also called the aging hormone) is supposed to be calmed down with the release of DHEA (the youth hormone). If your cortisol levels are on all the time, your DHEA levels are off all the time. You wear your body out. Choosing to be angry is illogical.

Being relaxed increases DHEA levels. So do certain foods and activities. Your mind is clearer when you are relaxed. If you have a lot to think about, the best thing you can do is sleep, or rest, on it. Being relaxed makes your work more productive, with fewer mistakes.

You can't rest if you are feeling aggressive. Aggression and competition are just tools. The tool will still be there when you need it again.

Here are some suggestions about how to use your 5 Common Senses as a team to alleviate stress/aggression in your body, mind, and spirit. Using at least one per category increases your Motivation, without burning out...choosing wisely increases stamina, not stimulation.

Touch

- Stay dry and warm
- Eight hugs, or touches, and/or prolonged period of eye contact a day

- Walk, especially therapeutic after eating
- Physical activity of any kind, keep moving
- Sunbathe, but not to the point of sweating. Rest in sunshine.
- Clean up an area of clutter in your your mind, spirit or surroundings
- Volunteer to spend time with people less fortunate than yourself. There is always someone out there that needs your time, or motivational skills.

Sight

- Have fun with color, wisely. Cool colored clothing of greens, blues, purples, or whites help keep you calmer.
- Go to a museum or exhibit that requires you to walk slowly to examine one piece at a time.
- Don't watch TV or play video games for an hour before you go to bed, on any screen, even tiny ones. Especially tiny ones. They make your eyes work even harder. Eyes need stamina too.
- Avoid watching video with a crawl of text on the bottom of the screen in general. One thing at a time.
- Put away things around you that are red, orange or yellow (whenever possible) until your life calms down. All have a stimulating effect on your mind.
- Use cooler colored flower arrangements of greens, blues, purples, and white make a difference during the summer, whenever your life is really busy, or when you are undergoing harsh western medical treatments like chemo and/or steroids.

Taste

- The main flavor for this category is **Bitter**
- (coffee, cacao, hops, citrus peel, dark leafy greens)

- A little bitter increases circulation and helps slow an overly active digestive system
- Too much bitter impairs digestion of vitamins and minerals in your food
- To reduce the harmful effects of too much bitter, use more salty flavors like soy sauce, seaweed and salt.
- Suggested food list for this category is found at the end of this chapter.

Smell

- Aromatherapy involves everything you smell in a day. Your sense of smell automatically sends information directly to the brain. The brain automatically works on identifying what that smell is and if you have smelled it before. If the smell is something that is alarming (like smoke you can't identify), an alert response is begun. The smell of coffee does the same thing because of procedural memory. You instantly have the motivation and energy to react to an emergency. If the smell is familiar or calming, a calming response is begun. You can use this automatic brain response for self-care.
- Some smells calm you down, like floral scents and sweetness. Some stir memories that have a calming or motivating response. Aromatherapy can be done with the smell of soup simmering on the stove, freshly cut citrus, line dried laundry, the smell after a rain or snowfall, or the steam coming off of your tea.
- Tending, weeding an herb garden of any size is aromatherapy. If the herb is used for stimulating your system, weeding it will release the oils and you will be energized while you work. If the herb is used for calming your system, weeding it will release the oils and you will be calmed while you work. Choose wisely.

- Best smells for calming are sandalwood, cypress, cedar and rosewood.

Hearing

- Feel safer. Take a news break from talk radio, the TV, iPad, iPhone, newspapers, magazines and/or action movies or dramas. They are designed to keep your attention in whatever way possible. News does it with fear. Sports do it with aggressive competition. Fear and competition sells products. Advertisers know it.
- Silence is golden. How long has it been since you've sat just five minutes in complete silence? It does wonders.
- Slow your music down a few beats, acoustic if possible, for a few days.
- Choose a style of listening with few or no commercial breaks. Let your mind rest without interruption by anyone, including a DJ or commercial. Don't you have enough words in your day already?
- Make a playlist of at least ten songs that make you smile just thinking about them. Preferably from a time before your first serious relationship or when you were toe-curling happy. No one has to know what is on it. Listen to it at least once a day.
- Turn down the volume. If you are using music for helping you multi-task, keep the volume low enough to hear someone else talk to you.
- If nearby sounds are louder than people can talk, you are damaging your ears.

General food guidelines for your Common Sense of Touch...

- Eat a cooling diet...like milk, cool drinks in the heat (ice

only in the hottest part of the year), cold juicy fruit and dates.
- Dry cereal and granola bars are wiser snack choices than anything with sugar in it. Sugar makes you hotter inside and out, and makes diarrhea worse.
- Plan menus around lightly spiced, lightly oiled dishes.
- Use chopped fresh herbs and lime instead.
- No sour fruit; eat sweet, juicy fruit instead like watermelons and peaches.
- Eat sweet and bitter, cooked vegetables like peas, spinach, chard, broccoli, asparagus, green beans, and Brussels sprouts. Eat avocados, uncooked.
- Eat something every two hours, a handful of something. Don't get hungry.

During chemo treatment cycles...

- Increase your stamina in body, mind and spirit before and after treatments. Eat easily digested, cooked, nutritious foods. Be focused on small, hands-on projects that you can work on during treatments. Laugh with friends and family...all add stamina.
- During chemo or radiation, drink a lot of water, clear soups, eat easily digested well–cooked vegetables. Omega 3-6-9 make your cell structure, veins, intestinal wall, and stomach lining stronger. Chemo makes tissue fragile.
- Be gentle on your body, mind, and spirit while your body is dealing with chemotherapy. Eat as much as you can. Drink a lot of water. Talk about the upcoming project that you are working on with friends and family. Laugh often.

THE FOLLOWING FOOD guideline is for helping you to choose your fuel wisely.

The Greeks advised to eat all things in moderation. True, if you are healthy. No symptoms, no problem.

If you are experiencing any symptoms of being overwhelmed, too busy, or undergoing chemotherapy...you need to eat wisely until you are feeling more yourself.

The key is to cool your body. If you are healthy, eat cooling foods to prevent burnout. If you are on chemo or have a symptom from this category, you need to cool down to alleviate the symptoms.

The listings include the name of the food; and what it does to your body. The last entry on the line is if you should, or how often you should, eat it.

ALCOHOL (HARD OR WINE) • Warming; edibility: No
    Alcohol (beer) • Warming; edibility: Rarely
    Allspice • Warming; edibility: No
    Almonds • Warming; edibility: No
    Almonds (w/o skin) • Neutral; edibility: Yes
    Almonds (with skin) • Warming; edibility: No
    Almond milk • Neutral; edibility: Yes
    Anise • Warming; edibility: No
    Apples (sweet) • Cooling; edibility: Yes
    Apple cider • Warming; edibility: No
    Applesauce • Cooling; edibility: Yes
    Apricots (dried) • Warming; edibility: No
    Apricots (sour) • Neutral ; edibility: No
    Apricots (sweet) • Cooling; edibility: Yes
    Artichokes • Warming; edibility: Yes
    Artichokes (Sunchokes) • Cooling; edibility: Yes
    Asparagus • Cooling; edibility: Yes
    Avocados • Cooling; edibility: Yes
    Bananas • Cooling; edibility: No
    Barley • Neutral; edibility: Yes
    Barley malt • Warming; edibility: Yes

Basil (dried) • Warming; edibility: No
Basil (fresh) • Cooling; edibility: Yes
Bay leaf • Warming No
Beans (adzuki) • Cooling; edibility: Yes
Beans (black) • Cooling; edibility: Yes
Beans (garbanzo) • Cooling ; edibility: Yes
Beans, green/string • Cooling; edibility: Yes
Beans (kidney) • Cooling; edibility: Yes
Beans (lima) • Cooling; edibility: Yes
Beans (mung) • Cooling; edibility: Yes
Beans (navy) • Cooling; edibility: Yes
Beans (pinto) • Cooling; edibility: Yes
Beans (white) • Cooling; edibility: Yes
Beef • Warming; edibility: No
Beet (greens) • Cooling; edibility: Maybe
Beets (cooked) • Cooling; edibility: Yes
Berries (sour) • Warming; edibility: No
Berries (sweet) • Cooling; edibility: Yes
Black–eyed peas • Cooling; edibility: Yes
Brazil nut • Warming; edibility: No
Bread (yeasted) • Warming; edibility: No
Broccoli • Cooling; edibility: Yes
Brussels sprouts • Cooling; edibility: Yes
Buckwheat • Neutral; edibility: No
Burdock root • Warming; edibility: No
Butter • Neutral; edibility: Yes
Buttermilk • Warming; edibility: No
Cabbage (cooked) • Neutral; edibility: Yes
Cabbage (red) • Warming; edibility: Maybe
Canola (oil) • Neutral; edibility: Yes
Caffeine (any) • Warming; edibility: No
Caraway • Warming; edibility: Maybe
Carbonated bev. (any) • Warming; edibility: No
Cardamom • Warming; edibility: Maybe
Carob • Neutral; edibility: Yes

Carrots (cooked) • Cooling; edibility: Yes
Carrots (raw) • Warming; edibility: Maybe
Cashews • Cooling; edibility: Maybe
Cauliflower (cooked) • Cooling; edibility: Yes
Cayenne • Warming; edibility: No
Celery • Neutral; edibility: Yes
Cereal (dry) • Warming; edibility: Maybe
Chai (hot, spiced milk) • Warming; edibility: Maybe
Chard • Cooling; edibility: Yes
Cheese (goat) • Warming; edibility: Yes
Cheese (hard) • Warming; edibility: No
Cheese (soft, not aged) • Warming; edibility: Yes
Cherries (sour) • Warming; edibility: No
Cherries (sweet) • Neutral; edibility: Yes
Chicken (dark) • Warming; edibility: No
Chicken (white) • Warming; edibility: Yes
Chili pepper • Warming; edibility: No
Chilies (green) • Warming; edibility: No
Chocolate • Warming; edibility: No
Chutney, mango (spicy) • Warming; edibility: No
Chutney, mango • Cooling; edibility: Maybe
Cilantro • Cooling; edibility: Yes
Cinnamon • Warming; edibility: Maybe
Clams • Neutral; edibility: Maybe
Cloves • Warming; edibility: No
Coconut milk • Warming; edibility: Yes
Coconut meat • Warming; edibility: Yes
Coconut oil • Cooling Yes; edibility:
Coffee • Warming; edibility: No
Coffee substitute • Cooling; edibility: Yes
Coriander (seeds) • Warming; edibility: Yes
Corn (oil) • Warming; edibility: No
Corn (dried) • Warming; edibility: No
Corn (fresh) • Cooling; edibility: Rarely
Cottage cheese • Cooling; edibility: Yes

Couscous • Neutral; edibility: Yes
Cranberries • Warming; edibility: No
Cucumber • Cooling; edibility: Yes
Cumin • Warming; edibility: Yes
Daikon radish • Warming; edibility: No
Dandelion greens • Cooling; edibility: Yes
Dates • Neutral; edibility: Yes
Dill (leaf) • Cooling; edibility: Yes
Dulse • Cooling; edibility: Yes
Duck • Warming; edibility: No
Egg (white) • Cooling; edibility: Yes
Egg (yolk) • Neutral; edibility: Maybe
Eggplant • Neutral ; edibility: Rarely
Fennel (bulb) • Warming; edibility: Yes
Fennel (seed) • Warming; edibility: Yes
Figs • Neutral Yes; edibility:
Filberts • Warming; edibility: No
Fish (mild) • Cooling; edibility:Yes
Fish (oily) • Warming; edibility: No
Flaxseed • Cooling; edibility: Yes
Flaxseed (oil) • Cooling; edibility: Yes
Fruit juice concentrates • Cooling; edibility: Yes
Garlic • Warming; edibility: No
Ghee • Cooling; edibility: Yes
Ginger (dried) • Warming; edibility: No
Ginger (fresh) • Warming; edibility: Maybe
Granola • Warming; edibility: Yes
Grapefruit • Neutral; edibility: No
Grapes (unripe) • Warming; edibility: No
Grapes (any color) • Cooling; edibility: Yes
Grape leaf • Cooling; edibility: Yes
Greens (leafy) • Cooling; edibility: Yes
Ham • Warming; edibility: No
Hazelnut • Warming; edibility: No
Honey (raw) • Neutral; edibility: Rarely

Horseradish • Warming; edibility: No
Ice cream • Cooling; edibility: Yes
Icy cold drinks • Cooling; edibility: Maybe
Juice, aloe vera • Cooling; edibility: Yes
Juice, apple • Cooling; edibility: Yes
Juice, apricot • Cooling; edibility: Yes
Juice, berry (sour) • Warming; edibility: No
Juice, berry (sweet) • Cooling; edibility: Yes
Juice, carrot • Warming; edibility: No
Juice, cherry (sour) • Warming; edibility: No
Juice, cherry (sweet) • Warming; edibility: Yes
Juice, cranberry • Warming; edibility: No
Juice, grape • Cooling; edibility: Yes
Juice, grapefruit • Warming; edibility: No
Juice, mango • Cooling; edibility: Yes
Juice, mixed vegetable • Cooling; edibility: Yes
Juice, orange • Warming; edibility: Maybe
Juice, papaya • Neutral; edibility: No
Juice, pear • Cooling; edibility: Yes
Juice, pineapple • Warming; edibility: No
Juice, prune • Cooling; edibility: Yes
Juice, tomato • Warming; edibility: No
Juice, V–8 • Warming; edibility: No
Kale • Cooling; edibility: Yes
Ketchup • Warming; edibility: No
Kiwi • Warming; edibility: Rarely
Kohlrabi • Warming; edibility: Rarely
Lamb • Warming; edibility: No
Leeks (cooked) • Neutral; edibility: Yes
Lemon • Cooling; edibility: Yes
Lemonade • Cooling; edibility: No
Lentil (brown) • Cooling; edibility: Yes
Lentil (red) • Cooling; edibility: Yes
Lettuce • Cooling; edibility: Yes
Lime • Warming; edibility: Maybe

Macadamia nut • Warming; edibility: No
Mace • Warming; edibility: No
Mango (ripe) • Cooling; edibility: Yes
Maple syrup • Cooling; edibility: Yes
Marjoram • Warming; edibility: No
Mayonnaise • Warming; edibility: No
Melon • Cooling; edibility: Yes
Milk (almond) • Cooling; edibility: Yes
Milk (chocolate) • Warming; edibility: No
Milk (cow) • Neutral; edibility: Yes
Milk (goat) • Cooling; edibility: Yes
Milk (rice) • Cooling; edibility: Yes
Milk (soy) • Cooling; edibility: Yes
Millet • Warming; edibility: No
Miso • Warming; edibility: No
Miso broth • Warming; edibility: Maybe
Molasses • Warming; edibility: No
Mushrooms • Cooling; edibility: Yes
Mustard (condiment) • Warming; edibility: No
Mustard (greens) • Warming; edibility: No
Mustard (seeds) • Warming; edibility: No
Nutmeg • Warming; edibility: No
Oat bran • Cooling; edibility: Yes
Oats (cooked) • Cooling ; edibility:Yes
Oats (dry) • Neutral; edibility: No
Okra • Neutral ; edibility:Yes
Olive oil • Cooling; edibility: Yes
Olives (black) • Cooling; edibility: Yes
Olives (green) • Warming; edibility: No
Onions (cooked) • Cooling; edibility: Yes
Onions (raw) • Warming; edibility: No
Orange (peel) • Warming; edibility: Maybe
Orange • Warming; edibility: Maybe
Oregano • Warming; edibility: No
Papaya • Warming; edibility: Maybe

Paprika • Warming; edibility: No
Parsley (dried) • Warming; edibility: Maybe
Parsley (fresh) • Cooling; edibility: Yes
Parsnip • Cooling; edibility: Yes
Pasta (wheat) • Neutral; edibility: Yes
Peach • Warming; edibility: No
Peanuts • Warming; edibility: No
Pear • Cooling; edibility: Yes
Peas • Neutral; edibility: Yes
Peas (dried) • Warming; edibility: Maybe
Pecans • Warming; edibility: No
Pepper (black) • Warming; edibility: Maybe
Peppers (hot) • Warming; edibility: No
Peppers (sweet) • Cooling; edibility: Yes
Peppermint • Warming; edibility: Yes
Perch • Warming; edibility: Maybe
Pickles • Warming; edibility: No
Pine nuts • Warming; edibility: No
Pineapple • Warming; edibility: Maybe
Pistachios • Warming; edibility: No
Plum (sweet) • Cooling; edibility: Yes
Pomegranate • Cooling; edibility: Yes
Popcorn (plain) • Warming; edibility: Maybe
Poppy seed • Warming; edibility: No
Pork • Neutral; edibility: No
Potato (sweet) • Warming; edibility: Yes
Potato (white) • Neutral; edibility: Yes
Prunes • Neutral; edibility: Yes
Pumpkin • Neutral; edibility: Yes
Pumpkin seeds • Neutral; edibility: Maybe
Quinoa • Neutral; edibility: No
Radish • Warming; edibility: No
Raisins • Neutral; edibility: Yes
Rhubarb • Cooling; edibility: No
Rice (basmati) • Neutral; edibility: Yes

Rice (brown) • Neutral; edibility: Maybe
Rice (white) • Warming; edibility: Yes
Rice (wild) • Neutral; edibility: Yes
Rice cakes (plain) • Neutral; edibility: Yes
Rice syrup • Warming; edibility: Yes
Rosemary • Warming; edibility: No
Rye • Warming; edibility: No
Safflower Oil • Warming; edibility: No
Saffron • Cooling; edibility: Yes
Sage • Warming; edibility: No
Salmon • Neutral Maybe; edibility:
Salt (in moderation) • Cooling; edibility: No
Sardines • Neutral; edibility: Maybe
Scallions • Warming; edibility: No
Sesame oil • Warming; edibility: No
Sesame seed • Neutral; edibility: No
Shellfish • Neutral; edibility: Yes
Shrimp • Warming; edibility: Maybe
Sour cream • Warming; edibility: No
Soy oil • Cooling; edibility:Yes
Soy cheese • Cooling; edibility: Yes
Soy sauce • Warming; edibility: No
Soy sausages • Warming; edibility: No
Soybeans (edamame) • Cooling; edibility: Yes
Spearmint • Cooling; edibility: Yes
Spinach (cooked) • Neutral; edibility: Yes
Spinach (raw) • Warming; edibility: Maybe
Sprouts • Cooling; edibility: Yes
Squash (spaghetti) • Cooling; edibility: Yes
Squash (summer) • Cooling; edibility: Yes
Squash (winter) • Warming; edibility: Maybe
Star Anise • Warming; edibility: No
Strawberry • Neutral; edibility: Maybe
Sugar, white • Warming; edibility: Rarely
Sunflower (oil) • Warming; edibility: Yes

Sunflower (seed) • Warming; edibility: Yes
Tahini • Warming; edibility: No
Tamari • Warming; edibility: Maybe
Tarragon • Warming; edibility: Maybe
Tea, black or green • Cooling; edibility: Yes
Tea, iced • Cooling; edibility: Maybe
Thyme • Warming; edibility: No
Tofu • Neutral; edibility: Yes
Tomatoes (dried) • Warming; edibility: No
Tomatoes (fresh) • Cooling; edibility: Maybe
Tomatoes (sauce) • Warming; edibility: No
Tuna • Warming; edibility: No
Turkey (dark) • Warming; edibility: No
Turkey (white) • Warming; edibility: Yes
Turnip • Neutral ; edibility: No
Turnip (greens) • Neutral ; edibility: No
Vanilla • Neutral ; edibility: Maybe
Venison • Warming; edibility: Yes
Vinegar (any) • Warming; edibility: No
Walnut oil • Warming; edibility: Rarely
Walnuts • Warming; edibility: No
Watercress • Cooling; edibility: Maybe
Watermelon • Cooling; edibility: Yes
Wheat • Warming; edibility: Yes
Wheat bran • Warming; edibility: Yes
Wintergreen • Cooling; edibility: Yes
Yogurt (plain) • Cooling; edibility: No
Zucchini • Cooling; edibility: Yes

6

YOUR COMMON SENSE OF SIGHT

Your common sense of Sight is your most enthusiastic of senses. It's where having fun in life comes from. Being able to enjoy all of your Common Senses comes from this category. This category is about enthusiasm for your life.

Being happy and healthy come from getting the most out of your lifestyles choices (rest, food, water, play, work, interacting with people), emotions and attitude.

Asian Medicines call this category different names and use different techniques to remedy symptoms found here...but the category itself is nearly identical in all three traditions.

Ayurveda: In India, this category is the Dosha Pitta–Vata
Traditional Tibetan–Mongolian Medicine: In Mongolia, this category is called the the Nyepa Bile
Traditional Chinese Medicine:
In China, this is The Element of Wood.

What your Common Sense of Sight does...
Each common sense plays an important (20%) role in your health. They all have very specific responsibilities. This one deals primarily with your liver, turning food into fuel power and harnessing an active mind.

- **Body:** Turning food into energy, metabolism, circulation, and moving your body AND everything involving your brain, spinal cord, waste management, and digestion
- **Mind:** Multi–tasking, spontaneity, enjoying a creative lifestyle
- **Spirit:** Enthusiasm

Your Common Sense of Sight Traits:
Creative, Multi-tasking, Inventive, Can talk to anyone, of any age; Physically active, but not competitive; Team player, Impulsive, Athletic, but not competitive; Loves puzzles and playing most games

Symptoms of too much enthusiasm: Jaundice, Hot flashes, Distracted more than usual, Obsessiveness, Boredom, Sadness, Sighing, Restlessness, Substance abuse, Migraine, Frequent but quick to heal rashes, Fever, Burning eyes, Insomnia, Controlling or critical of others

Activities of warming action movement:
Running–X Country, Skiing–slalom, Swimming laps, Crafts, Artwork of any kind, Birdwatching, Playing cards in a group, Photography, Dance

Meridians involved: Liver, Bladder

Season of most enthusiastic growth: Spring

Sight is the most enthusiastic of sense.

Having fun alone or with other people, learning new things, pursuing a goal, multi-tasking, working on a dream, flirting, sexuality, relationships of all kinds, dancing like nobody is looking, games of any kind, enjoying your physical senses, having pleasure of any kind, and spontaneity are all found in this category. Whew.

People with a majority of traits in this category are almost always happy and curious. They are never bored. Being bored would be a fairly serious symptom for them. They never seem to run out of enthusiasm for life. They don't need much sleep and wake up looking forward to the day.

There's a reason for that.

This is the Common Sense responsible producing happy hormones. This category is about having a healthy liver and metabolism. People with a majority of traits in this category naturally produce a lot of stress busting hormones.

They like to play. They have active minds and bodies. Physical movement creates happy hormones. So does playfully attaining goals. This built-in stress-busting frees up their minds to multi-task, invent new things, learn new things, solve puzzles of any sort and do emergency response work.

Everyone has this built-in stress buster system of hormones at their disposal. Everyone needs them to neutralize stress hormones. Happy hormones are all beneficial to brain function. Your brain needs to rest from stress just like muscles need to rest after a sprint.

When you don't produce enough of these happy hormones, your stress hormones don't get turned off. Your body stays on high alert all the time. Very tiring.

The four happy hormones are serotonin, dopamine, oxytocin, and endorphins. If you find yourself stressed all the time, your self-care choices should be focused on producing these necessary hormones to eliminate feeling stress in your life.

Serotonin makes you feel pleasure with your physical senses of touch, sight, taste, smell, and hearing. It's also in charge of your sleep cycles. Serotonin regulates your mood, prevents depression, makes you feel happy with life and where you're heading next.

To produce this hormone, your body needs a particular mix of vitamins and minerals. Think of it like having just the right things in your pantry. You need vitamins A, B1, B2, B3, B5, B6, B12, C, D, E, K, Biotin, and Folic Acid. See the vitamin list for details about what foods you need to eat for these. It's not as hard as it looks to eat them in a normal diet. Feeling happy with life is worth the effort.

Serotonin requires sunlight. Feel sunshine on your face as much as possible all year round. Its why everyone is happy to be outside for first warm sunshine day of spring. We are producing serotonin for the first time in a while.

All of the happy hormones require levels of physical movement. Serotonin requires low intensity exercise like tai chi, yoga, slow dancing, and walking.

What depletes it? Common lifestyle factors and choices. We are doing it to ourselves. Caffeine, nicotine, alcohol, stress, antidepressants, pesticides, heavy metals, and lack of sunshine on our faces.

Dopamine is why we get excited about working towards a goal. That great feeling of crossing a finish line, acing a deadline, spring cleaning, the excitement at the end of a close sporting event, cheering someone, or reaching a milestone in life.

Alcohol, caffeine, and sugar all prevent dopamine from being released. So do stress and obesity.

Symptoms of dopamine deficiency are craving sugar, depression, restless leg syndrome, oversleeping, procrastination, not feeling pleasure anywhere in your day, mood swings, not wanting to be around anyone, and feeling not good enough.

Your body needs a serving of B9 (folate), tyrosine and phenylalanine every day to produce dopamine. Easily done with a normal diet.

Heres just a few of the choices you have to get what you need: apples, asparagus, avocado, banana, beans, beef, beef liver, beets, bread/grains, broccoli, Brussel sprouts, chicken, citrus, dairy, dark chocolate, eggs, fish/seafood, leafy greens, legumes, nuts/seeds, papaya, parmesan cheese, pork, soy, turkey, turmeric, and wheat germ.

Dopamine is produced when doing exercise with a time limit, distance or counting reps to achieve a particular goal. It's the natural high reward for pushing your body to achieve a particular goal.

Oxytocin is the love hormone. Everyone needs it. It's produced when you touch someone, or they touch you. This is the hormone produced for a feeling of satisfaction, loving something or someone. It's the primary hormone released during orgasm. It assists a woman through childbirth, beginning breast feeding, and bonding with a baby. For men it's an ingredient in creating testosterone.

Oxytocin is released when you are touching someone else. Holding someones hand, getting a hug, cuddling on the couch with someone, this is the love between a child and their stuffed animal, and why a really great massage make you smile. They all release oxytocin in your system. It gives you a feeling of trust, safety. Close relationships make us happy for a reason. Physical contact produces a happy hormone needed to keep our lymph/immune systems healthy.

Symptoms of oxytocin deficiency are adrenal fatigue, burnout, loneliness, insomnia, detachment, depression, anxiety, being fearful, headaches, low sex drive, and rapid aging.

All made better with eight hugs a day.

You also need foods that have oxytocin. Bananas, beans, cashews, eggs, legumes, potatoes, quinoa, salmon, sesame seeds, walnuts, whole grain rice, and yogurt all contain oxytocin. Comfort foods.

Endorphins are your your built in pain blockers. It's released when you are pushing your body to the max. The runner's high, the high after eating a lot chili peppers is caused by this hormone. Relieving pain and stress caused by having to push the body that far. It's a state of bliss, pleasure, sensuality, sexuality. A rush.

Symptoms of low levels of endorphins are addictions, physical and emotional pain. Avoid processed foods, alcohol and caffeine to boost your endorphin levels.

You can also raise your endorphin levels with occasional strenuous exercise, laughing more, learning something new, or volunteering somewhere.

Foods that will help restore your endorphin levels are avocados, beans, berries, broccoli, cauliflower, citrus, coconut oil, dark chocolate, leafy greens, lentils, nuts/seeds, peas, olive oil, salmon, sardines, spinach, sprouted grains, squash, and sweet potatoes.

T<small>RADITIONAL</small> T<small>IBETAN</small>-M<small>ONGOLIAN</small> <small>MEDICINE</small> calls this category Bile.

They teach that the symptoms that are in this category are caused by a combination of Aggression and Attachment.

Vigorously working toward an unhealthy passion/attachment can make your life unhappy and cause symptoms.

Definition of **Attachment,** noun

1. *A feeling that binds one to a person, place, thing,*

Mongolian Om

cause, ideal, or the like; devotion, profound regard.

Aggression can be transformed into joyous, cautious attentiveness followed by well thought–out action.

Attachment can be transformed into a mind that is totally clear and unimpeded

Traditional Tibetan–Mongolian Medicine teaches that all disease is caused by misusing at least one of three strong emotions: Aggression (anger/competition of any kind), Attachment (to people, ideas, or things) and Ignorance (closed–mindedness, not wanting to know or change). They are the three root poisons to all illness. Each very useful when used wisely.

The symptoms most likely to occur in an enthusiastic, active lifestyle are those caused by Aggression and Attachment.

People that handle these emotions wisely as tools are creative, impulsive, reflective, interested in everything, and excitable. They are quick to sicken, quick to heal, passionate about righting wrongs and helping the downtrodden, deeply concerned about human rights, equality and freedom for all. They make everyone feel safe and are excellent at creating homes and communities. They are the storytellers, keepers of family history and heirlooms.

They use Aggression as motivation for finding physically energy to work on an idea. Attachment is used for staying committed to the project. It's a very handy combination for coming up with a good idea and seeing it all the way through to the finish line.

They are impulsive, especially go too far when having fun with a pet project. But there are a lot of reasons why hot disease happens to this happy go lucky category.

If it has been unseasonably warm, aggression and attachment tendencies get stronger. A very hot, dry summer will cause symptoms even if you have been doing everything else right.

Other causes for hot disease symptoms in this category would be too much hot, sour, salty, and/or greasy food, a recent cold, infection, or virus. A very common reason for some of these symptoms is keeping anger or envy hidden. Western psychology agrees.

Hidden/secret emotion in our culture is called keeping your cards close to your chest, holding a secret torch for someone, wanting very much to keep up with the Joneses. These simmering emotions causes hot disease.

No matter what the reason is behind hot disease symptoms...the advice is the same. Use all five of your Common Senses to cool yourself off.

Want to rid yourself of symptoms of too much Aggression and/or Attachments? Keep your life feeling fun for everyone in your life, including you.

This is the category that creates happiness in your life. Joy is a necessary nutrient.

Use negative emotions and situations to motivate you towards a passion or bliss...then let it go.

"Follow your bliss.

If you do follow your bliss, you put yourself on a kind of track that has been there all the while waiting for you, and the life you ought to be living is the one you are living.

When you can see that, you begin to meet people who are in the field of your bliss, and they open the doors to you.

I say, follow your bliss and don't be afraid, and doors will open where you didn't know they were going to be.

If you follow your bliss, doors will open for you that wouldn't have opened for anyone else."

— Joseph Campbell

Here are some suggestions about how to use your 5 Common Senses as a team. Using at least one per category increase your **Enthusiasm**, without burning out…its about building stamina, not stimulation.

Touch

- Physical touch is not an option for some people. People in this category need it. At least eight hugs a day, or touches on the arm, or prolonged eye contact. Especially true when they are sick. Too much physical isolation causes them stress. A feeling of restlessness, fidgeting, is a symptom found in this category…of needing to be with people. To play.
- Wash your hands in cooler water.
- Walk at a slower pace than usual.
- Use slightly less blankets at night than you normally would.
- Open a window. Feel a slight breeze on your face in at least one room or while driving, whenever possible.
- Skip. Whenever you can get away with it.
- Dance. To anything. The playful nature of dancing to music is calming.

Sight

- Cut back on gaming and/or screen time at least an hour before bed
- Either read or do crafts for that hour instead.
- Read for fun, nothing work related, nothing that will make you too introspective. Keep it positive, playful.
- Color deeply effects your body, mind and spirit. Red, Orange, Yellow and Green are warm colors. They perk up your eyes and mind. An active mind helps to perk up your body. An active mind and body make your spirit happy. Green, blue, indigo and white are cool colors. All pastels are cool colors because of the white. Green is both warming and calming because it's neutral...yellow and blue combined.
- If you are feeling stressed, restless, or overwhelmed...use cool colors throughout your day. If you are feeling a little bored, emotional or distracted...use warm colors. Seek them out.
- Count to seven on a walk. There are seven colors in a rainbow. Find an example of each of the colors before you stop walking. Make it a daily game with yourself. Do something fun for yourself as a reward if you get all seven.

Taste

- The most helpful flavor is **Sour** (vinegar, lemon, fermented foods).
- A little sour is good for your liver and helps digestion.
- Too much sour can damage your liver, overstimulate your digestion, weaken muscle tone, and slow metabolism, not good. The easiest way for most people is to cut back on yogurt, sour cream, and fermented drinks.
- To reduce the harmful effects of too much sour in your system, use **Pungent** (hot, spicy) foods.

- Try a new food. Learn to cook it.
- No brown plates of food. Keep it colorful.
- Invite someone to dinner...or find a new topic to talk about with dinner.
- Make an effort to create a setting. Different plates than usual. Sit in a different place. A change of pace during meals is fun.
- Suggested food list for this category is at the end of this chapter

Scent

- Best smells for headaches that are common with symptoms common to this category are chamomile, lavender, marjoram, peppermint, rose, and rosemary.
- Change the scents in your house. Find soaps, shampoos, candles, sprays, or essential oils that you've never used before. Smell them all. Only get the ones that make you smile.
- Write down your five favorite smells from childhood. How many are still in your life? Can they be replicated? If so, do it.
- Use an Aromatherapist to create your very own perfume. Nobody else will smell like this. Perfume smells differently on different people. Choose several vials of essential oils that make you smile. Don't stop blending until you can't stop smelling yourself.

Hearing

- Music that is upbeat, funny or heartwarming lyrics, but not too fast a tempo
- Singing, but not any sad songs
- Headphones help focus during chaos, life with a private soundtrack.

- Listen to music from the most fun period of your life. Nobody else has to hear it. Use the music to remember everything about the time. What did you wear? What food did you like? What was your routine like?
- Close your eyes occasionally during your day and just listen to your world for 30 seconds.

General food guidelines for your Common Sense of Sight...

- A cooling diet. Choose foods that are very nutritious and easy to digest.
- A well-cooked vegetable is easier to digest than a raw one. Steamed and chilled is okay when you have a need for broccoli, cauliflower, or peppers
- Stews, soups and long simmered one-pot dishes are perfect most of the year. Have stews on cold days, clearer or cold soups when it's warmer.
- Lightly spiced dishes are best. Use chopped fresh herbs instead.
- Just say no to fried food, eating on the run, caffeine, alcohol, sugar, processed foods, or cut back as far as you can.
- Just say no to fermented foods (including sour cream, yogurt, kefir, soy sauce, vinegars etc.) during stressful times or hot weather; they makes it worse.
- All things in moderation

ALCOHOL (HARD OR WINE) • Warming; edibility: No
    Alcohol (beer) • Warming; edibility: Rarely
    Allspice • Warming; edibility: Maybe
    Almonds • Warming; edibility: Maybe
    Almonds (w/o skin) • Neutral; edibility: Yes

Almonds (with skin) • Warming; edibility: Rarely
Almond extract • Warming; edibility: Yes
Almond milk • Neutral; edibility: Yes
Amaranth • Neutral; edibility: Yes
Anise • Warming; edibility: Maybe
Apples (sweet) • Cooling; edibility: Yes
Apple cider • Warming; edibility: Rarely
Applesauce • Cooling; edibility: Yes
Apricots (dried) • Warming; edibility: Maybe
Apricots (sour) • Neutral; edibility: No
Apricots (sweet) • Cooling; edibility: Yes
Artichokes • Warming; edibility: Yes
Artichokes (Sunchokes) • Cooling; edibility: Yes
Asparagus • Cooling Yes
Avocados • Cooling Yes
Bananas • Cooling Yes
Barley • Neutral; edibility: Yes
Barley malt • Warming; edibility: Yes
Basil (dried) • Warming; edibility: Maybe
Basil (fresh) • Cooling; edibility: Yes
Bay leaf • Warming; edibility: Maybe
Beans (adzuki) • Cooling; edibility: No
Beans (black) • Cooling; edibility: Maybe
Beans (garbanzo) • Cooling; edibility: No
Beans (green/string) • Cooling; edibility: Yes
Beans (kidney) • Cooling; edibility: Maybe
Beans (lima) • Cooling; edibility: No
Beans (mung) • Cooling; edibility: Yes
Beans (navy) • Cooling; edibility: No
Beans (pinto) • Cooling; edibility: No
Beans (white) • Cooling; edibility: No
Beef • Warming; edibility: Maybe
Beets (greens) • Cooling; edibility: Maybe
Beets (cooked) • Cooling; edibility: Yes
Berries (sour) • Warming; edibility: Maybe

Berries (sweet) • Cooling; edibility: Yes
Black–eyed peas • Cooling; edibility: Yes
Brazil nuts • Warming; edibility: Maybe
Bread (yeasted) • Warming; edibility: Rarely
Broccoli • Cooling; edibility: Yes
Brussels sprouts • Cooling; edibility: Yes
Buckwheat • Neutral; edibility: Rarely
Burdock root • Warming; edibility: Rarely
Butter • Neutral; edibility: Yes
Buttermilk • Warming No
Cabbage (cooked) • Neutral; edibility: Yes
Cabbage (red) • Warming; edibility: Yes
Canola (oil) • Neutral; edibility: Yes
Caffeine (any) • Warming; edibility: No
Caraway • Warming; edibility: Yes
Carbonated bev. (any) • Warming; edibility: No
Cardamom • Warming; edibility: Maybe
Carob • Neutral; edibility: Yes
Carrots (cooked) • Cooling; edibility: Yes
Carrots (raw) • Warming; edibility: Maybe
Cashews • Cooling; edibility: Maybe
Cauliflower (cooked) • Cooling; edibility: Yes
Cayenne • Warming; edibility: No
Celery • Neutral; edibility: Yes
Cereal (dry) • Warming; edibility: Yes
Chai (hot, spiced milk) • Warming; edibility: Maybe
Chard • Cooling; edibility: Yes
Cheese (goat) • Warming; edibility: Yes
Cheese (hard) • Warming; edibility: Rarely
Cheese (soft, not aged) • Warming; edibility: Yes
Cherries (sour) • Warming; edibility: No
Cherries (sweet) • Neutral; edibility: Yes
Chicken (dark) • Warming; edibility: Maybe
Chicken (white) • Warming; edibility: Yes
Chili pepper • Warming; edibility: No

Chilies (green) • Warming; edibility: No
Chocolate • Warming; edibility: Rarely
Cilantro • Cooling; edibility: Yes
Cinnamon • Warming; edibility: Yes
Clams • Neutral; edibility: Yes
Cloves • Warming; edibility: Maybe
Coconut milk • Warming; edibility: Yes
Coconut meat • Warming; edibility: Yes
Coconut oil • Cooling; edibility: Yes
Coffee (bean based) • Warming; edibility: No
Coffee (grain) • Cooling; edibility: Yes
Coriander leaves • Cooling; edibility: Yes
Coriander seeds • Warming; edibility: Yes
Corn oil • Warming; edibility: Rarely
Corn (dried) • Warming; edibility: Maybe
Corn (fresh) • Cooling; edibility: Maybe
Cottage cheese • Cooling; edibility: Yes
Couscous • Neutral; edibility: Yes
Cranberries • Warming; edibility: No
Cucumber • Cooling; edibility: Yes
Cumin • Warming; edibility: Yes
Daikon radishes • Warming; edibility: Maybe
Dandelion greens • Cooling; edibility: Yes
Dates • Neutral; edibility: Yes
Dill (leaf) • Cooling; edibility: Yes
Dulse • Cooling; edibility: Yes
Duck • Warming; edibility: No
Egg white • Cooling; edibility: Yes
Egg yolk • Neutral; edibility: Yes
Eggplant • Neutral; edibility: Maybe
Fennel bulb • Warming; edibility: Yes
Fennel seed • Warming; edibility: Yes
Figs • Neutral; edibility: Yes
Fish (mild) • Cooling; edibility: Yes
Fish (oily) • Warming; edibility: Maybe

Flaxseed • Cooling; edibility: Yes
Flaxseed oil • Cooling; edibility: Yes
Fruit juice concentrates • Cooling; edibility: Yes
Garlic • Warming; edibility: Maybe
Ghee • Cooling; edibility: Yes
Ginger (dried) • Warming; edibility: No
Ginger (fresh) • Warming; edibility: Maybe
Granola • Warming; edibility: Yes
Grapefruit • Neutral; edibility: No
Grapes (green) • Warming; edibility: Maybe
Grapes (red/purple) • Cooling; edibility: Yes
Grape leaf • Cooling; edibility: Yes
Greens (leafy) • Cooling; edibility: Yes
Ham • Warming; edibility: Rarely
Hazelnuts • Warming; edibility: Maybe
Honey (raw) • Neutral; edibility: Maybe
Horseradish • Warming; edibility: Rarely
Ice cream • Cooling; edibility: Yes
Icy cold drinks (any) • Cooling; edibility: Maybe
Juice, aloe vera • Cooling; edibility: Yes
Juice, apple • Cooling; edibility: Yes
Juice, apricot • Cooling; edibility: Yes
Juice, berry (sour) • Warming; edibility: No
Juice, berry (sweet) • Cooling; edibility: Yes
Juice, carrot • Warming; edibility: Yes
Juice, cherry (sour) • Warming; edibility: No
Juice, cherry (sweet) • Warming; edibility: Yes
Juice, cranberry • Warming; edibility: No
Juice, grape • Cooling; edibility: Yes
Juice, grapefruit • Warming; edibility: No
Juice, mango • Cooling; edibility: Yes
Juice, mixed vegetable • Cooling; edibility: Yes
Juice, orange • Warming; edibility: Maybe
Juice, papaya • Neutral; edibility: Yes
Juice, pear • Cooling; edibility: Yes

Juice, pineapple • Warming; edibility: No
Juice, prune • Cooling; edibility: Yes
Juice, tomato • Warming; edibility: Rarely
Juice, V–8 • Warming; edibility: Rarely
Kale • Cooling; edibility: Yes
Ketchup • Warming; edibility: Rarely
Kiwi • Warming; edibility: Maybe
Kohlrabi • Warming; edibility: Maybe
Lamb • Warming; edibility: No
Leeks (cooked) • Neutral; edibility: Yes
Lemon • Cooling; edibility: Maybe
Lemonade • Cooling; edibility: Maybe
Lentils (brown) • Cooling; edibility: Yes
Lentils (red) • Cooling; edibility: Yes
Lettuce • Cooling; edibility: Yes
Lime • Warming; edibility: Yes
Macadamia nuts • Warming; edibility: Maybe
Mace • Warming; edibility: Maybe
Mangos (ripe) • Cooling; edibility: Yes
Maple syrup • Cooling; edibility: Yes
Marjoram • Warming; edibility: Maybe
Mayonnaise • Warming; edibility: Rarely
Melon • Cooling; edibility: Yes
Milk (almond) • Cooling; edibility: Yes
Milk (chocolate) • Warming; edibility: No
Milk (cow) • Neutral; edibility: Yes
Milk (goat) • Cooling; edibility: Yes
Milk (rice) • Cooling; edibility: Yes
Milk (soy) • Cooling; edibility: Yes
Millet • Cooling; edibility: Yes
Miso • Warming; edibility: Rarely
Molasses • Warming; edibility: Maybe
Mushrooms • Cooling; edibility: Yes
Mustard (condiment) • Warming; edibility: Rarely
Mustard (greens) • Warming; edibility: Maybe

Mustard (seeds) • Warming; edibility: Rarely
Nutmeg • Warming; edibility: Maybe
Oat bran • Cooling; edibility: Yes
Oats (cooked) • Cooling; edibility: Yes
Oats (dry) • Neutral; edibility: Maybe
Okra • Neutral; edibility: Yes
Olive oil • Cooling; edibility: Yes
Olives (black) • Cooling; edibility: Yes
Olives (green) • Warming; edibility: No
Onions (cooked) • Cooling; edibility: Yes
Onions (raw) • Warming; edibility: No
Orange peel • Warming; edibility: Maybe
Oranges • Warming; edibility: Maybe
Oregano • Warming; edibility: Maybe
Papayas • Warming; edibility: Maybe
Paprika • Warming; edibility: Maybe
Parsley (dried) • Warming; edibility: Maybe
Parsley (fresh) • Cooling; edibility: Yes
Parsnip • Cooling; edibility: Yes
Pasta (wheat) • Neutral; edibility: Yes
Peaches • Warming; edibility: Maybe
Peanuts • Warming; edibility: Maybe
Pears • Cooling; edibility: Yes
Peas • Neutral; edibility: Yes
Peas (dried) • Warming; edibility: Maybe
Pecans • Warming; edibility: Maybe
Pepper (black) • Warming; edibility: Maybe
Peppers (hot) • Warming; edibility: No
Peppers (sweet) • Cooling; edibility: Yes
Peppermint • Warming; edibility: Yes
Perch • Warming; edibility: Maybe
Pickles • Warming; edibility: No
Pine nuts • Warming; edibility: Maybe
Pineapple • Warming; edibility: Maybe
Pistachios • Warming; edibility: Maybe

Plums (sweet) • Cooling; edibility: Yes
Polenta • Warming; edibility: Maybe
Pomegranates • Cooling; edibility: Yes
Popcorn (plain) • Warming; edibility: Yes
Poppy seed • Warming; edibility: Maybe
Pork • Neutral; edibility: Rarely
Potatoes (sweet/yams) • Warming; edibility: Yes
Potatoes (white) • Neutral; edibility: Yes
Prunes • Neutral; edibility: Yes
Psyllium seeds • Cooling; edibility: Yes
Pumpkins • Neutral; edibility: Yes
Pumpkin seeds • Neutral; edibility: Yes
Quinoa • Neutral; edibility: Maybe
Radishes • Warming; edibility: Maybe
Raisins • Neutral; edibility: Yes
Rhubarb • Cooling; edibility: Rarely
Rice (basmati) • Neutral; edibility: Yes
Rice (brown) • Neutral; edibility: Yes
Rice (white) • Warming; edibility: Yes
Rice (wild) • Neutral; edibility: Yes
Rice cakes (plain) • Neutral; edibility: Yes
Rice syrup • Warming; edibility: Yes
Rosemary • Warming; edibility: Maybe
Rutabaga • Cooling; edibility: Yes
Rye • Warming; edibility: Rarely
Safflower oil • Warming; edibility: Rarely
Saffron • Cooling; edibility: Yes
Sage • Warming; edibility: Maybe
Salmon • Neutral; edibility: Maybe
Salt (in excess) • Cooling; edibility: Rarely
Sardines • Neutral; edibility: Maybe
Scallions • Warming; edibility: Maybe
Seaweed • Cooling; edibility: Rarely
Seitan (wheat meat) • Neutral; edibility: Yes
Sesame oil • Warming; edibility: Maybe

Sesame seed • Neutral; edibility: Rarely
Shellfish (except shrimp) • Neutral; edibility: Yes
Shrimp • Warming; edibility: Maybe
Sour cream • Warming; edibility: No
Soy oil • Cooling; edibility: Yes
Soy cheese • Cooling; edibility: Yes
Soy flour • Warming; edibility: Yes
Soy powder • Cooling; edibility: Yes
Soy sauce • Warming; edibility: Rarely
Soy sausages • Warming; edibility: No
Soybeans • Cooling; edibility: Yes
Spearmint • Cooling; edibility: Yes
Spelt • Neutral; edibility: Yes
Spinach (cooked) • Neutral; edibility: Yes
Spinach (raw) • Warming; edibility: Maybe
Sprouts • Cooling; edibility: Yes
Sprouts (not spicy) • Cooling; edibility: Yes
Squash (spaghetti) • Cooling; edibility: Yes
Squash (summer) • Cooling; edibility: Yes
Squash (winter) • Warming; edibility: Maybe
Star Anise • Warming; edibility: Maybe
Strawberries • Neutral; edibility: Yes
Sugar, white • Warming; edibility: Rarely
Sunflower (oil) • Warming; edibility: Yes
Sunflower (seed) • Warming; edibility: Yes
Tahini • Warming; edibility: Rarely
Tamari • Warming; edibility: Maybe
Tapioca • Neutral; edibility: Yes
Tarragon • Warming; edibility: Maybe
Tea, black • Cooling; edibility: Yes
Thyme • Warming; edibility: Maybe
Tofu • Neutral; edibility: Yes
Tomatoes (dried) • Warming; edibility: Maybe
Tomatoes (fresh) • Cooling; edibility: Yes
Tomatoes (sauce) • Warming; edibility: Maybe

Turmeric • Warming; edibility: Yes
Tuna • Warming; edibility: Yes
Turkey (dark) • Warming; edibility: Rarely
Turkey (white) • Warming; edibility: Yes
Turnips • Neutral; edibility: No
Turnip greens • Neutral; edibility: No
Vanilla • Neutral; edibility: Yes
Venison • Warming; edibility: Yes
Vinegar (any) • Warming; edibility: No
Walnuts • Warming; edibility: Maybe
Watercress • Cooling; edibility: Yes
Watermelon • Cooling; edibility: Yes
Wheat • Warming; edibility: Yes
Wintergreen • Cooling; edibility: Yes
Yogurt (plain) • Cooling; edibility: No
Zucchini • Cooling; edibility: Yes

7
YOUR COMMON SENSE OF TASTE

- Your Common Sense of Touch is primarily about your body.
- Your Common Sense of **Taste** is primarily about your mind.
- Your Common Sense of Hearing is primarily about your spirit.

This category is the doorway between your spirit and your body. Mind makes your dreams into reality. This ability is the basis of all artistry and creativity.

Ayurveda: In India, this category is the Dosha, Vata

Traditional Tibetan–Mongolian Medicine: In Mongolia, this category is called the Nyepa, Wind

Traditional Chinese Medicine:
In China, this is The Element of Earth.

WHAT YOUR COMMON Sense of Taste does...

- **Body:** Anything involving your brain, spinal cord, waste management, and digestion
- **Mind:** Adapting to changes and handling your emotions calmly
- **Spirit:** Communication & feeling heard

Your Common Sense of Taste Traits: Energetic, Intuitive, Talkative, Team Player, Compassionate, Creative, Enjoy helping others, Nurturing, Adaptable, Enchanted by music and/or dance

Symptoms of too much Communication: Digestion problems, Sleep problems, Unhappy, but not depressed; Sudden fatigue, Cravings, Twitching, Joint pain, Weight management, Anxiety, Unable to finish anything

Activities of middle path (neutral action) movement: Distance running, Downhill skiing, Swimming for fun, Artwork, Cooking, Creating new games using cards; Playing a musical instrument

Meridians involved: Stomach, Spleen

Season of most change: Spring and Summer Equinoxes (3 weeks before and 3 weeks after actual equinox dates) Weather changes from warm to cold...and cold to warmth

Taste is the most adaptable sense.

This is the midway point, third of five, perfectly balanced...the middle path, common ground.

The ability to find common ground means you can see both sides of any situation. This makes compassion, forgiveness, communication, and unconditional nurturing possible.

This category also gives you the ability to change direction whenever you need to. It navigates around obstacles like wind around rocks.

The season found in this category is Equinox. It's the transition season when the weather changes from hot to cold, or cold to hot. The equinox season begins three weeks before the Equinox date and lasts until three weeks afterwards.

People born with a majority of traits in this category are natural mediators, caregivers, teachers, or any other profession that works directly with people. They really do enjoy talking to everyone and hearing their stories. They easily adapt their vocabulary and conversation to whoever they are talking to.

Their patient, empathic listening skills are strong, even as children. Compassionate listening makes people feel heard. Feeling heard calms your spirit and reduces stress hormones. Making other people feel heard and cared for is the art of nurturing.

People born in this category can create harmony in what looks and sounds like chaos. I remember watching my mother have six conversations with her children at once, while helping with our homework, while some of us were arguing.

She spoke with all of us and helped solve the arguments. We all felt completely heard by her. Each of us felt we had her complete attention, one at a time. We all felt heard and cared for.

Nurturing is a calming trait, given or received. Taking care of someone can be a moving meditation. After a busy day, I often calm down by cooking for family and friends. A simply prepared meal focuses my mind on them, not my day.

Cooking can be a creative expression. It's a way for me to have a bit of fun.

If you have had an emotionally difficult day, it's important to calm your mind and spirit. Stress hormones won't go away until your mind and spirit are calmed.

The fastest way to calm your mind is creative expression of some sort. It doesn't have to take a lot of time or prep. Children instinctively do it all the time. They play. Their minds get clearer, they become happier, with just a well chosen game or two. Adults need to remember to do the same.

If you only have five minutes...take seven deep breaths. Or get a pad of paper and quickly think of as many happy favorite childhood games or songs that you can in five minutes. Keep the list somewhere close so you can glimpse your childhood whenever you need it.

If you have more time...write, draw, make a playlist, throw clay, dance or cook something nurturing for yourself or your family.

If emotions overwhelm you on a regular basis, you have too little control over your emotions. Emotions are supposed to help you deal with a situation, not make it worse.

Symptoms of too little emotional control include choosing to dive into your studies or work, canker sores, water retention, swollen prostate, tender gums, inability to forgive, emotional numbness, jealousy, unclear memory, and being cold to the bone for no reason.

It is very important for people in this category to stay balanced during their day. They are prone to both hot and cold diseases. It depends on what is going on in their day.

Becoming too isolated, cold, or bored can tip them into cold disease. Being too stressed, hot or busy can tip them into hot disease.

Aim for the middle, a blend of two extremes, nothing so stimulating that you become stressed; nothing so calming that you become numb. Avoid extremes.

A tightrope walker uses a pole to counterbalance his steps. Consider one end of that pole to be stimulating events in your day. The other end of the long pole are calming events in your day. The wire is your day. As your day changes, so does your need for balance in one direction or the other.

Make a point of stopping every few hours for a ten minute break. During that break close your eyes and imagine yourself on a tightrope with a balancing pole. How balanced do you feel? If you are either too busy or too calmed for your particular comfort zone, adjust balance with self-care.

Use your mind to make sure that you're not slipping to one side of that tightrope pole or the other. Make sure you have enough stamina to keep up with your busy day. Rest, drink enough water, laugh often and choose your food wisely.

Stay in the middle. If you are beginning to feel too stressed or hot, use your common senses to cool off. If you are feeling too isolated, overly emotional or cold, use your common senses to warm up.

A perfectly smoothly running day can change in a blink. Adapting to a new situation requires keeping your balance, probably the most important trait found in this category.

TRADITIONAL TIBETAN-MONGOLIAN MEDICINE *calls this category Wind.*

They teach that the symptoms in this category are caused by unhealthy amounts of Attachment.

Definition of **Attachment,** noun

1. A feeling that binds one to a person, place, thing, cause, ideal, or the like; devotion, profound regard.

Attachment can be transformed into a mind that is totally clear and unimpeded.

Attachment is a strong emotional tool that keeps us interested in something. You can be attached to something physically, mentally, or spiritually. An attachment is only unhealthy if you can't step away from it when you need to, have too many interests at once, or can't finish anything you start. Lack of attachment is lack of commitment.

Starting any new interest (whether it is an idea, activity, person, place or thing) is fun, stimulating, and creative...but it takes passion and commitment to finish what you start. That's why there's a happy hormone that kicks in when you accomplish a goal.

This category is called Wind in traditional Tibetan–Mongolian medicine. Wind is a wonderful analogy for the attachment category. We are blown from interest to interest throughout our day like a kite on a string. Keeping a strong tether to reality prevents being carried away by random breezes or strong gusts.

- If we have too many interests at once, our little kite is constantly changing direction and incapable of going higher.
- If we are too interested, we become obsessive and possessive. Like a kite stuck in a strong gust of wind, steering the kite is next to impossible without damaging your tether.
- If we aren't interested enough, our kite doesn't even get off the ground. Our commitment/attachment is what makes the wind move.

Lacking wind in your life brings symptoms like sighing, loss of strength, lack of energy, talking less than normal, feeling clogged up, unclear memory, melancholy, and feeling cold to the bone for no reason.

Common causes for too little wind are too little activity, being too cozy, very hot dry summer or windy days, sitting in a cold draft, or being made to feel powerless.

You can increase wind in your life with weight–bearing exercise, sitting near heat, sunbathing, dressing warmly and using dim lighting and candles more often. Laugh with friends more often.

Too much wind/interest is just as problematic. If there is too much momentum, it becomes difficult for a kite to change direction...or stop. Too much wind/attachment is only healthy for very short amounts of time.

Symptoms of too much attachment in your life are greed, obsession, talking more than normal, dizziness, restlessness, shopaholic behavior, obsessive and negative thoughts.

Common causes are too much bitter food, lack of sleep or food, being too active, being overwhelmed by any of the five common senses and windy days.

You can decrease the wind in your life by sitting in cool places, swimming or washing in cool water, eating warm nutritious food, and walking. While doing all of these things, try to only think about no more than two things. Quiet your mind, quiet the wind.

People in this category are amazing when healthy. Their minds are creative, impulsive, reflective, interested, excitable. They are full of energy, highly intuitive, and very willing to help others. They have strong bodies that they stay healthy with a diet of fresh fruit and vegetables, a little meat and dairy food.

They love to sing and to argue, enjoy taking risks, and need drama in their lives. They can be naive and sentimental. They are enchanted by music and dance, and are happiest when exploring their spiritual potential.

However, they are also most likely to be thrown off balance by their self-care choices. Body, mind, and/or spirit symptoms happen whenever they are either too stimulated, or too calm. It's almost always fixed by a better diet.

Poor diet choices cause symptoms of being anxious, paranoid, controlling, manipulative, behaving like a drama queen, can't finish anything, sighing, have developed a twitch, breathing problems, lots of energy followed by deep fatigue, pins and needles sensations in hands/feet or strong cravings for food, alcohol, drugs, or people.

A huge warning flag is if you enjoy meddling in other peoples lives or live vicariously through your children/relatives. Your life really should be enough to keep you busy and happy.

If you feel like there is too much time to kill in your day, or if you find yourself watching more than three hours of TV/device screen at a time, you need to build up other interests in your life. Start by no TV or screen time an hour before you go to bed.

Learn a new craft that you can do instead of screen time, like knitting or carving. Practice an hour a night of no screen. Listen to music or audiobooks while keeping your hands busy. After a week, increase no screen time to two hours before bed, then three.

You will sleep better.

Here are some examples of how you can use your 5 Common Senses to support, or increase, your ability to adapt. Use at least one per category a day if you are either dominant in this sense, or if you are experiencing symptoms from this category.

Touch

- Avoid extremes in temperature. Wear layers. If you are a bit warm, take a layer off. If you just a bit cool, add a layer. Don't wait until you are either sweaty or cold.
- Stretching exercise, qi gong, tai chi, or yoga poses
- Keep your ears, neck, upper chest and shoulders out of drafts or wind.
- Eight hugs a day. No exceptions. It's not as hard as you think it might be. Most people want the contact.
- Walk. Especially if you need to vent some steam or gather your thoughts.

Sight

- Use extreme color contrasts in your clothing or artwork choices sparingly.
- Go for a walk and try to find all seven colors of the rainbow before going back inside.
- Pull the drapes on a windy day...or balance its effects on your concentration.

- If it's cold, or you are somewhat spacey feeling, light a candle or two. Each flame is a tiny campfire.
- If it's hot, or you are feeling overwhelmingly busy, choose pastels whenever possible.
- Avoid TV, especially any channels with crawls at the bottom of the screen.

Taste

- The most helpful flavor is **sweet** (sugar, processed flour, grains, fruits)
- A little sweet can nourish your spirit, enrich your blood and help heal worry
- Too much sweet leads to more worry, slows your ability to clean out bacteria and viruses from your blood. Particularly important for recovering from an infection.
- To reduce the harmful effects of too much sweet in your system, use **sour** (vinegar, lemon, fermented foods).

Scent

- Best smells for stabilizing are rose, geranium, lemon balm, hyssop, rosewood, chamomile, and jasmine.
- Best smells for easing pain of emotions are basil, geranium, jasmine, rose, sandalwood, and ylang-ylang.
- Choose your timing of scent wisely. The internet makes this a simple keyword search. Aromatherapy sites are plentiful. Use the scents you already have in your home to either stimulate or calm when needed.
- Discard all scent used during an unpleasant relationship or emotionally traumatic event. Nothing brings it all back like scent. It is directly related to memory functions. Get more after the memories are no longer painful to think about.

- Have a personal scent made after you have undergone a dramatic change in your life, or choose a brand new one off the shelf. Much more fun if you have an aromatherapist or a perfume specialist in the department store help you make your choice. Try a lot of them. Choose the one that makes you smile every time you catch a whiff of yourself.

Hearing

- If you are having any symptoms of being too busy, calm your system with slower music. Fewer words make music less stimulating. If there are lyrics, make sure that they are happy ones, no drama.
- If you are having symptoms of fatigue in body, mind and/or spirit, stimulate your system with faster tempo music. No sad lyrics. If there are lyrics, keep it fun. Very beneficial to use music from your childhood. Anything that makes you smile or want to dance, skip, keep time, or hum.
- Use ambient sound when feeling easily distracted either during your day or while trying to sleep. Many people use headphones to screen out distracting noises with either silence of music. Choose wisely.
- Limit the amount of words you hear in a day.

General food guidelines for your Common Sense of Taste...

- Dried, dehydrated and foods that cause gas should be avoided.
- All spices are good, in moderation. Balance spicy hot foods with cooling side dishes and condiments
- Just say no to carbonated drinks of any kind, they will make you a bit spacey. Try tea blends or juices instead.
- Just say no to raw vegetables. They are harder to digest.

- Try cooking or steaming all your vegetables for a salad and chilling them instead.
- Just say no to fermented foods (including sour cream, yogurt, kefir, soy sauce, vinegars, etc.) during stressful times or hot weather, they make it worse.
- All things in moderation. No symptoms, no problem.
- If you feel too warm, cool off.
- If you feel too cool, warm up.

Alcohol (hard or wine) • Warming; edibility: Maybe
Alcohol (beer) • Warming; edibility: Maybe
Almonds • Warming; edibility: Yes
Almonds (w/o skin) • Neutral; edibility: Yes
Almonds (with skin) • Warming; edibility: Yes
Almond extract • Warming; edibility: Yes
Almond milk • Neutral; edibility: Yes
Amaranth • Neutral; edibility: Yes
Anise • Warming; edibility: Yes
Apple (cooked) • Cooling; edibility: Yes
Apples (raw) • Cooling; edibility: No
Apple cider • Warming; edibility: Yes
Applesauce Cooling; edibility: Yes
Apricots (dried) • Warming; edibility: No
Apricots (sour) • Neutral; edibility: Yes
Apricots (sweet) • Cooling; edibility: Yes
Artichokes • Warming; edibility: No
Artichoke (Sunchokes) • Cooling; edibility: Yes
Asparagus • Cooling; edibility: Yes
Avocados • Cooling; edibility: Yes
Bananas • Cooling; edibility: Yes
Barley • Neutral ; edibility: No
Barley malt • Warming; edibility: Yes
Basil (dried) • Warming; edibility: Yes
Basil (fresh) • Cooling; edibility: Yes
Bay leaf • Warming; edibility: Yes

Beans (adzuki) • Cooling; edibility: No
Beans (black) • Cooling; edibility: No
Beans (garbanzo) • Cooling; edibility: No
Beans (green/string) • Cooling; edibility: Yes
Beans (kidney) • Cooling; edibility: No
Beans (lima) • Cooling; edibility: No
Beans (mung) • Cooling; edibility: Yes
Beans (navy) • Cooling; edibility: No
Beans (pinto) • Cooling; edibility: No
Beans (white) • Cooling; edibility: No
Beef • Warming; edibility: Yes
Beet greens • Cooling; edibility: Rarely
Beets (cooked) • Cooling; edibility: Yes
Berries (sour) • Warming; edibility: Yes
Berries (sweet) • Cooling; edibility: Yes
Black-eyed peas • Cooling; edibility: No
Brazil nuts • Warming; edibility: Yes
Bread (yeasted) • Warming; edibility: No
Broccoli • Cooling; edibility: No
Brussels sprouts • Cooling; edibility: Yes
Buckwheat • Neutral; edibility: No
Butter • Neutral; edibility: Yes
Buttermilk • Warming; edibility: Yes
Cabbage (cooked) • Neutral; edibility: Yes
Cabbage (red) • Warming; edibility: Yes
Canola (oil) • Neutral ; edibility: Yes
Caffeine (any) • Warming; edibility: No
Caraway • Warming; edibility: Yes
Carbonated bev. (any) • Warming; edibility: No
Cardamom • Warming; edibility: Yes
Carob • Neutral; edibility: Maybe
Carrots (cooked) • Cooling; edibility: Yes
Carrots (raw) • Warming; edibility: Maybe
Cashews • Cooling; edibility: Maybe
Cauliflower (cooked) • Cooling ; edibility: Maybe

Cayenne • Warming; edibility: Yes
Celery • Neutral; edibility: No
Cereal (dry) • Warming; edibility: No
Chai (hot, spiced milk) • Warming; edibility: Yes
Chard • Cooling; edibility: Yes
Cheese (goat) • Warming; edibility: Yes
Cheese (hard) • Warming; edibility: Maybe
Cheese (soft, not aged) • Warming; edibility: Yes
Cherries (sour) • Warming; edibility: Yes
Cherries (sweet) • Neutral; edibility: Yes
Chicken (dark) • Warming; edibility: Yes
Chicken (white) • Warming; edibility: Yes
Chili peppers • Warming; edibility: Yes
Chilies (green) • Warming; edibility: Yes
Chocolate • Warming; edibility: No
Chutney, mango (spicy) • Warming; edibility: Yes
Chutney, mango (sweet) • Cooling; edibility: Yes
Cilantro • Cooling; edibility: Yes
Cinnamon • Warming; edibility: Yes
Clams • Neutral; edibility: Yes
Cloves • Warming; edibility: Yes
Coconut (milk) • Warming; edibility: Yes
Coconut (meat) • Warming; edibility: Yes
Coconut (oil) • Cooling ; edibility: Yes
Coffee (bean– based) • Warming; edibility: No
Coffee (grain) • Cooling ; edibility: Yes
Coriander (seeds) • Warming; edibility: Yes
Corn (oil) • Warming; edibility: Rarely
Corn (dried) • Warming; edibility: Maybe
Corn (fresh) • Cooling; edibility: Rarely
Cottage cheese • Cooling; edibility: Yes
Couscous • Neutral; edibility: No
Cranberries • Warming; edibility: No
Cucumber • Cooling; edibility: Yes
Cumin • Warming; edibility: Yes

Daikon radishes • Warming; edibility: Maybe
Dandelion greens • Cooling ; edibility: No
Dates • Neutral; edibility: No
Dill (leaf) • Cooling; edibility: Yes
Dulse • Cooling; edibility: Yes
Duck • Warming; edibility: Yes
Egg white • Cooling; edibility: Yes
Egg yolk • Neutral ; edibility: Yes
Eggplant • Neutral ; edibility: No
Fennel (bulb) • Warming; edibility: Yes
Fennel (seed) • Warming; edibility: Yes
Figs (dry) • Neutral ; edibility: No
Fish (mild) • Cooling; edibility: Yes
Fish (oily) • Warming; edibility: Yes
Flaxseed • Cooling ; edibility: No
Flaxseed oil • Cooling; edibility: Yes
Fruit juice concentrates • Cooling; edibility: Yes
Garlic • Warming; edibility: Maybe
Ghee • Cooling ; edibility: Yes
Ginger (dried) • Warming; edibility: No
Ginger (fresh) • Warming; edibility: Maybe
Granola • Warming; edibility: No
Grapefruit • Neutral; edibility: Yes
Grapes (green) • Warming; edibility: Yes
Grapes (red/purple) • Cooling; edibility: Yes
Grape leaf • Cooling; edibility: Yes
Greens (leafy) • Cooling; edibility: Yes
Ham • Warming; edibility: Rarely
Hazelnut • Warming; edibility: Yes
Honey (raw) • Neutral; edibility: Yes
Horseradish • Warming; edibility: Rarely
Ice cream • Cooling; edibility: Maybe
Icy cold drinks (any) • Cooling; edibility: No
Juice, aloe vera • Cooling; edibility: Yes
Juice, apple • Cooling ; edibility: No

Juice, apricot • Cooling; edibility: Yes
Juice, berry (sour) • Warming; edibility: Yes
Juice, berry (sweet) • Cooling ; edibility: Yes
Juice, carrot • Warming; edibility: Yes
Juice, cherry (sour) • Warming; edibility: Yes
Juice, cherry (sweet) • Warming; edibility: Yes
Juice, cranberry • Warming; edibility: No
Juice, grape • Cooling; edibility: Yes
Juice, grapefruit • Warming; edibility: No
Juice, mango • Cooling; edibility: Yes
Juice, mixed vegetable • Cooling; edibility: No
Juice, orange • Warming; edibility: Yes
Juice, papaya • Neutral; edibility: Yes
Juice, pear • Cooling; edibility: No
Juice, pineapple • Warming; edibility: Yes
Juice, prune • Cooling; edibility: Rarely
Juice, tomato • Warming; edibility: No
Juice, V-8 • Warming; edibility: No
Kale • Cooling; edibility: Yes
Ketchup • Warming; edibility: Yes
Kiwi • Warming; edibility: Maybe
Kohlrabi • Warming; edibility: No
Lamb • Warming; edibility: No
Leeks (cooked) • Neutral; edibility: Yes
Lemon • Cooling; edibility: Yes
Lemonade • Cooling ; edibility: Yes
Lentil (brown) • Cooling; edibility: Maybe
Lentil (red) • Cooling; edibility: Yes
Lettuce • Cooling ; edibility: Maybe
Lime • Warming; edibility: Yes
Mango (ripe) • Cooling; edibility: Yes
Maple syrup • Cooling; edibility: Yes
Mayonnaise • Warming; edibility: Yes
Melon • Cooling ; edibility: Yes
Milk (almond) • Cooling; edibility: Yes

Milk (chocolate) • Warming; edibility: No
Milk (cow) • Neutral ; edibility: Yes
Milk (goat) • Cooling; edibility: Yes
Milk (rice) • Cooling; edibility: Yes
Milk (soy) • Cooling; edibility: No
Millet • Warming; edibility: No
Miso broth • Warming; edibility: Yes
Molasses • Warming; edibility: Yes
Mushrooms • Cooling; edibility: No
Mustard (condiment) • Warming; edibility: Yes
Mustard greens • Warming; edibility: Maybe
Mustard seeds • Warming; edibility: Rarely
Nutmeg • Warming; edibility: Yes
Oat bran • Cooling; edibility: No
Oats (cooked) • Cooling ; edibility: Yes
Oats (dry) • Neutral ; edibility: No
Okra • Neutral; edibility: Yes
Olive oil • Cooling ; edibility: Yes
Olives (black) • Cooling; edibility: Yes
Olives (green) • Warming; edibility: No
Onions (cooked) • Cooling; edibility: Maybe
Onions (raw) • Warming; edibility: No
Orange peel • Warming; edibility: Yes
Oranges • Warming; edibility: Yes
Oregano • Warming; edibility: Yes
Papaya • Warming; edibility: Yes
Paprika • Warming; edibility: Yes
Parsley (dried) • Warming; edibility: Yes
Parsley (fresh) • Cooling; edibility: Maybe
Parsnip • Cooling; edibility: Yes
Pasta (wheat) • Neutral ; edibility: Maybe
Peaches • Warming; edibility: Maybe
Peanuts • Warming; edibility: Maybe
Pears • Cooling; edibility: No
Peas (cooked) • Neutral; edibility: Yes

Peas (dried) • Warming; edibility: No
Pecans • Warming; edibility: Yes
Peppers (black) • Warming; edibility: Maybe
Peppers (hot) • Warming; edibility: No
Peppers (sweet, ripe) • Cooling; edibility: No
Peppermint • Warming; edibility: Yes
Perch • Warming; edibility: Yes
Pickles • Warming; edibility: Yes
Pine nuts • Warming; edibility: Yes
Pineapple • Warming; edibility: Yes
Pistachios • Warming; edibility: Yes
Plums (sweet) • Cooling; edibility: Yes
Polenta • Warming; edibility: Rarely
Pomegranates • Cooling ; edibility: No
Popcorn (plain) • Warming; edibility: Yes
Poppy seed • Warming; edibility: Yes
Pork • Neutral; edibility: No
Potatoes (sweet/yams) • Warming; edibility: Yes
Potato (white) • Neutral ; edibility: Maybe
Prunes • Neutral ; edibility: No
Psyllium seeds • Cooling ; edibility: Yes
Pumpkins • Neutral ; edibility: Yes
Pumpkin seeds • Neutral; edibility: Yes
Quinoa • Neutral ; edibility: Yes
Radishes • Warming; edibility: No
Raisins • Neutral ; edibility: No
Rhubarb • Cooling; edibility: Yes
Rice (basmati) • Neutral; edibility: Yes
Rice (brown) • Neutral; edibility: Yes
Rice (white) • Warming; edibility: Yes
Rice (wild) • Neutral; edibility: Yes
Rice cakes (plain) • Neutral; edibility: No
Rosemary • Warming; edibility: Maybe
Rutabaga • Cooling; edibility: Yes
Rye • Warming; edibility: No

Safflower oil • Warming; edibility: No
Saffron • Cooling; edibility: Yes
Sage • Warming; edibility: Yes
Salmon • Neutral; edibility: Yes
Salt (in moderation) • Cooling; edibility: Yes
Sardines • Neutral; edibility: Yes
Scallions • Warming; edibility: Yes
Seaweed • Cooling; edibility: Yes
Seitan (wheat meat) • Neutral; edibility: Yes
Sesame oil • Warming; edibility: Yes
Sesame seed • Neutral; edibility: Rarely
Shellfish (not shrimp) • Neutral; edibility: Yes
Shrimp • Warming; edibility: Maybe
Sour cream • Warming; edibility: No
Soy cheese • Cooling; edibility: Yes
Soy flour • Warming; edibility: No
Soy powder • Cooling ; edibility: No
Soy sauce • Warming; edibility: Maybe
Soy sausages • Warming; edibility: No
Soybeans • Cooling; edibility: No
Spearmint • Cooling; edibility: Yes
Spinach (cooked) • Neutral; edibility: Maybe
Spinach (raw) • Warming; edibility: Maybe
Sprouts • Cooling; edibility: Yes
Sprouts (not spicy) • Cooling; edibility: Maybe
Squash (spaghetti) • Cooling; edibility: Yes
Squash (summer) • Cooling; edibility: Yes
Squash (winter) • Warming; edibility: Yes
Star Anise • Warming; edibility: Yes
Strawberries • Neutral; edibility: Yes
Sugar, white • Warming; edibility: No
Sunflower oil • Warming; edibility: Yes
Sunflower seed • Warming; edibility: Yes
Tahini • Warming; edibility: Yes
Tamari • Warming; edibility: Yes

Tapioca • Neutral; edibility: Yes
Tarragon • Warming; edibility: Yes
Tea, black • Cooling; edibility: Yes
Tea, iced • Cooling; edibility: No
Thyme • Warming; edibility: Yes
Tofu • Neutral; edibility: Maybe
Tomatoes (dried) • Warming; edibility: Rarely
Tomatoes (fresh) • Cooling ; edibility: No
Tomatoes (sauce) • Warming; edibility: Rarely
Turmeric • Warming; edibility: Yes
Tuna • Warming; edibility: Yes
Turkey (dark) • Warming; edibility: Yes
Turkey (white) • Warming; edibility: No
Turnips • Neutral; edibility: No
Turnip greens • Neutral; edibility: Yes
Vanilla • Neutral; edibility: Yes
Venison • Warming; edibility: No
Vinegar (any) • Warming; edibility: Yes
Walnuts • Warming; edibility: Yes
Watercress • Cooling; edibility: Yes
Watermelon • Cooling ; edibility: No
Wheat • Warming; edibility: Yes
Wheat bran • Warming; edibility: Yes
Yogurt (plain) • Cooling; edibility: No
Zucchini • Cooling; edibility: Yes

8

YOUR COMMON SENSE OF SMELL

Your Common Sense of Smell is your watchful sense. It notifies your mind of anything that is out of the ordinary. Ever notice how easily you get used to smells around you? Its called habituation.

Let's say you walk into a room from outdoors. A strong smell, good or bad, nearly knocks you over. An hour later you can barely smell it because you're used to it.

Once your mind has determined that a scent is safe, you can't smell it as strongly as you did the first time. This makes it easier for your sense of Smell to be on alert for the next new smell.

Personality traits from this category do the same thing. This is where boundaries are determined by your memories. What's harmful to your life, and what you prefer to believe, are all boundaries for keeping you safe.

All three Asian Medicines agree. This category is where memory, grudges, and belief systems are formed...and kept. The trick to keeping this Common Sense healthy is being flexible enough to update those boundaries when necessary.

Ayurveda: In India, this cautious, calming, methodical Dosha is called Vata–Kapha

Traditional Tibetan–Mongolian Medicine: In Mongolia, this category is the slower moving Nyepa is called Phlegm

Traditional Chinese Medicine: In China, this gentle, routine loving category is The Element of Metal.

WHAT THIS CATEGORY DOES...

Body: Anything involving your brain, spinal cord, waste management, and digestion & Structure, strength and regeneration of cells, mucus, muscles, bones, and tendons

Mind: Letting go, boundaries, pattern recognition

Spirit: Contentment

Your Common Sense of Smell Traits: Methodical, Disciplined, Gentle, Reserved, Wry sense of humor, Logical, to a fault, Self-controlled, Deep love of nature, Appreciates routines, Physically Strong

Symptoms of too much routine: Spacey, Sighing, Judgmental, Compulsive, Respiratory illness, Coughs, Dehydration, Skin problems, not a rash, Pins & needles feeling, General unhappiness, but not depressed

Activities for calming: Hiking, Skiing–slow cross country, Playing in water, Doing jigsaw puzzles, Flower arranging, Playing a card game built for two, Writing

Meridians involved: Lung, Large Intestine

Season related to your Common Sense of Smell: Autumn

Smell is the most protective sense.

Your sense of smell protects you. Smells alert the mind whenever something is different. Your mind tries to identify the new smell. If you have a pleasant memory of the smell, you relax. If alarming memories are triggered, your stress hormones prepare your body for danger. Smell uses memory wisely.

I moved 23 times in my first 22 years. Each place had its own smell. When we first arrived in a new town, new aromas seemed to be around every corner. Stores and restaurants smelled of different types of food. The air outside smelled of different kinds of trees, plants and even dirt. Clay smells differently than tidewater sandy soil, dusty soil from the Midwest, the forest loam of the Northeast or the deep mossy smell of the Northwest.

After a week, I could no longer noticed any of the aromas that fascinated me the week before. The smells were still there, but my nose had to work much harder to catch a whiff of them. My mind simply didn't care as much.

Your Common Sense of Smell determines what's normal and what's not. Not just smells, but any life situation.

When something new is noticed, your entire mind works on identification. Normal events are judged as important or not important in nanoseconds. Unidentified events have your complete attention until your memory or boundaries declare safety, then lets it go.

If something arises that challenges a boundary or a comfortable belief, it is dealt with as suspicious and dangerous. If your boundaries cannot flex around a new concept, stress hormones are released into your bloodstream because your mind is on alert.

Not being able to wrap your head around a new concept, or loss of faith in an old concept, you are no longer in your comfort zone... and symptoms to begin.

This category is all about absorbing information from your lifestyle and letting go of all that you no longer need. You are supposed to breathe in new ideas and situations, then release all that is unnecessary for your body, mind, and spirit.

Being able to let go of past issues, people, ideas, places or things is how you grow and change throughout your life. Nothing stays the same. People and situations come into your life for a season, a reason, or a lifetime. You don't know which one it is until your life is done.

Dreams, ideas, things, people, pets, life lessons all change your life in some way. When they are no longer part of your life, let them go. Remember the experience fondly, keep the best of what you learned from it and move on. Doing otherwise causes symptoms.

People with either a majority of traits found in this category are thoughtful, loyal, quiet and gentle. Deeply understanding nature and sharing nature with others are part of this category. They respect traditions but have no problem ripping them down and building new ones when convinced it's necessary.

It takes a lot of context and thought before they adapt or form a new boundary. Change is not easy for them. Spontaneity is not their forte.

When researching something new, or having to make an important decision, information is sought from everywhere. They read, take notes, read another perspective and compare them. They are looking for a pattern in the data. The new piece of information has to fit into a bigger picture on the subject.

Foundation beliefs are what you know to be true. Dreams, goals, information, religion, family values and traditions are all important, but can change in a blink.

How open-minded you are is determined by how easy it is for you to change as life does. Flexibility is the determining factor. If you aren't flexible, you feel defensive when a personal truth is threatened or changed. Stress begins as soon as you feel defensive.

Change doesn't harm your belief, it expands and deepens your understanding of that belief or idea. Letting go of obsolete information is important to the learning process. It's okay to become wiser. Protect your ideas, don't cage them.

Being too rigid in your thinking cools your body, mind, and

spirit too much. Cold disease symptoms for not letting go include greed, congestion, detachment, sluggishness, asthma, allergies, frequent colds, bowel disease, delicate skin, shortness of breath, headaches from sadness or disappointment, loss of body hair, clammy hands/feet, sweat easily, varicose veins, enlarged lymph nodes, sneezing or coughing when humid, and clinical depression.

If you have these symptoms frequently, you need to adapt more in your life. Change your routine. Eat new foods. Read something new. Forgive people. Grudges cause symptoms. Learn something new. Spend more time with people. Chinese Medicine teaches that eight hugs a day and three belly laughs are required for good health. This is especially true for these symptoms. If not hugs, try for prolonged eye contact with another person, eight times a day.

Letting go of too much, or being too flexible, means you have no real opinions of your own. Always changing your life, opinion and/or beliefs leads to hot diseases like feeling spacey, sighing, judgmental, compulsive, allergies, chronic cough, frequent dehydration, skin problems, but not a rash, pins and needles feeling in hands and/or feet, general happiness but not really depressed, and insomnia.

All of these hot disease symptoms are alleviated by getting a grip on your life and figuring out who you are…not who you are expected to be by others. Begin learning what is important to you and celebrate your unique point of view. This requires stamina and a clear mind.

- Keeping a schedule of some sort every day is the easiest way to clear your mind.
- Set some fundamental boundaries of meal times and bedtimes.
- Say "no" more often.
- Prioritize your time. Make time for yourself every day.
- Have to do lists per day.
- Include thirty minutes of every day to do something that

makes you smile. No exceptions, this is one part of your schedule that is carved in stone. You need it.

As kids we had to eat well three times a day. We were made to go to bed at the same time every night. It worked. We were so healthy that we were capable of bursting out of bed every morning. All this energy and we would beg to stay up a little longer every night. We had more energy than we could use up in a day. We didn't need to nap.

As children, we had no problem letting go of issues. We would happily skip away from them. We were required to learn something new every day. We had to constantly update our information, not stressing about having to do so. We were healthy. We were inspired to learn, and let go of anything we no longer needed.

Feel that way again. Eat well, sleep regularly, keep an open mind and play outside as often as possible.

TRADITIONAL TIBETAN-MONGOLIAN MEDICINE calls this category Phlegm. Symptoms from this category stem from too much *attachment* to people places or things and *ignorance*. Ignorance in this instance means choosing not to know.

Attachment (to people, places, things or dreams) can be transformed into a mind that is totally clear and unimpeded by greed.

Ignorance (closed mindedness) can be transformed into a necessary awareness of a bigger picture. Learning more about new things allows you to be comfortable with the ever changing nature of life.

Mongolian Om

Traditional Asian medicine believes there are eleven stages of grief...with emphasis on recovering from, and learning from the whole experience.

Asian stages of grief are:
1. Shock
2. Denial
3. Anger
4. Guilt about your involvement
5. Sadness
6. Acceptance
7. Growth
8. Experiencing the pain
9. Forgiveness of yourself and others
10. Taking care of yourself

and the last stage is the most important to your health…

11. Taking active steps to create a new life, celebrating a new start. Use the experience used as an opportunity to grow.

Everyone grieves at their own pace. If the loss was an integral part of who they believed themselves to be, there is a lot of emotional and spiritual reconstruction needed; not patching, reconstruction. This takes time.

Be with them, remind them of their strengths, joys and virtues. They don't need to be alone, but they need quiet. Be supportive of their new choices. Help them get their new life choices started with friendship and humor. Be kind. Every new life adventure should begin that way.

If there are symptoms of ignorance or attachment, help them through it, gently.

Ignorance (closed mindedness) happens when someone chooses to hang onto an original foundation belief no matter what. They do not want it changed in any way. They do not want to know of an updated version. They do not want to be inspired in a new direction.

Being closed minded is a difficult way to live, especially in a culture that changes all the time. This age of information requires a lot of updating. Changing your mind can be done without damaging your integrity. Choose your battles. Some foundations should not changed without a fight, like compassion for family, friends, community and humanity.

Traditional Tibetan–Mongolian Medicine appropriately calls this category of traits and symptoms the Phlegm nyepa. Not letting go enough causes congestion.

Congestion of body, mind, and/or spirit causes symptoms like greed, coughing, breathing problems, physical and mental sluggishness, constipation, general unhappiness, sudden fatigue, dementia, joint pain, and cravings for food, alcohol, drugs, or people.

These symptoms aren't all because of being stubborn about change. Common causes for too much Phlegm traits are oversleeping; too much bitter, sweet, heavy and/or greasy foods; relaxing too much after eating; not enough physical activity; too much of a daily routine; or being in a cold, damp place for too long.

Easy ways to **decrease Phlegm** traits and symptoms are to stay warm, especially your hands, feet and torso; learn something new or update your information about something you used to know; keep moving; and play, remember to try for at least three belly laughs a day, given or received.

Laughing is a wonderful way to inspire yourself to move forward of and through anything that you are having a difficult time letting go.

You cannot overdose on laughter, or warm conversation with friends, during a hard time. It really is what friends and family are for. They are safe places to expand boundaries, grow and change without judgement.

Go for a walk to clear your head of distractions. Go for a walk to inspire your new direction in thought or lifestyle choices. Go for a walk to remember who you are, and what you really like about yourself. Consider all of the things that make you proud of yourself. Consider the good you have done for others and positive differences you have made in the lives of others.

On the way back, think about how you can be even better than you were because you're older/wiser now. Be proud of what you had to learn a lot to accomplish what you did. You had to change, and it was a good thing.

When you are having symptoms of not being able to let go, it's time to change or update something in your life again.

Mayans say, "It isn't easy, it isn't difficult. It is necessary."

Here are some suggestions about how to use your Common Senses to keep your sense of Smell healthy. Use at least one per category, every day, to keep your mind calmed...but flexible.

Touch

- Move.
- Go for a walk.
- Dress warmly.
- Sit in warm, dry places.
- Play a game you love
- Eight hugs/four belly laughs a day, given or received.

Sight

- Photography
- Read, study something new
- Visit an art gallery
- Take a different route to a regular place.
- Wear at least one bright thing every day.
- Birdwatching

Taste

- The most helpful flavor is **pungent** (hot & spicy)
- A little pungent can get your energy, digestion and circulation moving. Its a tonic for your lungs, eases sadness and grief.
- Too much pungent will case your body to sweat. This cools you down instead.

- To reduce effects of too much pungent in your system, use **bitter** (coffee, hops, cacao, citrus peel, dark leafy greens).

Smell

- Best smells to build energy are frankincense, lemon balm, and geranium.
- Write 5 smells from childhood that still make you smile.
- Try something new. Don't buy any aroma you're used to.
- Identify any grudges. Forgive them.
- Forgive yourself of past mistakes. Fix what you can and move on.

Hearing

- No sad lyrics
- No dramatic movies
- Limit conversations with people more depressed than you are.
- Fill your quiet time with soft music that makes you smile.
- Learn to identify birds by their song

General food guidelines for your Common Sense of Smell...

- Nuts are good, in moderation, no more than a handful a day.
- Fish and chicken are good. Cook them with fresh herbs for lightness.
- Prepare nutritious food that is easily digested.
- Most veggies are good. Just make sure they are well-cooked.
- Warm drinks, warm food.
- Fruit is good, just don't keep it in the fridge.
- Fruit should be cooked and spiced in the winter.

- Just say no to canned, processed, fast food, ice cold drinks and sugar in most of its forms. These foods are responsible for your mind and body feeling spacey. Even your mind feels clogged up.
- Just say no to dairy foods, they add more moisture and mucus to your system than you need.
- All spices are good (except salt!).
- Eat several small meals with fruit snacks.

The following food guideline is for helping you to choose your fuel wisely. The Greeks advised to eat all things in moderation. True, if you are healthy. No symptoms, no problem.

The listings include the name of the food; and what it does to your body. The last entry on the line is if you should, or how often you should, eat it.

Alcohol (hard or wine) • Warming; edibility: Rarely
Alcohol (beer) • Warming; edibility: Rarely
Allspice • Warming; edibility: Yes
Almonds (w/o skin) • Neutral; edibility: Yes
Almonds (with skin) • Warming; edibility: Maybe
Almond extract • Warming; edibility: Yes
Almond milk • Neutral; edibility: Rarely
Apples (cooked) • Cooling; edibility: Yes
Apple (raw) • Cooling; edibility: Yes
Apple cider • Warming; edibility: Yes
Applesauce • Cooling; edibility: Yes
Apricots (dried) • Warming; edibility: Yes
Apricots (sweet) • Cooling; edibility: Yes
Artichokes • Warming; edibility: Maybe
Artichoke (Sunchokes) • Cooling; edibility: Yes
Asparagus • Cooling; edibility: Yes
Avocados • Cooling; edibility: Maybe
Bananas • Cooling; edibility: Maybe
Barley • Neutral; edibility: Maybe
Barley malt • Warming; edibility: Rarely

Basil (dried) • Warming; edibility: Yes
Basil (fresh) • Cooling; edibility: Yes
Bay leaf • Warming; edibility: Yes
Beans (black) • Cooling; edibility: No
Beans (garbanzo) • Cooling; edibility: No
Beans, green • Cooling ; edibility: Yes
Beans (kidney) • Cooling; edibility: No
Beans (lima) • Cooling; edibility: No
Beans (mung) • Cooling; edibility: No
Beans (navy) • Cooling; edibility: No
Beans (pinto) • Cooling; edibility: No
Beans (white) • Cooling; edibility: No
Beef • Warming; edibility: No
Beet greens • Cooling; edibility: Maybe
Beets (cooked) • Cooling; edibility: Yes
Berries (sour) • Warming; edibility: Yes
Berries (sweet) • Cooling; edibility: Yes
Black–eyed peas • Cooling; edibility: Maybe
Brazil nuts • Warming; edibility: Maybe
Bread (yeasted) • Warming; edibility: No
Broccoli • Cooling; edibility: Maybe
Brussels sprouts • Cooling; edibility: Yes
Buckwheat • Neutral; edibility: Yes
Butter (salted) • Neutral; edibility: Rarely
Butter (unsalted) • Neutral ; edibility: Maybe
Buttermilk • Warming; edibility: Maybe
Cabbage (cooked) • Neutral; edibility: Yes
Cabbage (red) • Warming; edibility: Yes
Canola (oil) • Neutral; edibility: Yes
Caffeine (any) • Warming; edibility: Rarely
Caraway • Warming; edibility: Yes
Carbonated bev. (any) • Warming; edibility: No
Cardamom • Warming; edibility: Yes
Carob • Neutral; edibility: Yes
Carrots (cooked) • Cooling; edibility: Yes

Carrots (raw) • Warming; edibility: No
Cashews • Cooling; edibility: Maybe
Cauliflower (cooked) • Cooling; edibility: Yes
Cayenne • Warming; edibility: Yes
Celery • Neutral; edibility: Maybe
Cereal (dry) • Warming; edibility: Maybe
Chai (hot, spiced milk) • Warming; edibility: Maybe
Chard • Cooling; edibility: Yes
Cheese (goat) • Warming; edibility: Yes
Cheese (hard) • Warming; edibility: Rarely
Cheese (soft, not aged) • Warming; edibility: Maybe
Cherries (sour) • Warming; edibility: Maybe
Cherries (sweet) • Neutral; edibility: Yes
Chicken (dark) • Warming; edibility: Maybe
Chicken (white) • Warming; edibility: Yes
Chili peppers • Warming; edibility: Maybe
Chilies (green) • Warming; edibility: Yes
Chocolate • Warming; edibility: Rarely
Chutney, mango (spicy) • Warming ; edibility: Maybe
Chutney, mango (sweet) • Cooling; edibility: Rarely
Cilantro • Cooling; edibility: Yes
Cinnamon • Warming; edibility: Yes
Clams • Neutral; edibility: Yes
Cloves • Warming; edibility: Yes
Coconut milk • Warming; edibility: Maybe
Coconut meat • Warming; edibility: Maybe
Coconut oil • Cooling; edibility: Maybe
Coffee (bean-based) • Warming; edibility: Rarely
Coffeelike (grain bev.) • Cooling; edibility: Yes
Coriander • Warming; edibility: Yes
Corn oil • Warming; edibility: Yes
Corn (dried) • Warming; edibility: Yes
Corn (fresh) • Cooling; edibility: Yes
Cottage cheese • Cooling; edibility: No
Couscous • Neutral; edibility: Yes

Cranberries • Warming ; edibility: Rarely
Cucumbers • Cooling; edibility: Rarely
Cumin • Warming; edibility: Yes
Daikon radishes • Warming; edibility: Yes
Dandelion greens • Cooling; edibility: Maybe
Dates • Neutral; edibility: Rarely
Dill leaf • Cooling; edibility: Yes
Dulse • Cooling; edibility: Maybe
Duck • Warming; edibility: No
Egg white • Cooling; edibility: Yes
Egg yolk • Neutral; edibility: Yes
Eggplants • Neutral; edibility: Yes
Fennel bulb • Warming; edibility: Yes
Fennel seed • Warming; edibility: Yes
Figs (dry) • Neutral; edibility: Maybe
Filberts • Warming; edibility: Maybe
Fish (mild) • Cooling; edibility: Yes
Fish (oily) • Warming; edibility: No
Flaxseed • Cooling; edibility: Yes
Flaxseed oil • Cooling; edibility: Rarely
Garlic • Warming; edibility: Yes
Ghee • Cooling; edibility: Yes
Ginger (dried) • Warming; edibility: Yes
Ginger (fresh) • Warming; edibility: Yes
Granola • Warming; edibility: Yes
Grapefruit • Neutral; edibility: No
Grapes (red/purple) • Cooling; edibility: Maybe
Grape leaf • Cooling ; edibility: Yes
Greens (leafy) • Cooling; edibility: Yes
Ham • Warming; edibility: No
Hazelnuts • Warming; edibility: No
Honey (raw) • Neutral ; edibility: Yes
Horseradish • Warming; edibility: Yes
Ice cream • Cooling; edibility: No
Icy cold drinks (any) • Cooling; edibility: No

Juice, aloe vera • Cooling; edibility: Yes
Juice, apple • Cooling; edibility: Maybe
Juice, apricot • Cooling; edibility: Yes
Juice, berry (sour) • Warming; edibility: Yes
Juice, berry (sweet) • Cooling; edibility: Yes
Juice, carrot • Warming; edibility: Yes
Juice, cherry (sour) • Warming; edibility: No
Juice, cherry (sweet) • Warming; edibility: Yes
Juice, cranberry • Warming; edibility: No
Juice, grape • Cooling; edibility: Yes
Juice, grapefruit • Warming; edibility: No
Juice, mango • Cooling; edibility: Yes
Juice, mixed vegetable • Cooling; edibility: No
Juice, orange • Warming; edibility: No
Juice, papaya • Neutral; edibility: No
Juice, pear • Cooling; edibility: Yes
Juice, pineapple • Warming; edibility: Maybe
Juice, prune • Cooling; edibility: Yes
Juice, tomato • Warming; edibility: No
Juice, V–8 • Warming; edibility: No
Kale • Cooling ; edibility: Yes
Ketchup • Warming; edibility: Rarely
Kiwis • Warming; edibility: No
Kohlrabis • Warming; edibility: Yes
Lamb • Warming; edibility: No
Leeks (cooked) • Neutral; edibility: Yes
Lemons • Cooling ; edibility: Maybe
Lemonade • Cooling ; edibility: No
Lentils • Cooling; edibility: Yes
Lettuce • Cooling ; edibility: Yes
Limes • Warming; edibility: Maybe
Macadamia nuts • Warming; edibility: No
Mace • Warming; edibility: Yes
Mangos (ripe) • Cooling ; edibility: Rarely
Maple syrup • Cooling ; edibility: No

Marjoram • Warming; edibility: Yes
Mayonnaise • Warming; edibility: No
Melons • Cooling; edibility: No
Milk (almond) • Cooling; edibility: No
Milk (chocolate) • Warming; edibility: No
Milk (cow) • Neutral; edibility: No
Milk (goat) • Cooling; edibility: Yes
Milk (rice) • Cooling; edibility: No
Milk, soy (cold) • Cooling; edibility: No
Milk, soy (hot, spiced) • Cooling; edibility: Yes
Millet • Warming; edibility: Yes
Miso broth • Warming; edibility: No
Molasses • Warming; edibility: No
Mushrooms • Cooling; edibility: Yes
Mustard (condiment) • Warming; edibility: Maybe
Mustard greens • Warming; edibility: Yes
Mustard seeds • Warming; edibility: Yes
Nutmeg • Warming; edibility: Yes
Oat bran • Cooling; edibility: Yes
Oats (cooked) • Cooling; edibility: No
Oats (dry) • Neutral; edibility: Yes
Okra • Neutral; edibility: Yes
Olive oil • Cooling; edibility: No
Olives (black) • Cooling; edibility: No
Olives (green) • Warming; edibility: No
Onions (cooked) • Cooling; edibility: Yes
Onions (raw) • Warming; edibility: Yes
Orange peel • Warming; edibility: Yes
Oranges • Warming; edibility: No
Oregano • Warming; edibility: Yes
Papayas • Warming; edibility: No
Paprika • Warming Yes; edibility:
Parsley (dried) • Warming; edibility: Yes
Parsley (fresh) • Cooling; edibility: Yes
Parsnips • Cooling; edibility: Yes

Pasta (wheat) • Neutral; edibility: Rarely
Peaches • Warming; edibility: Yes
Peanuts • Warming; edibility: No
Pears • Cooling; edibility: Yes
Peas (cooked) • Neutral; edibility: Yes
Peas (dried) • Warming; edibility: Yes
Pecans • Warming; edibility: Yes
Pepper (black) • Warming; edibility: Yes
Peppers (hot) • Warming; edibility: Yes
Peppers (sweet) • Cooling; edibility: Yes
Peppermint • Warming; edibility: Yes
Perch • Warming; edibility: Yes
Persimmons • Warming; edibility: Yes
Pickles • Warming; edibility: No
Pine nuts • Warming; edibility: No
Pineapples • Warming; edibility: No
Pistachios • Warming; edibility: No
Plum (sweet) • Cooling; edibility: No
Polenta • Warming; edibility: Yes
Pomegranates • Cooling; edibility: Yes
Popcorn (plain) • Warming; edibility: Yes
Poppy seed • Warming; edibility: Yes
Pork • Neutral; edibility: No
Potato (sweet) • Warming; edibility: No
Potato (white) • Neutral; edibility: Yes
Prunes • Neutral; edibility: Yes
Psyllium seeds • Cooling; edibility: No
Pumpkin • Neutral; edibility: No
Pumpkin seeds • Neutral; edibility: Maybe
Quinoa • Neutral; edibility: Maybe
Radishes • Warming; edibility: Yes
Raisins • Neutral; edibility: Yes
Rhubarb • Cooling; edibility: No
Rice (basmati) • Neutral; edibility: Yes
Rice (brown) • Neutral; edibility: No

Rice (white) • Warming; edibility: No
Rice (wild) • Neutral; edibility: Yes
Rice cakes (plain) • Neutral; edibility: Rarely
Rosemary • Warming; edibility: Yes
Rutabagas • Cooling; edibility: Yes
Rye • Warming; edibility: Yes
Safflower oil • Warming; edibility: No
Sage • Warming; edibility: Yes
Salmon • Neutral; edibility: Yes
Salt (in moderation) • Cooling; edibility: No
Sardines • Neutral; edibility: No
Scallions • Warming; edibility: Yes
Seaweed • Cooling; edibility: Maybe
Seitan (wheat meat) • Neutral; edibility: Yes
Sesame oil • Warming; edibility: No
Sesame seed • Neutral; edibility: No
Shellfish (not shrimp) • Neutral; edibility: No
Shrimp • Warming; edibility: Yes
Sour cream • Warming; edibility: No
Soy cheese • Cooling ; edibility: No
Soy flour • Warming; edibility: No
Soy powder • Cooling; edibility: No
Soy sauce • Warming; edibility: Yes
Soy sausages • Warming; edibility: No
Soybeans • Cooling; edibility: No
Spearmint • Cooling; edibility: Yes
Spelt • Neutral; edibility: Yes
Spinach (cooked) • Neutral; edibility: Yes
Spinach (raw) • Warming; edibility: Yes
Sprouts • Cooling; edibility: Yes
Squash (spaghetti) • Cooling; edibility: Yes
Squash (summer) • Cooling; edibility: Yes
Squash (winter) • Warming; edibility: No
Strawberries • Neutral; edibility: Maybe
Sugar, white • Warming; edibility: No

Sunflower oil • Warming; edibility: Yes
Sunflower seed • Warming; edibility: Maybe
Tahini • Warming; edibility: No
Tamari • Warming; edibility: No
Tapioca • Neutral; edibility: Yes
Tarragon • Warming; edibility: Yes
Tea, black • Cooling; edibility: Yes
Tea, iced • Cooling; edibility: No
Thyme • Warming; edibility: Yes
Tofu (cold) • Neutral; edibility: No
Tofu (hot) • Neutral; edibility: Yes
Tomatoes (dried) • Warming; edibility: Yes
Tomatoes (fresh) • Cooling; edibility: No
Tomatoes (sauce) • Warming; edibility: Yes
Turmeric • Warming; edibility: Yes
Tuna (fresh) • Warming; edibility: Yes
Turkey (dark) • Warming; edibility: No
Turkey (white) • Warming; edibility: Yes
Turnips • Neutral; edibility: Yes
Turnip greens • Neutral; edibility: Yes
Vanilla • Neutral; edibility: Yes
Venison • Warming; edibility: Yes
Vinegar (any) • Warming; edibility: No
Walnut oil • Warming; edibility: No
Walnuts • Warming; edibility: No
Watercress • Cooling; edibility: Yes
Watermelons • Cooling; edibility: No
Wheat • Warming; edibility: Yes
Wheat bran • Warming; edibility: Yes
Yogurt (plain) • Cooling; edibility: No
Zucchinis • Cooling; edibility: No

9

YOUR COMMON SENSE OF HEARING

Your common sense of Hearing is primarily about your spirit.

Your innermost thoughts are part of your most calming of senses. This category is about the quietest part of you.

This is where being grounded comes from. Being spiritually grounded is the basis physical stamina and mental serenity.

This category cools the heat of body and mind like water on a hot day.

Ayurveda: In India, this is the most cooling Dosha, called Kapha

Traditional Tibetan–Mongolian Medicine: In Mongolia, this category is the Nyepa called Yellow Water (Lymph)
Traditional Chinese Medicine:
In China, this is The Element of Water

WHAT THIS CATEGORY DOES...
Body: Structure, strength, regeneration of cells, mucus, muscles, bones and tendons
Mind: Having no judgment of others. Everyone is different, but equally human. All having emotional experiences similar to yours.
Spirit: Inspiration
Your Common Sense of Hearing Traits: Peaceful, Tolerant, Traditional, Introspective, Watchful, Thrifty, Philosophical, Curious, Long memories, Slow metabolism
Symptoms of too much quiet: Depression, Sluggishness, Lots of colds /flu, Sinus congestion, Bronchitis/Pneumonia, Water retention, Eye problems, Eating disorders, Skin outbreaks, Isolationism, Judgmental
Activities with cooling action: Walking, Snow shoeing, Wading in shallow water, Reading, Listening to music, Playing solitaire, Research
Meridians involved: Central, Kidney, Bladder
Most calming season: Winter

Hearing is the most calming sense.

Shakespeare said, "To thine own self, be true."
In this culture, we call it being grounded. If you are confident and happy about who you are and your place in the world, you are grounded...in every way.
Being grounded means not much rattles you. Everything is handled as it comes, cheerfully taken in stride. Feeling that way means all five of your senses are grounded at the same time.

Your spirit needs all five categories to be completely grounded and healthy. When your spirit is completely grounded, stress hormones and symptoms disappear.

No physical or mental stress means more stamina, flexibility and strength.

- Being grounded in your sense of Touch means you are confident and comfortable with physical movement and mental focus you use in your life.
- Being grounded in your sense of Sight means you truly enjoy your life. You feel playfully committed to a life full of diverse interests and community.
- Being grounded in your sense of Taste means you calmly adapting to changes and have compassionate emotional control in your life.
- Being grounded in your sense of Smell means your life is kept in order with healthy boundaries, and you can change them when necessary.
- Being grounded in your sense of Hearing means you are comfortable listening to your inner self. Following your conscience and doing the right thing are part your quiet strength...spirit.

If you have tried everything and a symptom just won't go away, chances are pretty good that it's a spiritual issue. Symptoms are clues. They will help identify what part of your spirit needs grounding.

Find your symptoms in the following listing. Then read what your life might need beyond foods and mental exercises.

Find out what your spirit still needs to be added to your lifestyle. You don't need to accomplish everything in the list. Your intuition will tell you which ones are the right ones to work on.

Your spirit will tell you.

Your Common Sense of Touch needs grounding if you are... Anxious, restless, insomnia, talking too much or more rapidly than normal, nervous laughter, easily stimulated, profuse/frequent perspiration (your body trying to cool the body as fast as possible), flushed face, red eyes, irregular or rapid heartbeat, painful urination, strong but erratic pulse, overheats easily, tooth pain, mouth infections, mouth sores, tongue sores, cold sores, blistered lips, dry painful eczema, dizziness, headache, and feeling hot when it isn't.

*Spiritual issues to work on...*Optimism, feeling safe, daily tasks are effortless, joy of life, comfortable in your own skin, graceful, feelings flow freely, enthusiasm, creativity, enjoy intimacy, a passion for life, able to bounce back from stress, spontaneity

Your Common Sense of Sight needs grounding if you are... Arrogant, controlling, angry disposition, workaholic, pain just below the ribs, hernias, migraines, high blood pressure, oily skin/hair, boils, cramps of long muscles, hands, feet; vertigo, ringing in ears, constipation with cramps/spasms, sciatica, heartburn, difficult swallowing, eye/ear pain, shingles, awkward or accident-prone, hard thick nails, breast pain, tendon injuries, jaundice, quick to hunger, feeling hot when it isn't, fever, hot flashes

*Spiritual issues to work on...*Feelings flow freely, enthusiasm, creativity, enjoy intimacy, a passion for life, able to bounce back from stress, spontaneity, charisma, healthy self–esteem, appreciates uniqueness in others, complete control of your emotions and thoughts, decisive, committed, radiate joy

Your Common Sense of Taste needs grounding if you are... Overworking– especially studying or intellectual work, canker sores, conjunctivitis, excess appetite, water retention, swollen prostate, tender gums, PMS (with lethargy, aching, hunger and swelling), sores on scalp, heavy head and eyes, sticky eyelids, sticky mucus in nose and throat, sticky saliva and perspiration, swollen, sensitive spleen or liver, greed, constipation, talking more than normal, dizziness, loss of strength, sighing, restlessness, obsessive/negative thoughts

*Spiritual issues to work on...*Charisma, healthy self–esteem, appreciates uniqueness in others, complete control of your emotions and thoughts, decisive, committed, radiate joy, patient, compassionate, empathy, unconditional love, trusting, accepting, forgiveness, okay spending time alone, no problem expressing hopes and dreams, confident, honest, wise, strong sense of freedom, discrete, independent, feeling heard

Your Common Sense of Smell needs grounding if are... Overly critical, trouble letting go, rashes, eczema and problems with sweating, dry cough with tight chest, sinus headache, nasal polyps, dry hair, dry skin, dry mucous membranes, no perspiration, stiff spine/neck and posture, constipation with tense intestine, dry, cracked nails and lips, scanty urine, dry nose–throat, tight muscles, paranoia, over involvement to the point of isolating friends and/or family, fearful of deadlines and/or making a mistake, writing obsessively detailed to-do lists

*Spiritual issues to work on...*No problem expressing hopes and dreams, confident, honest, wise, strong sense of freedom, discrete, independent, intuitive, focused, concentration, feels in control of life, comfortable in your own skin, no need for others in order to feel happy and whole, patterns are easily seen

Your Common Sense of Hearing needs grounding if you have... Ringing in ears, hot flashes, oversensitive vision and/or hearing, headaches above eyes, lack of sweat and urine, hardening of blood vessels and cartilage, rigidity of joints and muscles, kidney and bladder stones, Bony tumors, weak digestion, shrinking gums, needs little sleep, hypertension, skin outbreaks (sores), eye problems, bone disorders, diarrhea, muscle atrophy, sweating, cynical/pessimistic outlook, memory loss

*Spiritual issues to work on...*Honoring your intuition, focus, easy concentration, feeling in control of life, comfortable in your own skin, no need for others in order to feel happy and whole, patterns are easily seen, respectful of many perspectives for every situations, treats ALL people equally, selfless, no judgment felt or given, trusting and trustworthy, inspired, joyful, unconditionally compassionate.

∽

TRADITIONAL TIBETAN-MONGOLIAN MEDICINE *calls this category Yellow Water (lymph).* Symptoms in this category come from what they call ignorance. It isn't about intellect. This is about a willingness to see things differently than you have before. Being stubborn or having a grudge are symptoms.

Ignorance (closed mindedness) can be transformed into a necessary awareness of a bigger picture. Learning more about new things allows you to be comfortable with the ever changing nature of life.

The primary function of the Lymph Nyepa is about structure in your Body, Mind and Spirit

Mongolian Om

Body: regeneration of your cells, mucus, muscles, bones and tendons

Mind: emotion management, **letting go,** knowing which problems are your life lessons in progress and when they are for intended for someone else

Spirit: walking the talk of being joyfully present, compassionate and tolerant. Nobody is better or worse than you are. We all have more to learn.

This is the part of you that constantly thinks new thoughts. This is where philosophy, inventions, and imagination come from.

Spirit never sleeps. It keeps inspiring through the night in your dreams. Let me sleep on it. Everyone has had the feeling of waking up with a solution. Spirit works when your body and mind are quiet.

This wellspring of fresh ways to new ways of looking at life needs to keep moving. If your inner voice gets too quiet, or isn't heard, cold disease symptoms of congestion begin.

There are many reasons for your Common Sense of Hearing to become congested. Symptoms from this category like depression, bronchitis, pneumonia, or hormonal trouble can happen out of the blue.

Sometimes its the weather. Cold, rainy, dark, windy will cause you to catch cold or become depressed. Cold disease symptoms. Other causes are from sitting too long in a damp place, not dressing warmly enough, an allergy to dust/wool or liver trauma.

When you have a cold disease symptom everything slows down. Your body doesn't want to move. Your mind is foggy and your spirit is uninspired. You just don't want to do anything but lay there.

All cold disease symptoms are alleviated with warmth. Warm your body with all five of your senses. Warm your mind with becoming enthusiastic about something new or finishing a project. Warm your spirit with being with other people, helping someone else.

My very logical father told me recently that the most important thing he had learned in life was to remain happily curious about everything. The rest is easy.

Asian medicine agrees with him.

Remaining happily curious about what life has to offer next is the real fountain of youth. It keeps your spirit warm and constantly inspired.

Being happy and grounded in your life creates stamina used by body, mind and spirit.

Spiritual stamina is the basis of wellness.

HERE ARE some suggestions about how to use your Common Senses as a team to maintain a calming lifestyle without becoming too calm. There is such a thing as too much meditation or having too much calmness in your life.

The trick about effective meditation, or any kind of resting, is knowing when to get up and use the stamina you just got from your break.

Touch

- Stay dry and warm
- Eight hugs, or touches, and/or prolonged period of eye contact a day

- Walk, especially therapeutic after eating
- Physical activity of any kind, keep moving
- Sunbathe, or bask in a warm window when feeling low on energy
- Clean up an area of clutter in your your mind, spirit or surroundings
- Volunteer to spend time with people less fortunate than yourself

Sight

- Make eye contact with everyone in your day
- Surround yourself with at least one of every color, in every room: Red, Orange, Yellow, Emerald green, Sky blue, Indigo blue and Violet
- Paint, organize photographs, do collages of things you'd like to do
- Go on photography walks
- Go birdwatching

Taste

- Salty (Salt, soy sauce, seaweeds) slows emotional management. A little salty can calm you down by slowing circulation of qi, reduces inflammation and helps rid the body of toxins.
- Too much salt weakens bones and muscle tone, incontinence and being emotionally overwhelmed.
- Pungent (hot and spicy) gets you moving, but don't overdo it.
- Use Sweet (sugars, grains, fruit) to reduce the harmful effects of too much pungent in your system but don't overdo it...too much sugar creates too much mucus.

Scent

- Aromatherapy teaches that the best smells to clear negative emotions are lemon, orange, lavender, frankincense, geranium, pine, rose and cedar

Hearing

- No sad sounding lyrics, instrumentals, conversations, movies, timelines, tweets or texts
- No dramatic conversations unless it is with an uplifting person
- Silence is golden, to a point
- Listen to your quietest self with respect for whatever you find there. Intuition and inspiration are from this category, believe in your own wisdom.

General food guidelines for your Common Sense of Hearing...

- No sweet or sour fruit
- Eat astringent fruit instead
- Just say no to sweet and juicy vegetables
- Eat pungent and bitter vegetables instead
- Just say no to nuts.
- Just say no to dairy foods, they add more moisture to your system than you need.
- Just say no to fatty or oil foods, eat light dry foods instead.
- All spices are good (except salt)!
- If you feel too warm, cool off. If you feel too cool, warm up.

The following food guideline is for helping you to choose your fuel wisely. The Greeks advised to eat all things in moderation. True, if you are healthy. No symptoms, no problem.

The listings include the name of the food; and what it does to your body. The last entry on the line is if you should, or how often you should, eat it.

ALCOHOL (HARD OR WINE) • Warming; edibility: No
Alcohol (beer) • Warming; edibility: Yes
Allspice • Warming; edibility: Yes
Almonds • Warming; edibility: No
Almonds (w/o skin) • Neutral; edibility: Rarely
Almonds (with skin) • Warming; edibility: No
Almond extract • Warming; edibility: Yes
Almonds milk • Neutral; edibility: No
Amaranth • Neutral; edibility: Maybe
Anise • Warming; edibility: Yes
Apples (cooked) • Cooling; edibility: Yes
Apples (raw) • Cooling; edibility: Yes
Apple cider • Warming; edibility: Yes
Applesauce • Cooling; edibility: Yes
Apricots (dried) • Warming; edibility: Yes
Apricots (sour) • Neutral; edibility: Yes
Apricots (sweet) • Cooling; edibility: Yes
Artichokes • Warming; edibility: Yes
Artichoke (Sunchokes) • Cooling Yes
Asparagus • Cooling; edibility: Yes
Avocados • Cooling; edibility: No
Bananas • Cooling ; edibility: No
Barley • Neutral; edibility: Yes
Barley malt • Warming; edibility: No
Basil (dried) • Warming; edibility: Yes
Basil (fresh) • Cooling; edibility: Yes
Bay leaf • Warming; edibility: Yes
Beans (adzuki) • Cooling; edibility: Yes
Beans (black) • Cooling; edibility: Yes
Beans (garbanzo) • Cooling; edibility: Yes
Beans (green/string) • Cooling; edibility: Yes

Beans (kidney) • Cooling; edibility: No
Beans (lima) • Cooling; edibility: Yes
Beans (mung) • Cooling; edibility: Yes
Beans (navy) • Cooling; edibility: Yes
Beans (pinto) • Cooling; edibility: Yes
Beans (white) • Cooling; edibility: Yes
Beef • Warming; edibility: No
Beet greens • Cooling; edibility: Yes
Beets (cooked) • Cooling; edibility: Yes
Berries (sour) • Warming; edibility: Yes
Berries (sweet) • Cooling; edibility: Yes
Black-eyed peas • Cooling; edibility: Yes
Brazil nuts • Warming; edibility: No
Bread (yeasted) • Warming; edibility: No
Broccoli • Cooling; edibility: No
Brussels sprouts • Cooling; edibility: Yes
Buckwheat • Neutral Yes
Burdock root • Warming No
Butter (salted) • Neutral No
Butter (unsalted) • Neutral Yes
Buttermilk • Warming Maybe
Cabbages (cooked) • Neutral Yes
Cabbages (red) • Warming Yes
Canola (oil) • Neutral Yes
Caffeine (any) • Warming Maybe
Caraway • Warming; edibility: Yes
Carbonated bev. (any) • Warming; edibility: No
Cardamom • Warming; edibility: Yes
Carob • Neutral; edibility: Yes
Carrots (cooked) • Cooling; edibility: Yes
Carrots (raw) • Warming; edibility: Yes
Cashews • Cooling; edibility: No
Cauliflower (cooked) • Cooling; edibility: Yes
Cayenne • Warming; edibility: Yes
Celery • Neutral; edibility: Yes

Cereal (dry) • Warming; edibility: Yes
Chai (hot, spiced milk) • Warming; edibility: Maybe
Chard • Cooling; edibility: Yes
Cheese (goat) • Warming; edibility: Yes
Cheese (hard) • Warming; edibility: No
Cheese (soft, not aged) • Warming; edibility: No
Cherries (sour) • Warming; edibility: Yes
Cherries (sweet) • Neutral; edibility: Yes
Chicken (dark) • Warming; edibility: No
Chicken (white) • Warming; edibility: Yes
Chili peppers • Warming; edibility: Yes
Chilies (green) • Warming; edibility: Yes
Chocolate • Warming; edibility: Maybe
Chutney, (spicy) • Warming; edibility: Yes
Chutney, (sweet) • Cooling; edibility: No
Cilantro • Cooling; edibility: Yes
Cinnamon • Warming; edibility: Yes
Clams • Neutral; edibility: Yes
Coconuts • Warming; edibility: No
Coffee (bean) • Warming; edibility: Maybe
Coriander leaves • Cooling; edibility: Yes
Coriander seeds • Warming; edibility: Yes
Corn oil • Warming; edibility: Yes
Corn (dried) • Warming; edibility: Yes
Corn (fresh) • Cooling; edibility: Yes
Cottage cheese • Cooling; edibility: No
Couscous • Neutral; edibility:Yes
Cranberries • Warming; edibility: Yes
Cucumbers • Cooling; edibility: No
Cumin • Warming; edibility: Yes
Daikon radishes • Warming; edibility: Yes
Dandelion greens • Cooling; edibility: Yes
Dates • Neutral; edibility: No
Dill (leaf) • Cooling; edibility: Yes
Dulse • Cooling; edibility: Yes

Duck • Warming; edibility: No
Egg white • Cooling; edibility: Yes
Egg yolk • Neutral; edibility: Yes
Eggplants • Neutral; edibility: Yes
Fennel bulb • Warming; edibility: Yes
Fennel seed • Warming; edibility: Yes
Figs (dry) • Neutral; edibility: Maybe
Filberts • Warming; edibility: No
Fish (mild) • Cooling; edibility: Yes
Fish (oily) • Warming; edibility: Yes
Flaxseed • Cooling; edibility: Yes
Flaxseed oil • Cooling; edibility: Yes
Fruit juice concentrates • Cooling; edibility: Yes
Garlic • Warming; edibility: Maybe
Ghee • Cooling; edibility: Yes
Ginger (dried) • Warming; edibility: Maybe
Ginger (fresh) • Warming; edibility: Maybe
Granola • Warming; edibility: Maybe
Grapefruit • Neutral; edibility: No
Grapes (unripe) • Warming; edibility: Yes
Grapes (red/purple) • Cooling; edibility: Yes
Grape leaf • Cooling; edibility: Yes
Greens (leafy) • Cooling; edibility: Yes
Ham • Warming; edibility: Rarely
Hazelnuts • Warming; edibility: Maybe
Honey (raw) • Neutral; edibility: Yes
Horseradish • Warming; edibility: Maybe
Ice cream • Cooling; edibility: Rarely
Icy cold drinks (any) • Cooling; edibility: No
Juice, apple • Cooling; edibility: Yes
Juice, apricot • Cooling; edibility: Yes
Juice, berry (sour) • Warming; edibility: Yes
Juice, berry (sweet) • Cooling; edibility: Yes
Juice, carrot • Warming; edibility: Yes
Juice, cherry (sour) • Warming; edibility: Maybe

Juice, cherry (sweet) • Warming; edibility: Yes
Juice, cranberry • Warming; edibility: Maybe
Juice, grape • Cooling; edibility: Yes
Juice, grapefruit • Warming; edibility: No
Juice, mango • Cooling; edibility: Yes
Juice, mixed vegetable • Cooling; edibility: Rarely
Juice, orange • Warming; edibility: No
Juice, papaya • Neutral; edibility: Rarely
Juice, pear • Cooling; edibility: Yes
Juice, pineapple • Warming; edibility: Yes
Juice, prune • Cooling; edibility: Yes
Juice, tomato • Warming; edibility: Maybe
Juice, V–8 • Warming; edibility: Maybe
Kale • Cooling; edibility: Yes
Ketchup • Warming; edibility: Rarely
Kiwis • Warming; edibility: No
Kohlrabis • Warming; edibility: Yes
Lamb • Warming; edibility: No
Leeks (cooked) • Neutral; edibility: Yes
Lemons • Cooling; edibility: Maybe
Lemonade • Cooling; edibility: No
Lentils • Cooling; edibility: Yes
Lettuce • Cooling; edibility: Maybe
Limes • Warming; edibility: Maybe
Macadamia nuts • Warming ; edibility: Maybe
Mace • Warming; edibility: • Yes
Mango (ripe) • Cooling; edibility: Rarely
Maple syrup • Cooling; edibility: Maybe
Marjoram • Warming; edibility: Yes
Mayonnaise • Warming; edibility: No
Melons • Cooling; edibility: Maybe
Milk (almond) • Cooling; edibility: Maybe
Milk (chocolate) • Warming; edibility: No
Milk (cow) • Neutral; edibility: No
Milk (goat) • Cooling; edibility: Yes

Milk (rice) • Cooling; edibility: Maybe
Milk, soy • Cooling; edibility: Maybe
Millet • Warming; edibility: Yes
Miso • Warming; edibility: Maybe
Molasses • Warming; edibility: Rarely
Mushrooms • Cooling; edibility: Yes
Mustard (condiment) • Warming; edibility: Yes
Mustard greens • Warming; edibility: Yes
Mustard seeds • Warming; edibility: Yes
Nutmeg • Warming; edibility: Yes
Oat bran • Cooling; edibility: Yes
Oats (cooked) • Cooling; edibility: Maybe
Oats (dry) • Neutral; edibility: Yes
Okra • Neutral; edibility: Yes
Olive oil • Cooling; edibility: Yes
Olives (black) • Cooling; edibility: Maybe
Olives (green) • Warming; edibility: Rarely
Onions (cooked) • Cooling; edibility: Yes
Onions (raw) • Warming; edibility: No
Orange peel • Warming; edibility: Yes
Oranges • Warming; edibility: Maybe
Oregano • Warming; edibility: Yes
Papayas • Warming; edibility: Rarely
Parsley (dried) • Warming; edibility: Yes
Parsley (fresh) • Cooling; edibility: Yes
Parsnips • Cooling; edibility: Maybe
Pasta (wheat) • Neutral; edibility: Maybe
Peaches • Warming; edibility: Yes
Peanuts • Warming; edibility: Maybe
Pears • Cooling; edibility: Yes
Peas (dried) • Warming; edibility: Yes
Pecans • Warming; edibility: Maybe
Pepper (black) • Warming; edibility: Yes
Peppers (hot) • Warming; edibility: Yes
Peppers (sweet) • Cooling; edibility: Yes

Peppermint • Warming; edibility: Yes
Perch • Warming; edibility: Yes
Pickles • Warming; edibility: No
Pine nuts • Warming; edibility: Maybe
Pineapples • Warming; edibility: Rarely
Pistachios • Warming; edibility: Maybe
Plums (sweet) • Cooling; edibility: Maybe
Polenta • Warming; edibility: Yes
Pomegranates • Cooling; edibility: Yes
Popcorn (plain) • Warming; edibility: Yes
Poppy seed • Warming; edibility: Yes
Pork • Neutral; edibility: No
Potato (sweet/yams) • Warming; edibility: Maybe
Potato (white) • Neutral; edibility: Yes
Prunes • Neutral; edibility: Yes
Psyllium seeds • Cooling; edibility: No
Pumpkins • Neutral; edibility: No
Pumpkin seeds • Neutral; edibility: Maybe
Quinoa • Neutral; edibility: Maybe
Radishes • Warming; edibility: Yes
Raisins • Neutral; edibility: Yes
Rhubarb • Cooling; edibility: Rarely
Rice (basmati) • Neutral; edibility: Yes
Rice (brown) • Neutral; edibility: Rarely
Rice (white) • Warming; edibility: Rarely
Rice (wild) • Neutral; edibility: Yes
Rice cakes (plain) • Neutral ; edibility: Rarely
Rosemary • Warming; edibility: Yes
Rutabagas • Cooling; edibility: Yes
Rye • Warming; edibility: Yes
Safflower Oil • Warming; edibility: No
Sage • Warming; edibility: Yes
Salmon • Neutral; edibility: Yes
Salt • Cooling; edibility: Rarely
Sardines • Neutral ; edibility: Yes

Scallions • Warming; edibility: Yes
Seaweed • Cooling; edibility: Maybe
Seitan (wheat meat) • Neutral; edibility: Yes
Sesame oil • Warming; edibility: Maybe
Sesame seed • Neutral; edibility: Maybe
Shellfish • Neutral; edibility: Yes
Shrimp • Warming; edibility: Yes
Sour cream • Warming; edibility: No
Soy cheese • Cooling; edibility: Rarely
Soy flour • Warming; edibility: Rarely
Soy powder • Cooling; edibility: Rarely
Soy sauce • Warming; edibility: Yes
Soy sausages • Warming; edibility: Rarely
Soybeans • Cooling; edibility: Maybe
Spearmint • Cooling; edibility: Yes
Spelt • Neutral; edibility: Yes
Spinach (cooked) • Neutral; edibility: Yes
Spinach (raw) • Warming; edibility: Maybe
Sprouts • Cooling; edibility: Maybe
Squash (spaghetti) • Cooling; edibility: Yes
Squash (summer) • Cooling; edibility: Yes
Squash (winter) • Warming; edibility: Maybe
Star Anise • Warming; edibility: Yes
Strawberries • Neutral; edibility: Maybe
Sugar, white • Warming; edibility: No
Sunflower oil • Warming; edibility: Yes
Sunflower seed • Warming; edibility: Maybe
Tahini • Warming; edibility: Maybe
Tamari • Warming; edibility: Rarely
Tapioca • Neutral; edibility: Yes
Tarragon • Warming; edibility: Yes
Tea, black • Cooling ; edibility: Yes
Tea, iced Cooling; edibility: No
Thyme • Warming; edibility: Yes
Tofu (cold) • Neutral; edibility: Maybe

Tofu (hot) • Neutral; edibility: Yes
Tomatoes (dried) • Warming; edibility: Yes
Tomatoes (fresh) • Cooling; edibility: Rarely
Tomatoes (sauce) • Warming; edibility: Yes
Tuna • Warming; edibility: Yes
Turkey (dark) • Warming; edibility: Rarely
Turkey (white) • Warming; edibility: Yes
Turnips • Neutral; edibility: Yes
Turnip greens • Neutral; edibility: Yes
Vanilla • Neutral; edibility: Yes
Venison • Warming; edibility: Maybe
Vinegar (any) • Warming; edibility: No
Walnuts • Warming; edibility: Maybe
Watercress • Cooling; edibility: Yes
Watermelons • Cooling; edibility: Maybe
Wheat • Warming; edibility: Yes
Wheat bran • Warming; edibility: Yes
Wintergreen • Cooling; edibility: Yes
Yogurt (plain) • Cooling; edibility: No
Zucchini • Cooling; edibility: No

10

FIVE KINDS OF SYMPTOMS

All symptoms are clues. Which Common Sense category it belongs to is a big clue. It determines whether you are dealing with a hot or cold disease.

The next few pages are a listing of common symptoms that are fairly easily remedied with self-care. Circle all the symptoms that you either currently have, or have had many times.

Is there a pattern? Are several of the symptoms in the same Common Sense? Are the same meridians presenting different symptoms?

~

IF YOU HAVE BEEN SUFFERING from several symptoms within a particular Common Sense, read its chapter for insights and suggested remedies. Chances are pretty good that eating from the food list for that category will either clear up most of your problem. If it doesn't, at least your immune system will be a bigger help in fixing it.

Which meridian involved is also a big clue. The Chinese meridians are wonderful for pinpointing remedies for a symptom. Read more about them in chapters 18 and 19.

If most of your symptoms are from a particular meridian, you're in luck. Each meridian has its own food tonics list that can be found in most supermarkets. Add those suggested foods to the Common Sense list you are using. Eat at least one of the suggested tonic foods with every meal for a week.

If your symptoms aren't better after a week of eating well, or as soon as it seems to be getting worse, contact your health care provider. Never try to self-heal something you think might be beyond your scope. If intuition says call someone, do it.

Knowing which meridian is responsible for your symptom, and what you've tried so far, is invaluable time-saving information for your Naturopath or Acupuncturist. Your Western care doctor will also benefit from hearing the progression of your symptom and what you did for it.

1. Abdominal distention • Sense: Smell; meridian: Large Intestine/Spleen
2. Abdominal pain • Hearing; meridians: Central, Large Intestine, Spleen
3. Abdominal rumbling • Sense: Taste; meridian: Stomach
4. Aggression • Sense: Sight; meridian: Liver
5. Appetite loss • Sense: Taste; meridian: Spleen
6. Arm, inner–pain/weakness • Sense: Touch; meridian: Heart
7. Armpit pain or swelling • Sense: Touch; meridian: Pericardium
8. Arrogance • Sense: Sight; meridian: Liver
9. Asthma • Sense: Smell; meridian: Lung
10. Back–weak low back • Sense: Hearing; meridian: Bladder
11. Bladder–sore Hearing; meridian: Bladder
12. Blood flow–irregular • Sense: Touch; meridian: Heart
13. Blood vessel disorders • Sense: Touch; meridian: Heart
14. Breath–disorders • Sense: Smell; meridian: Lung
15. Breath–shortness • Sense: Smell; meridian: Lung

16. Bronchitis • Sense: Smell; meridian: Lung
17. Bunions • Sense: Taste; meridian: Spleen
18. Bursitis • Sense: Smell; meridian: Large Intestine
19. Cardiac disorders • Sense: Touch; meridian: Heart
20. Carpal tunnel • Sense: Smell; meridian: Lung
21. Carpal tunnel • Sense: Touch; meridian: Pericardium
22. Cervical pain • Sense: Touch; meridian: Small Intestine
23. Chest pains • Sense: Touch; meridian: Heart
24. Chest tightness • Sense: Smell; meridian: Lung
25. Chest tightness • Sense: Taste; meridian: Stomach
26. Complexion–poor • Sense: Touch; meridian: Heart
27. Constipation • Sense: Touch; meridian: Heart
28. Coughing • Sense: Hearing; meridian: Kidney
29. Coughing • Sense: Smell; meridian: Lung
30. Cramps–menstrual • Sense: Touch; meridian: Pericardium
31. Delirium • Sense: Touch; meridian: Heart
32. Depression • Sense: Touch; meridian: Pericardium
33. Diaphragm tightness • Sense: Sight; meridian: Liver
34. Digestive pain • Sense: Taste; meridian: Stomach
35. Digestive trouble • Sense: Taste; meridian: Stomach
36. Dreaming–excessive • Sense: Touch; meridian: Heart
37. Eczema • Sense: Hearing; meridian: Central
38. Elbow–spasm • Sense: Touch; meridian: Pericardium
39. Elbow–tennis • Sense: Smell; meridian: Large Intestine
40. Elbow–tennis • Sense: Smell; meridian: Lung
41. Emphysema • Sense: Smell; meridian: Lung
42. Eye pain • Sense: Touch; meridian: Governing Vessel
43. Eyes –red • Sense: Sight; meridian: Liver
44. Eyes –red • Sense: Touch; meridian: Heart
45. Eyesight–dim • Sense: Touch; meridian: Small Intestine
46. Fatigue–limbs • Sense: Taste; meridian: Spleen
47. Feet–painful soles • Sense: Hearing; meridian: Kidney
48. Finger (index) stiffness • Sense: Smell; meridian: Large Intestine

49. Flatulence • Sense: Sight; meridian: Gall Bladder
50. Forearm-pain • Sense: Smell; meridian: Large Intestine
51. Forearm-spasm • Sense: Touch; meridian: Pericardium
52. Forearm-stiff • Sense: Smell; meridian: Lung
53. Frustration • Sense: Sight; meridian: Liver
54. Gastritis • Sense: Taste; meridian: Stomach
55. Genital pain and swelling • Sense: Hearing; meridian: Central
56. Glands-swollen • Sense: Touch; meridian: Heart
57. Glaucoma • Sense: Sight; meridian: Liver
58. Hand pain • Sense: Smell; meridian: Large Intestine
59. Hand weakness • Sense: Smell; meridian: Large Intestine
60. Head colds • Sense: Hearing; meridian: Bladder
61. Headache-side of head • Sense: Taste; meridian: Stomach
62. Headaches • Sense: Sight; meridian: Gall Bladder
63. Hearing loss • Sense: Touch; meridian: Small Intestine
64. Heart disorders due to stress • Sense: Touch; meridian: Pericardium
65. Heart palpitations • Sense: Touch; meridian: Heart
66. Heartbeat-rapid • Sense: Touch; meridian: Pericardium
67. Hemorrhoids • Sense: Hearing; meridian: Bladder
68. Hemorrhoids • Sense: Touch; meridian: Governing
69. Hernias • Sense: Sight; meridian: Liver
70. Hernias • Sense: Touch; meridian: Governing
71. Hip pain or arthritis • Sense: Sight; meridian: Gall Bladder
72. Hip stiffness • Sense: Hearing; meridian: Bladder
73. Hot flashes • Sense: Hearing; meridian: Central
74. Hot flashes Touch; meridian: • Sense: Pericardium
75. Hunger-frequent • Sense: Taste; meridian: Stomach
76. Impatience • Sense: Sight; meridian: Liver
77. Impotent • Sense: Touch; meridian: Governing
78. Incontinence • Sense: Touch; meridian: Governing
79. Indigestion • Sense: Sight; meridian: Gall Bladder
80. Insomnia • Sense: Touch; meridian: Heart

81. Intestinal disorders • Sense: Smell; meridian: Large Intestine
82. Intestinal rumbling • Sense: Smell; meridian: Large Intestine
83. Joint pain–generalized • Sense: Sight; meridian: Gall Bladder
84. Kidney–ache • Sense: Hearing; meridian: Kidney
85. Kidney–pain • Sense: Hearing; meridian: Bladder
86. Kidney–sore • Sense: Hearing; meridian: Bladder
87. Knee stiffness • Sense: Hearing; meridian: Bladder
88. Lung congestion • Sense: Hearing; meridian: Kidney
89. Lung disorders • Sense: Smell; meridian: Large Intestine
90. Menstrual disorders • Sense: Hearing; meridian: Central
91. Mouth–bitter taste • Sense: Sight; meridian: Gall Bladder
92. Nausea • Sense: Taste; meridian: Spleen
93. Neck–stiff • Sense: Smell; meridian: Large Intestine
94. Neck–stiff • Sense: Taste; meridian: Stomach
95. Neck–stiff • Sense: Touch; meridian: Governing
96. Nose disorders • Sense: Smell; meridian: Large Intestine
97. Nosebleed • Sense: Hearing; meridian: Bladder
98. Palm–hot • Sense: Touch; meridian: Pericardium
99. Palm pain • Sense: Touch; meridian: Heart
100. Pelvic complaints • Sense: Sight; meridian: Liver
101. Pelvic complaints • Sense: Taste; meridian: Spleen
102. Pelvic congestion • Sense: Taste; meridian: Stomach
103. Pelvic pain • Sense: Taste; meridian: Stomach
104. Pelvic pain and swelling • Sense: Hearing; meridian: Central
105. Pericarditis • Sense: Touch; meridian: Pericardium
106. Prostate trouble • Sense: Touch; meridian: Pericardium
107. Pulse–irregular • Sense: Touch; meridian: Heart
108. Rib pain or tightness • Sense: Sight; meridian: Liver
109. Rib tightness • Sense: Sight; meridian: Gall Bladder
110. Ribcage pain (below right) • Sense: Sight; meridian: Gall Bladder

111. Sexual difficulties • Sense: Touch; meridian: Pericardium
112. Shoulder pain • Sense: Smell; meridian: Large Intestine
113. Shoulder pain • Sense: Smell; meridian: Lung
114. Shoulder pain • Sense: Touch; meridian: Small Intestine
115. Sinus-clogged • Sense: Hearing; meridian: Bladder
116. Sinus-pain • Sense: Taste; meridian: Stomach
117. Sinusitis • Sense: Smell; meridian: Large Intestine
118. Speech-slurred • Sense: Touch; meridian: Heart
119. Spinal pain • Sense: Hearing; meridian: Kidney
120. Spinal pain and stiffness • Sense: Hearing; meridian: Bladder
121. Spinal pain or spasm • Sense: Touch; meridian: Governing
122. Sterility • Sense: Touch; meridian: Governing
123. Stiffness • Sense: Touch; meridian: Small Intestine
124. Stomach complaints • Sense: Taste; meridian: Stomach
125. Stomach pain (in pit) • Sense: Hearing; meridian: Central
126. Stubbornness • Sense: Sight; meridian: Liver
127. Sweating-spontaneous • Sense: Smell; meridian: Lung
128. Swelling • Sense: Touch; meridian: Small Intestine
129. Talking fast • Sense: Touch; meridian: Heart
130. Teeth disorders Smell; meridian: Large Intestine
131. Thigh pain • Sense: Taste; meridian: Stomach
132. Thirst • Sense: Touch; meridian: Heart
133. Throat-plum pit feeling • Sense: Sight; meridian: Liver
134. Throat-sore • Sense: Touch; meridian: Small Intestine
135. Throat-swollen • Sense: Taste; meridian: Stomach
136. Throat disorders • Sense: Smell; meridian: Lung
137. Throat disorders • Sense: Touch; meridian: Heart
138. Throat obstruction • Sense: Hearing; meridian: Central
139. Throat pain • Sense: Sight; meridian: Gall Bladder
140. TMJ • Sense: Touch; meridian: Small Intestine
141. Tongue-dry • Sense: Hearing; meridian: Kidney
142. Tongue-hot • Sense: Hearing; meridian: Kidney
143. Tongue-Pale or purple • Sense: Touch; meridian: Heart

144. Tongue–stiffness at base • Sense: Taste; meridian: Spleen
145. Tongue–ulcers • Sense: Touch; meridian: Heart
146. Trachea disorders • Sense: Smell; meridian: Lung
147. Trapeziums pain • Sense: Smell; meridian: Large Intestine
148. Trapeziums stiffness • Sense: Sight; meridian: Gall Bladder
149. Ulnar neuropathy • Sense: Touch; meridian: Small Intestine
150. Vocal cord disorders • Sense: Smell; meridian: Lung
151. Voice difficulties • Sense: Smell; meridian: Lung
152. Wrist disorders • Sense: Smell; meridian: Lung
153. Wrists–weak • Sense: Touch; meridian: Heart

11

EVERYBODY NEEDS VITAMINS & MINERALS

All humans need vitamins and minerals to be healthy. Everyone. No exceptions. They're the ingredients your body needs to make everything you need to be happy. If your body, mind, and spirit are healthy...you are happy.

Ever tried to make a cake without all of the ingredients in the recipe? It isn't going to work. The same is true if your body doesn't have the right ingredients for a happy hormone.

Symptoms are how your body to tells you that an ingredient is missing in either your lifestyle or diet.

Sometimes a simple habit, like drinking coffee, causes symptoms. Caffeine alone costs you Vitamin A, B Complex, B1, B2, B3, B6, B12, Folic Acid, Iron, Magnesium and Potassium. Can you spare any of these ingredients? Apparently not...if you have symptoms.

No symptoms, no problem. If you love your coffee, but not the vitamin loss...you have to start including foods in your diet that have those vitamins. I prefer using foods over supplements.

The following list is an overview of why you need to read those nutrition labels. You really are what you eat.

Vitamin A

What it does... Vitamin A repairs bodily tissues and organs. It also maintains night vision, foundational for creating healthy hair, skin, bones and teeth.

Just a few symptoms of when you don't have enough... Frequent infections, allergies, loose teeth, brittle hair/nails, no appetite.

*Things that erase Vitamin A from your system...*Alcohol, caffeine, excessive iron, mineral oil

*Foods with Vitamin A...*Apple, apricot, asparagus, banana, beans (string), beet, blackberry, blueberry, broccoli, butter, cabbage, cantaloupe, carrot, cashews, cauliflower, celery, cheese (all), cherry, chicken, clam, cod (all mild fish), corn, crab, cucumber, dates, egg yolks, eggplant, fig, grape, grapefruit, greens, leeks, lemon, lentils, lettuce, mackerel (all oily fish), milk, mushrooms, mussels, mustard green.

Nectarine, oats, okra, olive, onion, orange, oyster, papaya, parsley, peas, peach, pecan, persimmon, pineapple, potato (sweet), prunes, pumpkin, pumpkin seed, radish, raisins, raspberry, rhubarb, salmon, sardine, shrimp, spinach, squash (summer), squash (winter), strawberry, sunflower seed, tangerine, tomato, trout, tuna, turkey, walnut, watercress, watermelon, wheat, wheat bran, wheat germ, wheat berries, yogurt.

Vitamin B Complex

B Complex includes B_1 (thiamine), B_2 (riboflavin), B_3 (niacin), B_6 (pyridoxine), B_{12} (cyanocobalamin), B_{13} (orotic acid), B_{15} (pangamic acid), B_{17} (laetrile), biotin, choline, folic acid, inositol, PABA (para-aminobenzoic acid) and pantothenic acid.

What they do... They are needed by your body for converting carbs into glucose. Your body uses glucose to produce energy. B complex vitamins are your body's regulator for metabolism, nervous system functions, healthy eyes, hair, liver and skin. It is also responsible for a normally functioning Gastro–Intestinal (GI) tract.

Just a few symptoms of when you don't have enough... Acne, anemia, poor appetite, constipation, depression, dry skin, exhaustion, insomnia and unusual irritability.

Things that erase B Complex vitamins from your system... Alcohol, caffeine, birth control pills, stress, excessive sugar, sleeping pills and any sulfa drugs

Foods with B complex vitamins... All of the B complex vitamins are found in brewers yeast and whole grain cereals.

Vitamin B1 ... Thiamine

What it does... Vitamin B_1 regulates the appetite and assimilation of food. It converts carbohydrates into glucose and insulates nerves. It is responsible for your and GI (Gastro–Intestinal) muscle tone as well as maintaining pulmonary muscle tone. This vitamin quickens the healing process, maintains healthy eyes, hair, liver and mouth.

Just a few symptoms of when you don't have enough... Loss of appetite, exhaustion, numbness in hands and/or feet, unusual nervousness, shortness of breath, constipation, depression, weakness, forgetfulness, cardiac troubles and impaired growth in children.

Things that erase Vitamin B_1 from your system... Alcohol, caffeine, fever, smoking, stress and surgery of any kind.

Foods with Vitamin B1... Almond, amaranth, apple, apricot, asparagus, banana, barley, bean (kidney), bean (string), beet, blackberry, blueberry, cabbage, cantaloupe, carrot, cashews, cauliflower, celery, cheese, cherry, chicken, clam, corn, crab, dates, egg yolk, eggplant, grape, grapefruit, leeks, lettuce, mackerel (all fish), milk, mushrooms.

Orange, oysters, parsley, peas, peanut, pear, pecan, perch persimmon, potato, pumpkin seed, raisins, raspberry, rice (brown), rye, salmon, sardines, sesame seeds, shrimp, spinach strawberry, sunflower seeds, tomato, trout, tuna, turkey, walnut, wheat, wheat bran, yogurt.

Vitamin B2 ...Riboflavin

What it does... Vitamin B_2 is necessary for forming antibodies, and red blood cells. It maintains healthy skin, hair, eyes, nails and liver. You need it to metabolize carbohydrates, fats and proteins. You need B_2 for enzymes to provide oxygen to all of your cells. Your cells need oxygen to break down sugar. Breaking down sugar produces the energy you need.

Just a few symptoms of when you don't have enough... Mouth cankers, skin problems, excessive hair loss, flaky skin around nose and forehead, dizziness

Things that erase Vitamin B_2 from your system... Alcohol, caffeine, processed sugar and smoking

*Foods with Vitamin B2...*Almond, apricot, avocado, banana, barley, blackberry, broccoli, cashews, cauliflower, cheese (all), cherry, chestnut, chicken, egg yolk, fig, greens (dark leafy), leeks, lentils, mackerel (all fish), milk (cow), mushrooms.

Oats, okra, peas, peanut, perch, potato, prunes, pumpkin, pumpkin seeds, raisins, raspberry, rye bread, salmon, seaweed, shrimp, spinach, squash (summer), squash (winter), strawberry, sunflower seeds, tangerine, trout, tuna, walnut, watermelon, wheat, wheat bran, wheat germ, wheat berries, yogurt.

Vitamin B3 ...Niacin

What it does... Vitamin B_3 reduces cholesterol. It is responsible for the metabolization of the fat–carbohydrate–protein cycle. It also insulates the nerves, maintains healthy skin and digestive system.

Just a few symptoms of when you don't have enough... Muscle soreness for no reason, muscle cramping, insomnia, mouth sores, loss of appetite, dry skin

Things that erase Vitamin B_3 from your system... Alcohol, caffeine, too much sugar and starches, and antibiotics.

*Foods with Vitamin B3...*Almond, apricot, asparagus, banana, barley, bean (navy), blackberry, blueberry, broccoli, buckwheat, carrot, cashews, cauliflower, cheese (all), cherry, chicken, corn, crab, egg yolk, fig, grape, grapefruit.

Mackerel (all fish), mushrooms, mustard greens, oats, okra, onion, orange, oyster, parsley, peach, peanut, pineapple, prunes, pumpkin seeds, raisins, raspberry, rice (brown), rye, salmon, shrimp, squash (summer), squash (winter), strawberry, sunflower seeds, tuna, turkey, walnut, watercress, wheat, wheat bran, wheat germ, yogurt.

Vitamin B6 ...Pyridoxine

What it does... Vitamin B_6 regulates the metabolism of fats, carbohydrates and protein. It is needed for producing red blood cells and antibodies. It is required for your body to be able to use any B_{12} that you may be trying to introduce into your diet. It also helps to regulate potassium and sodium.

Just a few symptoms of when you don't have enough... Unusual nervousness, hair loss, loss of mental function, dry mouth

Things that erase Vitamin B_6 from your system... Alcohol, caffeine, birth control pills and radiation.

*Foods with Vitamin B6...*Almond, apple, apricot, asparagus, banana, barley, bean (kidney), bean (string), beet, blackberry, blueberry, broccoli, cabbage, cantaloupe, carrot, cauliflower, celery, cheese (all), cherry, chicken, clams, corn, crab, dates, eggplant, fig, grape, grapefruit, leeks, lentils, lettuce, mackerel, mushrooms, mustard greens.

Nectarine, oats, onion, orange, oyster, parsley, pea, peach, peanut, pear, perch, pineapple, potato, raisins, raspberry, salmon, sardine, spinach, squash (summer), squash (winter), strawberry, tomato, trout, tuna, turkey, walnut, watercress, watermelon, wheat, wheat bran, wheat germ, yogurt.

Vitamin B12...Cyanocobalamin

What it does... Vitamin B_{12} regulates metabolism of carbohydrates, fats and proteins. Maintains healthy cells and nervous system, responsible for the formation of red blood cells. It also helps your body assimilate iron.

Just a few symptoms of when you don't have enough... Anemia, poor appetite, brain damage, unusual nervousness, general fatigue, unusual leg weakness and difficulty speaking.

Things that erase Vitamin A from your system... Alcohol, caffeine, laxatives, smoking and birth control pills.

Foods with Vitamin B12... Amaranth, banana, chicken, corn, cottage cheese, crab, cream, egg yolk, milk, peas, yogurt.

Biotin

What it does... This is essential for producing the fat your body needs for energy. Helps with being able to use proteins and vitamins in your diet. It is responsible for growth. You need it for healthy muscles, hair and skin.

Just a few symptoms of when you don't have enough... Poor skin color, depression, insomnia, muscle aches for no reason, constant skin trouble, loss of appetite and exhaustion.

Foods with Biotin Acid... Almonds, amaranth, American cheese, apples, asparagus, bananas, bean sprouts, beets, cabbage, cantaloupe, carrots, cauliflower, cheddar cheese, chicken, corn, cornmeal, cow's milk, egg yolk, grapefruit, green beans, hazelnuts, herring, lentils.

Mackerel, mushrooms, onions, oranges, oysters, peas, peaches, peanuts, pecan, raisins, salmon, sardines, strawberries, sweet potatoes, tuna, turkey, turnip greens, walnuts, watermelon.

Vitamin C ...Ascorbic Acid

What it does... Vitamin C is important for many, many reasons. It is needed for you to assimilate iron and vitamins, builds your resistance to infection, forms/maintains healthy teeth, gums and bones, strengthens blood vessels, and heals skin of wounds and burns.

It also removes heavy metals from the body, reduces oxidized cholesterol and is a strong antioxidant.

Just a few symptoms of when you don't have enough... Bleeding gums, frequent infections, bruise easily, nosebleeds, anemia

Things that erase Vitamin C from your system... Aspirin, antibiotics, sulfa drugs, cortisone, stress, smoking and surprisingly, baking soda.

*Foods with Vitamin C...*Amaranth, apple, apricot, asparagus, banana, blackberry, blueberry, broccoli, cabbage, cantaloupe, carrot, cauliflower, cherry, chicken, clams, corn, crab, fig, grape, grapefruit, greens (dark leafy–all), herring, lemon, milk.

Oats, orange, oyster, papaya, peas, peach, peanut, pear, pineapple, potato, prunes, pumpkin, raspberry, spinach, squash (summer), squash (winter), strawberry, tomato, tuna, turkey, watercress, watermelon, yogurt.

Calcium

What it does... Everyone knows that Calcium maintains healthy bones and teeth. It also regulates muscle responses and the rhythms of your heart. It regulates the level of acidity in your blood, helps to use iron in your diet and helps to prevent arthritis/rheumatism.

Just a few symptoms of when you don't have enough... Muscle cramps, joint pain, insomnia, blood slow to clot, heart palpitations, frequent tooth decay

Things that erase Calcium from your system... Chocolate, stress, lack of exercise, not enough vitamins C and D, not enough magnesium

*Foods with Calcium...*Too many to put here, trust me. Good rule of thumb is to find it in all grains, dairy products, meats, fresh fish and seafoods.

Choline

What it does... Metabolizes your body's fat and cholesterol. This is what keeps fat out of your liver and kidneys. It also insulates nerve endings.

Just a few symptoms of when you don't have enough... Cirrhosis of the liver, fatty deposits on the liver, bleeding stomach ulcers, high blood pressure and hardening of the arteries.

Things that erase Choline from your system... Alcohol, coffee, sugar, processed flour

Foods with Choline... Most effective if used with vitamins A and B12...Amaranth, apples, asparagus, bean sprouts, brown rice, cabbage, cheddar cheese, chicken, chickpeas, cornmeal, cow's milk, eggnog, egg yolk, grapefruit, green beans, goat's milk, lentils.

Molasses, mustard greens, peas, peanuts, pecans, potatoes, soy flour, wheat flour, wheat germ, whole wheat bread.

Copper

What it does... Copper is important for producing red blood cells. It helps assimilate vitamin C, aids amino acid function and making elastin for your body to use. Elastin maintains muscle tone and muscular responses.

Just a few symptoms of when you don't have enough... Anemia, edema, respiration troubles, dermatitis and overall weakness.

Things that erase Copper from your system... Excessive zinc and chronic diarrhea.

Foods with Copper... Almonds, apple, apricot, banana, blackberry, blueberry, broccoli, cantaloupe, cheese, cherries, cottage cheese, crab, cream, dates, egg yolk, grape, grapefruit, greens (dark leafy), lentils, mackerel, milk, mushrooms.

Oats, oranges, oyster, parsley, peanuts, pears, pecan, perch, potato, prunes, raisins, rye, salmon, sesame seeds, squash (summer), squash (winter), sunflower seeds, tomato, trout, turkey, walnut, wheat, wheat germ.

Vitamin D…Cholecalciferol

What it does… Everyone knows that Vitamin D is required for building strong bones and teeth in children. The same is true for adults. You need it in order for your body to absorb any calcium and phosphorus that you are trying to include in your diet. It is just as important for maintaining a healthy thyroid, nervous system and helps your blood to clot.

Just a few symptoms of when you don't have enough… Loss of energy, diarrhea, unusual nervousness, rickets in children, phosphorus build up in the kidneys, myopia, poor metabolism, diabetes.

Things that erase Vitamin A from your system… Mineral oil

Foods with Vitamin D… Amaranth, banana, butter, chicken, egg yolk, fish oil, milk, salmon, sardines, tuna.

Vitamin E…Tocopherol

What it does… Vitamin E maintains healthy muscles and nerves, slows the aging process, increases male potency, dilates blood vessels, protects adrenal and pituitary hormones, prevents edema, prevents miscarriage, protects your retention of fat-soluble vitamins and defends your body against toxins in your food.

Just a few symptoms of when you don't have enough… Heart disease, enlarged prostate, kidney and liver damage, gastrointestinal troubles, dull hair, impotency, miscarriages, anemia in babies, male sterility.

Things that erase Vitamin E from your system… Birth control pills, chlorine and mineral oils.

Foods with Vitamin E… Apple, banana, cabbage, cantaloupe, carrot, chicken, cream, egg yolk, grapefruit, greens (dark leafy), oranges, parsley, peanuts, rice (brown), shrimp, spinach, strawberry, turkey, wheat germ.

Folic Acid

What it does... Folic Acid is necessary for creating healthy red blood cells and nucleic acid. Nucleic acid promotes normal growth and reproduction of cells. It is essential for liver function and prevents intestinal parasites.

Just a few symptoms of when you don't have enough... Anemia, graying hair, gastrointestinal troubles, poor vitamin assimilation, learning disabilities

Things that erase Folic acid from your system... Alcohol, caffeine, smoking, sulfa drugs, streptomycin, stress.

Foods with Folic Acid... Almonds, apple, apricot, asparagus, banana, barley, blackberry, blueberry, broccoli, cabbage, cantaloupe, cauliflower, cheese, cherries, chicken, cottage cheese, crab, eggplant, egg yolk, grape, grapefruit, honey, lettuce.

Mackerel (all oily fish), oats, onion, orange, parsley, peach, peanut, pecan, pineapple, raisins, rice (brown), rye, salmon, spinach, strawberry, tuna, turkey, walnuts, wheat.

Iodine

What it does... Iodine regulates hormones from the thyroid. It is chiefly responsible for maintaining healthy hair, nails, skin tone, and teeth.

Just a few symptoms of when you don't have enough... Cold hands and feet, unusual nervousness, brittle nails, heart palpitations, unusually dry hair

Things that erase Iodine from your system... Too many nuts or nut products in your diet.

Foods with Iodine... There are traces of iodine in many foods. The best sources found in foods are in fish oil, kelp, iodized salt, salmon, and turkey.

Iron

What it does... Iron regulates how your body metabolizes protein. It forms hemoglobin in the blood and myoglobin in muscle tissues. It is also key in preventing infections and viruses.

Just a few symptoms of when you don't have enough... Anemia, brittle/weak nails, constipation, respiratory troubles, fatigue, frequent colds.

Things that erase Iron from your system... Caffeine, excessive phosphorus and zinc. You also lose iron from a lack of hydrochloric acid.

Hydrochloric acid is necessary for breaking food down in your stomach. You can find hydrochloric acid in cider vinegar, lemon juice, black olives, celery and spinach.

Foods with Iron... Almond, amaranth, apple, apricot, asparagus, banana, barley, beef, bean (sprouts), blackberry, blueberry, cabbage, cantaloupe, broccoli, cashews, cauliflower, cheese, cherries, chestnuts, chicken, clams, coffee beans, crab, dates, egg yolk, eggplant, grape, grapefruit, greens (dark leafy), lentils, lettuce, mackerel, milk, mushrooms.

Nectarines, oats, orange, oyster, papaya, parsley, peas, peach, peanut, pear, pecan, perch, pineapple, pork, potato, potato (sweet), prunes, pumpkin, pumpkin seeds, raisins, raspberry, rye, salmon, sardines, sesame seeds, shrimp, spinach, strawberry, sunflower seeds, tomato, tuna, turkey, walnuts, watermelon, wheat.

Vitamin K ...Phylloquinone

What it does... Vitamin K is required for a healthy liver. It is necessary for regulating blood clotting.

Just a few symptoms of when you don't have enough... Hemorrhaging, diarrhea, nosebleeds, colitis, blood slow to clot

Things that erase Vitamin K from your system... Radiation, antibiotics, mineral oil and aspirin.

Foods with Vitamin K... Asparagus, banana, chicken, egg yolk, milk (and cream), oats, orange, peach, raisins, strawberry, wheat, wheat germ.

Magnesium

What it does... Magnesium helps the body use the B complex, Vitamins C and E. It strengthens muscle functions, including your heart muscles. It's important for insulating nerves and regulates the balancing of acid and alkaline.

Just a few symptoms of when you don't have enough... Kidney stones, unusual nervousness, loss of muscle control, vascular blood clots, heart disease and calcification of blood vessels.

Things that erase Magnesium from your system... Alcohol, caffeine, excessive iron, mineral oil

Foods with Magnesium... Almonds, amaranth, apple, apricot, banana, barley, beet, blackberry, blueberry, broccoli, buckwheat, carrot, cashews, cauliflower, cheese, cherries, chicken, clam, corn, crab, dates, egg yolk, eggplant, fig, grape, grapefruit, greens (dark leafy), milk.

Onions, orange, oyster, peas, peach, peanut, pecan, perch, pineapple, potato, prunes, raisins, raspberry, rice (brown), rye, salmon, sesame seeds, shrimp, squash (summer), squash (winter), strawberry, sunflower seeds, tomato, tuna, turkey, walnut, watermelon, wheat, wheat germ.

Pantothenic Acid

What it does... It stimulates growth. From the growing of antibodies to skin regeneration. This is what makes skin shine and joints remain loose. The regeneration of healthy cells of all sorts.

Just a few symptoms of when you don't have enough... Dull hair, skin and nails. Itchy skin, hair loss, low blood sugar, frequent respiratory infections, depression, ulcers, constipation, fatigue

Things that erase Pantothenic Acid from your system... Alcohol, baking soda, coffee and vinegar

*Foods with Pantothenic Acid...*Most effective when taken with some folic acid, vitamins B_6, B_{12}, and C...Almonds, American cheese, apples, bananas, barley, broccoli, brown rice, Brussel sprouts, buckwheat flour, cabbage, cashews, cauliflower, cheddar cheese, cherries, chicken, clams, cornmeal, cottage cheese, corn, cow's milk, crabmeat, cream, dates, eggnog, egg yolk, eggplant, elderberries, goat's milk, grapefruit, halibut, ice cream, lentils, lobster.

Mushrooms, oranges, oysters, peas, peanuts, perch, pineapple, potatoes, pumpkin, raspberries, rye bread, salmon, sardines, shrimp, strawberries, sunflower seeds, turkey, watermelon, wheat flour, wheat germ, whole wheat bread, yogurt.

Phosphorus

What it does... It maintains nerve responses, helps with cell regeneration, regulates hormones and metabolism.

Just a few symptoms of when you don't have enough... Exhaustion, obesity, loss of appetite, arthritis, trouble with bones and teeth, gum disease, trouble breathing, constant nervousness.

Things that erase Phosphorus from your system... Too much sugar.

*Foods with Phosphorus...*Best taken with Calcium, Vitamins A and D...Phosphorus can be found in all dairy products, most grains, meats, seafood, nuts, fruits and vegetables. Eating a basic diet with little or no junk food will help. Just step away from the sugar.

Potassium

What it does... Potassium is important for normal kidney function, muscle contractions (including the heart), nerve insulation and regulation of proper acid and alkaline ratios.

Just a few symptoms of when you don't have enough... Cardiac arrest, slowed heart rate, overall weakness, dry skin, constipation, unusual nervousness or excitability, digestive troubles and insomnia.

Things that erase Potassium from your system... Alcohol, caffeine, diuretics, excessive sugar, long term diarrhea or excessive sweating.

Foods with Potassium... Apples, apricots, almonds, amaranth, apple apricot, banana, bean (sprouts), bean (string), beet, blackberry, blueberry, broccoli, cabbage, carrot, cashews, cauliflower, cheese, chicken, clams, corn, cottage cheese, cream, dates, egg yolk, grape, grapefruit, greens (dark leafy), lemon.

Mushrooms, nectarines, onion, orange, oyster, papaya, parsley, peas, peach, peanuts, pear, pecan, perch pineapple, potato, prunes, pumpkin, raisins, raspberry, salmon, shrimp, spinach, squash (summer), squash (winter), strawberry, sunflower seeds, tomato, tuna, turkey, walnut , watermelon.

12

VITAMIN & MINERAL LOSS HAPPENS HOW?!?

Everything you put into your mouth effects your body. Vitamin deficiency is usually caused by every day choices.

The most fun way to replace vitamins is with food. Cut back on things that are causing symptoms if you can. If the vitamin loss is from a necessary treatment or prescription, eating better will help with side effects.

Please read the previous chapter for foods that contain the vitamins/minerals you need to replace, and why your body needs all of them.

Make it fun. Choose foods you like anyway, but put them together in a new kind of menu. You'll be surprised at how much better you feel in less than a week.

Alcohol

- *Vitamin A:* Frequent infections, allergies, loose teeth, brittle hair and nails, loss of appetite.
- *B Complex:* Acne, anemia, no appetite, constipation, depression, dry skin, exhaustion, insomnia and irritability.

- *B1 Thiamine:* Loss of appetite, exhaustion, numbness in hands and/or feet, unusual nervousness, shortness of breath, constipation, depression, weakness, forgetfulness, cardiac troubles and impaired growth in children.
- *B2 Riboflavin:* Mouth cankers, skin problems, excessive hair loss, flaky skin around nose and forehead, dizziness
- *B3 Niacin:* Muscle soreness for no reason, muscle cramping, insomnia, mouth sores, no appetite, dry skin
- *B6 Pyridoxine:* Unusual nervousness, hair loss, loss of mental function, dry mouth
- *B12 Cyanocobalamin:* Anemia, poor appetite, brain damage, unusual nervousness, general fatigue, unusual leg weakness and difficulty speaking.
- *Choline:* Cirrhosis of the liver, fatty deposits on the liver, bleeding stomach ulcers, high blood pressure and hardening of the arteries.
- *Folic Acid:* Anemia, graying hair, gastrointestinal troubles, poor vitamin assimilation, learning disabilities
- *Magnesium:* Kidney stones, unusual nervousness, loss of muscle control, vascular blood clots, heart disease and calcification of blood vessels.
- *Pantothenic Acid:* Dull hair, skin and nails. Itchy skin, hair loss, low blood sugar, frequent respiratory infections, depression, ulcers, constipation, fatigue
- *Potassium:* Cardiac arrest, slowed heart rate, overall weakness, dry skin, constipation, unusual nervousness or excitability, digestive troubles and insomnia.

Antibiotics

- *B3 Niacin:* Muscle soreness for no reason, muscle cramping, insomnia, mouth sores, no appetite, dry skin
- *Vitamin C (Ascorbic Acid):* Bleeding gums, frequent infections, bruise easily, nosebleeds, anemia

- *Vitamin K (Phylloquinone):* Hemorrhaging, diarrhea, nosebleeds, colitis, blood slow to clot

Aspirin

- *Vitamin C (Ascorbic Acid):* Bleeding gums, frequent infections, bruise easily, nosebleeds, anemia
- *Vitamin K (Phylloquinone):* Hemorrhaging, diarrhea, nosebleeds, colitis, blood slow to clot

Baking Soda

- *Vitamin C (Ascorbic Acid):* Bleeding gums, frequent infections, bruise easily, nosebleeds, anemia
- *Pantothenic Acid:* Dull hair, skin and nails. Itchy skin, hair loss, low blood sugar, frequent respiratory infections, depression, ulcers, constipation, fatigue

Birth Control Pills

- *B Complex:* Acne, anemia, poor appetite, constipation, depression, dry skin, exhaustion, insomnia and unusual irritability.
- *B6 Pyridoxine:* Unusual nervousness, hair loss, loss of mental function, dry mouth
- *B12 Cyanocobalamin:* Anemia, poor appetite, brain damage, unusual nervousness, general fatigue, unusual leg weakness and difficulty speaking.
- *Vitamin E (Tocopherol):* Heart disease, enlarged prostate, kidney and liver damage, gastrointestinal troubles, dull hair, impotency, anemia in babies, male sterility.

C Vitamin (not enough)

- *Calcium:* Muscle cramps, joint pain, insomnia, blood slow to clot, heart palpitations, frequent tooth decay

Caffeine

- *Vitamin A:* Frequent infections, allergies, loose teeth, brittle hair and nails, loss of appetite.
- *B Complex:* Acne, anemia, poor appetite, constipation, depression, dry skin, exhaustion, insomnia and unusual irritability.
- *B1 Thiamine:* Loss of appetite, exhaustion, numbness in hands and/or feet, unusual nervousness, shortness of breath, constipation, depression, weakness, forgetfulness, cardiac troubles and impaired growth in children.
- *B2 Riboflavin:* Mouth cankers, skin problems, excessive hair loss, flaky skin around nose and forehead, dizziness
- *B3 Niacin:* Muscle soreness for no reason, muscle cramping, insomnia, mouth sores, loss of appetite, dry skin
- *B6 Pyridoxine:* Unusual nervousness, hair loss, loss of mental function, dry mouth
- *B12 Cyanocobalamin:* Anemia, poor appetite, brain damage, unusual nervousness, general fatigue, unusual leg weakness and difficulty speaking.
- *Folic Acid:* Anemia, graying hair, gastrointestinal troubles, poor vitamin assimilation, learning disabilities
- *Iron:* Anemia, brittle/weak nails, constipation, respiratory troubles, fatigue, frequent colds.
- *Magnesium:* Kidney stones, unusual nervousness, loss of muscle control, vascular blood clots, heart disease and calcification of blood vessels.

- *Potassium:* Cardiac arrest, slowed heart rate, overall weakness, dry skin, constipation, unusual nervousness or excitability, digestive troubles and insomnia.

Chlorine

- *Vitamin E (Tocopherol):* Heart disease, enlarged prostate, kidney/liver damage, gastrointestinal troubles, dull hair, impotency, miscarriages, anemia in babies, male sterility.

Chocolate

- *Calcium:* Muscle cramps, joint pain, insomnia, blood slow to clot, heart palpitations, frequent tooth decay

Coffee

- *Choline:* Cirrhosis of the liver, fatty deposits on the liver, bleeding stomach ulcers, high blood pressure and hardening of the arteries.
- *Pantothenic Acid:* Dull hair, skin and nails. Itchy skin, hair loss, low blood sugar, frequent respiratory infections, depression, ulcers, constipation, fatigue

Complex Carbs (excessive)

- *B3 Niacin:* Muscle soreness for no reason, muscle cramping, insomnia, mouth sores, loss of appetite, dry skin

Cortisone

- *Vitamin C (Ascorbic Acid):* Bleeding gums, frequent infections, bruise easily, nosebleeds, anemia

D Vitamin Deficiency

- *Calcium:* Muscle cramps, joint pain, insomnia, blood slow to clot, heart palpitations, frequent tooth decay

Diarrhea (chronic)

- *Copper:* Anemia, edema, respiration troubles, dermatitis and overall weakness.
- *Potassium:* Cardiac arrest, slowed heart rate, overall weakness, dry skin, constipation, unusual nervousness or excitability, digestive troubles and insomnia.

Diuretics

- *Potassium:* Cardiac arrest, slowed heart rate, overall weakness, dry skin, constipation, unusual nervousness or excitability, digestive troubles and insomnia.

Exercise (too little) Calcium

- *Calcium:* Muscle cramps, joint pain, insomnia, blood slow to clot, heart palpitations, frequent tooth decay

Fever

- *B1 Thiamine:* Loss of appetite, exhaustion, numbness in hands and/or feet, unusual nervousness, shortness of breath, constipation, depression, weakness, forgetfulness, cardiac troubles and impaired growth in kids.

Flour (white, processed/modern wheat)

- *Choline:* Cirrhosis/fatty deposits of the liver, bleeding ulcers, high blood pressure and hardening arteries.

Iron (too much)

- *Vitamin A:* Frequent infections, allergies, loose teeth, brittle hair and nails, loss of appetite.
- *Magnesium:* Kidney stones, unusual nervousness, loss of muscle control, vascular blood clots, heart disease and calcification of blood vessels.

Laxatives

- *B12 Cyanocobalamin:* Anemia, poor appetite, brain damage, unusual nervousness, general fatigue, unusual leg weakness and difficulty speaking.

Magnesium (not enough)

- *Calcium:* Muscle cramps, joint pain, insomnia, blood slow to clot, heart palpitations, frequent tooth decay

Mineral Oil

- *Vitamin A:* Frequent infections, allergies, loose teeth, brittle hair and nails, loss of appetite.
- *Vitamin E (Tocopherol):* Heart disease, enlarged prostate, kidney and liver damage, gastrointestinal troubles, dull hair, impotency, miscarriages, anemia in babies, male sterility.
- *Vitamin K (Phylloquinone):* Hemorrhaging, diarrhea, nosebleeds, colitis, blood slow to clot
- *Magnesium:* Kidney stones, unusual nervousness, loss of muscle control, vascular blood clots, heart disease and calcification of blood vessels.

Nuts (too much)

- *Iodine:* Cold hands and feet, unusual nervousness, brittle nails, heart palpitations, unusually dry hair

Phosphorus (too much)

- *Iron:* Anemia, brittle/weak nails, constipation, respiratory troubles, fatigue, frequent colds.

Radiation

- *B6 Pyridoxine:* Unusual nervousness, hair loss, loss of mental function, dry mouth
- *Vitamin K (Phylloquinone):* Hemorrhaging, diarrhea, nosebleeds, colitis, blood slow to clot

Sleeping Pills

- *B Complex:* Acne, anemia, poor appetite, constipation, depression, dry skin, exhaustion, insomnia and unusual irritability.

Smoking

- *B Riboflavin:* Mouth cankers, skin problems, excessive hair loss, flaky skin around nose and forehead, dizziness
- *B12 Cyanocobalamin:* Anemia, poor appetite, brain damage, unusual nervousness, general fatigue, unusual leg weakness and difficulty speaking.
- *Vitamin C (Ascorbic Acid):* Bleeding gums, frequent infections, bruise easily, nosebleeds, anemia
- *Folic Acid:* Anemia, graying hair, gastrointestinal troubles, poor vitamin assimilation, learning disabilities

Streptomycin (antimycobacterial) antibiotic

- *Folic Acid:* Anemia, graying hair, gastrointestinal troubles, poor vitamin assimilation, learning disabilities

Stress

- *B Complex:* Acne, anemia, poor appetite, constipation, depression, dry skin, exhaustion, insomnia and unusual irritability.
- *B1 Thiamine:* Loss of appetite, exhaustion, numbness in hands and/or feet, unusual nervousness, shortness of

breath, constipation, depression, weakness, forgetfulness, cardiac troubles and impaired growth in kids.
- *Vitamin C (Ascorbic Acid):* Bleeding gums, frequent infections, bruise easily, nosebleeds, anemia
- *Folic Acid:* Anemia, graying hair, gastrointestinal troubles, poor vitamin assimilation, learning disabilities

Sugar (too much)

- *B Complex:* Acne, anemia, poor appetite, constipation, depression, dry skin, exhaustion, insomnia and unusual irritability.
- *B3 Niacin:* Muscle soreness for no reason, muscle cramping, insomnia, mouth sores, loss of appetite, dry skin
- *Phosphorus:* Exhaustion, obesity, loss of appetite, arthritis, trouble with bones and teeth, gum disease, trouble breathing, constant nervousness.
- *Potassium:* Cardiac arrest, slowed heart rate, overall weakness, dry skin, constipation, unusual nervousness or excitability, digestive troubles and insomnia.

Sugar (white, processed)

- *B2 Riboflavin:* Mouth cankers, skin problems, excessive hair loss, flaky skin around nose and forehead, dizziness
- *Choline:* Cirrhosis of the liver, fatty deposits on the liver, bleeding stomach ulcers, high blood pressure and hardening of the arteries.

Sulfa Drugs

- *B Complex:* Acne, anemia, poor appetite, constipation, depression, dry skin, exhaustion, insomnia and unusual irritability.
- *Vitamin C (Ascorbic Acid):* Bleeding gums, frequent infections, bruise easily, nosebleeds, anemia
- *Folic Acid:* Anemia, graying hair, gastrointestinal troubles, poor vitamin assimilation, learning disabilities

Surgery of any kind

- *B1 Thiamine:* Loss of appetite, exhaustion, numbness in hands and/or feet, unusual nervousness, shortness of breath, constipation, depression, weakness, forgetfulness, cardiac troubles and impaired growth in kids.

Sweating (excessive)

- *Potassium:* Cardiac arrest, slowed heart rate, overall weakness, dry skin, constipation, unusual nervousness or excitability, digestive troubles and insomnia.

Vinegar

- *Pantothenic Acid:* Dull hair, skin and nails. Itchy skin, hair loss, low blood sugar, frequent respiratory infections, depression, ulcers, constipation, fatigue

Zinc (excessive)

- *Copper:* Anemia, edema, respiration troubles, dermatitis and overall weakness.
- *Phosphorus:* Exhaustion, obesity, loss of appetite, arthritis, trouble with bones and teeth, gum disease, trouble breathing, constant nervousness.

13

NATURE BATS LAST

Everyone has to adapt to the weather. Is it hot? Is it windy? Is is cold? You choose clothing to adapt to whatever is going on outside. Whether you know it or not, you're using your sense of Touch for self-care.

Your sense of Sight has a lot to do with daylight hours. The more daylight hours there are in a day, the more stimulated you are. Less daylight is naturally calming. Your eyes are connected to your brain. Use them as part of your self-care. Choose the colors of your clothes as daily color therapy. Warm colors stimulate your system. Cool colors calm you down. Print patterns are stimulating. Solid colors are calming.

Using your sense of Taste for self-care means more than eating well. By all means, use tonic foods for keeping your body healthier. But your sense of taste needs to be used to keep your mind and spirit healthy, too. Clear, optimistic, truthful, compassionate communication with everyone around you is as important as food.

Everyone uses aromatherapy every day. Whether you want to or not. Everything you smell effects you. Your sense of Smell gets your mind involved in self-care. Certain smells bring back memories in a way that photographs can't. I loved the smell of campfire when I was a child. I still feel about ten years old when I get a whiff of a warm fire on a cold day. Happy memory smells calm your spirit and mind...your body relaxes.

Do you listen to a lot of music or like to have background noise like a talk radio or TV? Do you prefer the quiet so you can hear yourself think instead? What you listen to matters to your sense of Hearing. There are some tunes that have made me dance since I was seven. Others music is perfect for really concentrating. After a day full of words all I want is quiet. It all depends on what I need.

Your self-care changes as your life does. Use all five of your common senses to stay healthy and happy throughout the seasons of the year. When life or the weather is too warm, cool off. When it is windy and full of changes, stay grounded and balanced. When your life or the weather is too cold, warm up.

Timing is everything. The seasons effect your body. Choosing wisely throughout the year keeps your immune system healthy. Your immune system can keep your body healthy all by itself. How you dress, eat and play for each of the seasons makes a difference.

Spring

- Rising sunlight hours, *warming* influence.
- Warmer temperatures, *warming* influence.
- More time to play outside, *warming* influence.

It's easy to get caught up in Spring momentum. If you are working and playing more outside, or your schedule is getting crazier by the day, remember to cool it down with your other senses before this wonderful season makes you sick.

Summer

- Rising sunlight hours, *warming* influence.
- Hotter temperatures, *warming* influence.
- More time to play outside, *warming* influence.

Summer is the time to bask like a lizard. The days are long and full of activity. Use all five of your senses to beat the heat.

The warmer the weather gets, or the busier your schedule gets, cool down accordingly. Do physical work as early in the day as possible. Use a wide brimmed hat to keep the sun off of your head, neck and ears. Seek the shade, use cooler colors, eat cooling foods, use cooling aromatherapies, listen to slower temp music, or quiet.

Autumn

- Rising moonlight hours, *cooling* influence.
- Cooler temperatures, *cooling* influence.
- Less time to play outside, *cooling* influence.

Autumn is abundant in food and colors. All warming colors until the leaves are abruptly gone. Cool nights draw you to a quieter lifestyle. Life is slowing down a bit more every day.

It can be hot during the day and cold in the evening. Eat that way. Have a salad with protein for lunch in the warm sun. The nights may be cool enough for you to eat something to warm your bones, like stew.

Conversely, it can be cold and rainy during the day and warm in the evening. Eat accordingly. If it feels summery, eat that way. If it feels colder, eat THAT way.

Winter

- Rising moonlight hours, *cooling* influence.
- Colder temperatures, *cooling* influence.
- Less time to play outside, *cooling* influence.

Winter is another season that you either love or hate. It can be a relief from the heat and the busy lifestyle of summer. The trick is staying warm inside and out. Laugh, play, enjoy company.

A time to look forward to traditions, weekly routines and quiet evenings. Even winter sports are over at an early enough hour to have a quiet evening.

If you live in a warm climate, it's rainier and darker than the rest of the year. Staying warm and dry with friends and family will keep all of you healthier.

I spent 40 winters in Vermont. My favorite part were all of the quiet snowy walks and warm reading by the fire.

Either climate, its about staying warm, dry, and cheerful.

The Equinoxes

- Weather changes daily
- Daylight changes daily
- Wind, a lot of wind.

Three weeks before, and three weeks after an equinox is viewed as an official season in Traditional Chinese Medicine. I agree. Those times aren't quite spring or fall yet.

The transition time between winter into spring, or summer into autumn, can be either season without warning. The only constant during this transition time is wind.

Hot one day and cold the next is hard on your immune system. The wider the temperature swing, the harder it is for your body to adapt. Your immune system is hard at work keeping up with the demands of warming you with slight shivers on cold days, then cooling you with sweat the next.

In western culture, this is called the flu/cold season for a reason. Most people don't adapt their self-care choices to the transition time. Inappropriate self-care weakens your immune system and you are susceptible to whatever illness is in the air because you are either too hot, too cold, not enough sleep, and cultural activities are very busy at these times of year.

Winter turning into the Spring Equinox is a time of preparing gardens, spring cleaning, being outside more, less darkness means less sleep, and wanting to have sunshine on your skin means a change into lighter, less warm, clothing.

Summer turning into Autumn Equinox is a time of harvesting and closing the gardens for the year, preparing your house for being inside, the beginning of the academic schedules, more darkness means less time to get things done after work, and colder weather means wearing heavier clothes.

Here are a few suggestions for staying healthy during changeable weather. The climate is unpredictable these days. Use all five of your senses to keep your balance through the winds of change.

Touch: Wear layers. Be prepared to add or remove a layer depending on the weather of the day. Don't rely on the calendar to tell you what to wear, use the thermometer. Fifty degrees may feel really warm during the winter, but you would need a jacket if it were summer. Wear a jacket.

Sight: Daylight hours change dramatically during the equinox season. Keep a regular schedule of mealtimes and bedtime. It stabilizes your mind.

This is a very good time to have a candle going at the same times every day. I light one when I get up in the morning and about an hour before sunset. A tiny campfire when your mind thinks it should be lighter/darker really helps

Taste: This is the category that deals with change. Eat according to the weather of the day. If it's cold outside, only eat warm food. If it's warm outside, eat lighter.

A huge piece of advice is about the ever present wind of the Equinoxes. Keep your throat covered with either a high collered shirt, scarf, or wrap of some sort. The number one issue with for your immune system is dealing with the cold. Your throat is the most sensitive to it.

Smell: This is the category of boundaries and methodical routines. Use those to keep you steady during times of change. People with a majority of traits in this category have the hardest time with the Equinox season. Change is not their favorite, but this time of year gives them no choice.

This is a time of fluctuating schedules. Eat and sleep at regular times. Practice saying no whenever possible to overloading your schedule. If your instincts say it would be to much look yourself in the mirror and say NO. People will get over it better than you think they will.

Hearing: Seasonal disorders are caused by changes in daylight. Depression is common in the darkening autumn, as well as in the early spring after a long winter. Use cheerful music and warm conversation with friends to help get through it. No sad lyrics, no dealing with people that either make you sad or angry.

There is such a thing as too much mediation or quiet. If you meditate regularly, change the time frame into taking a walk or any other kind of moving meditation like artwork/crafting. Being too quiet deepens depression.

14

ASIAN MEDICINE...IN A NUTSHELL

It is with the deepest respect and gratitude that I present the following material. It is not my intention to teach you these sacred practices.

These are merely tips of the iceberg compared to what wisdom practitioners and certified instructors can teach you. The following information is only intended for helping the reader with simple self-care.

This book uses a blended view of Asian Medicine...as I used them in my practice. The following chapters are a view into why I needed all three modalities.

I deeply respect all three traditions. They are the basis of western medicine. These traditions have been continually used for thousands of years because they still work.

People haven't changed much in 5,000 years but our resources have. My presentation of their food/herb tonics can all be found in most supermarkets.

15

CLASSICAL AYURVEDA

Classical Ayurveda Quoted from the Oxford English Dictionary:
    Definition of **Ayurveda,** noun
    The traditional Hindu system of medicine, which is based on the idea of balance in bodily systems and uses diet, herbal treatment and yogic breathing. From Sanskrit, Ayus 'life' + veda 'knowledge'

Ayurveda is the oldest known form of health care in the world. Originating in India over 5,000 years ago, it's often called the mother of all healing.

Ayuredic Om

It teaches that you are born with a sensitivity to certain symptoms. Those vulnerabilities remain with you for the rest of your days. These symptoms can be mental or physical and can be avoided by lifestyle choices like diet, meditation and exercise.

We are born with a unique tolerance for how much movement or stillness we require in a day to avoid being stressed. It isn't learned, it isn't even a choice. You just know. It's as personal as how warm or cold you like your bath/shower. When the water is too hot, or too cold, your body lets you know that it isn't happy. You have an automatic reaction. Same with symptoms.

All symptoms are categorized into three main types. The categories are called Doshas.

Each dosha is a set of traits/symptoms that can be alleviated with similar remedies…or avoided altogether with wise lifestyle choices. Each dosha deals with a particular set of bodily functions.

WHEN SOMEONE IS VERY busy and moving all the time, they have a tendency towards symptoms like heart trouble, migraines, high blood pressure, rashes, anger management and being critical of others. These are all symptoms found in the dosha called **Pitta**. I call this your Common Sense of Touch.

Pitta is Sanskrit for fire, or heat. Pitta means transformative fire. The parts of your body that are most effected by Pitta symptoms involve digestion, metabolism and having energy to move your body throughout your day. The more energy you have, the faster you can digest/move. If you have more energy/fire than you need, you develop Pitta symptoms.

WHEN SOMEONE IS in a life that requires adapting and changing all the time, creative, emotional, or caregiving all the time, there is another set of symptoms that are likely to occur.

These symptoms include never being able to finish anything, digestive trouble, constipation, insomnia, worry, addiction of any kind, cold hands and feet, a racing mind,

arthritis and unintended weight loss. The symptoms in this dosha are called **Vata**. I call this your Common Sense of Taste.

Vata is Sanskrit for wind. The invisible movement inside your body. Symptoms involve your mind, brain, spinal cord and how you eliminate all waste from your body. Managing wind direction is key. Imagine your body like a sailboat. A steady wind in your sails makes it easy to go from A to B without any stress.

If the wind is constantly changing speed or direction, you are constantly trying to keep up with those changes. An inefficient way to travel. When the wind in your life is changing too often, you develop Vata symptoms.

WHEN SOMEONE PREFERS A SLOWER, more orderly pace of life there are another set of symptoms that will need to be addressed at some point in their lives.

These symptoms include pneumonia, bronchitis, weight gain, water retention, sleeping a lot, allergies, depression, grudges and stubborn resistance to any sort of change. These symptoms are called **Kapha**. I call this your Common Sense of Hearing.

Kapha is Sanskrit for phlegm. Symptoms are about the part of the body that involves structure and protection of the organs. Cells holding together properly, the formation of mucus, muscles, fat, bones and tendons. Too much structure impedes movement. Too little movement will eventually become a Kapha symptom.

DOSHAS ARE sets of symptoms of certain bodily functions. Everyone has the same basic bodily functions. Everyone has to deal with symptoms from time to time.

If you have a tendency towards a particular set of symptoms, learn to avoid them. Every choice has a consequence. Ayurveda means Life Knowledge. It is focused on knowing how your life affects your health, mentally and physically.

There are two additional categories to Pitta, Vata, and Kapha.

The first blend is Pitta-Vata. It contains all the traits/symptoms of Pitta AND Vata. The symptoms are hot disease. I call this your Common Sense of Sight.

The second blend is Vata-Kapha. It contains all the traits/symptoms of Vata AND Kapha. The symptoms are cold disease. I call this your Common Sense of Smell.

No category is better than another, just different. Knowing which each of them do is important for healing a symptom. Making a symptom go away is just the first step. The goal is to be as healthy and productive for as long as possible. Prevention of getting sick at all is the real goal.

These are the five Doshas and what they do for your body:

Pitta: Symptoms would include all bodily functions involved with turning food into energy and movement of your body itself.

Pitta-Vata: Symptoms would include all bodily functions involved with turning food into energy and movement of your body itself. AND Symptoms involving your mind, brain, spinal cord and waste management of all sorts

Vata: Symptoms involving your mind, brain, spinal cord and waste management of all sorts

Vata-Kapha: Symptoms involving your mind, brain, spinal cord and waste management of all sorts AND Symptoms having to do with the physical structure of your cells, mucus, muscles, bones and tendons

Kapha: Symptoms having to do with the physical structure of your cells, mucus, muscles, bones and tendons

Here are descriptions of the Dosha categories and what they do for your body, mind, and spirit as a team.

PITTA

 Pitta: Fire: Transformative. The pitta fire transforms food to nutrients.
 AND Water: Prevents fire from becoming self destructive.
 Dosha Traits: Fiery in body and mind.
 They have a warm body temperature because of their excellent circulation. Pitta traits are responsible for transforming food into energy. Digestion, metabolism, endocrine system, liver, spleen, gall bladder, eyes, adrenal glands, digestive fire, blood, muscles. Abundant energy. Medium and/or athletic build. Orderly and decisive thinking. Intense, self-confident, creative, aggressive and competitive.
 Characteristics: Strong appetite, metabolism and digestion. Strong concentration. Alert, intelligent, logical, investigating minds. Organized and can become obsessive. Pittas are charismatic, ambitious, disciplined, aggressive and take charge easily.
 Warning Flags: When too many of these characteristics are active at once (or there is more energy created than the body can use), makes Pitta easily irritable, angered, hypercritical, bitter, judgmental, jealous, envious, prone to high blood pressure, heart diseases, headaches, fevers, inflammatory diseases, acid indigestion, excessive hunger, jaundice, burning eyes, colitis, sore throats, profuse perspiration, migraines, hot flashes, urethritis and insomnia.
 Pitta Do's: Slow down, Stabilizing, Plan free time daily, Spend time in nature, Walk in moonlight, Laugh

Suggested Foods for Pitta: Cooling, Sweet, Bitter, Astringent, Milk, butter & ghee, Olive, sunflower and coconut oils, Wheat, rice & barley

Pitta Don'ts: Don't add extra stress to your day in any way, Don't run unless you have to, Don't skip meals, Don't wait until you're hungry before eating, Snack Wisely

Suggested Foods to avoid: Pungent, Salty, Sour, Fermented dairy, Corn, rye, millet & brown rice. Avoid sesame, almond, and corn oil

Pitta-Vata

PITTA-VATA: Fire and water is Pitta. Wind and space is Vata.

Add them together and you get movement. Near constant movement in body and mind, especially the mind. People in this category never stop thinking.

Fire: Transformative. The pitta fire is what transforms food to nutrients.

Water: Prevents fire from becoming self destructive. Water adds stamina.

Wind: An active element. Expansive, irregular, changeable.

Space: The container of wind.

Dosha Traits: This is a combination of fire, water, wind and space. Constant change. This kind of mental and physical movement requires stamina. Lots of it. This is a fire in a changeable wind. When

Vata is dominant, there are a lot of ideas, but not a lot of follow through or concentration to finish.

Characteristics: Lean body build. The more Pitta influence in their mix, the more muscular they are. Less fiery than Pitta, but more focused than the distractible Vata traits.

Quick moving, friendly, talkative, enterprising and very intelligent. They run hot and cold. It is important for them to remember to stay on task, especially when they are under stress. Diet really helps.

Warning Flags: All of Pitta **AND** all of Vata Warning Flags.

Pitta-Vata Do's: Slow down, Consistency, Touch, and be touched, Plan free time daily, Light Exercise, Laugh

Suggested Foods for Pitta-Vata: Cooling, Sweet, Bitter, Astringent, Milk, butter & ghee, Olive, sunflower and coconut oils, Wheat, rice & barley

Pitta-Vata Don'ts: Don't take on more when already busy, Don't use all your energy at once, Don't skip meals, Avoid being too warm or too cold

Foods for Pitta-Vata to Avoid: Fermented dairy Corn, millet, and rye. Avoid sesame, almond & corn oil, Avoid uncooked fruit and vegetables

Vata

Vata: Wind: An active element. Expansive, irregular, changeable. **AND Space:** The container of wind.

Dosha Traits: Cold, Light, Dry, Irregular, Rough, Moving, Quick, Changeable.

Responsible for all communication and movement in the body and mind. Pumping heart, breathing lungs, elimination of wastes, mobility of bones, moving muscles and joints.

Without Vata, the other doshas are inactive. It brings movement to the transformation abilities of Pitta, and much needed movement for Kapha so ideas can begin moving towards manifestation

Characteristics: Usually in a rush. Enjoy travel, are physically active but are easily tired. Creative, intelligent, talkative, excited, impulsive, alert and quick to jump into the action - often without thinking first. They love change and try to keep their lives variable. They often feel unstable or ungrounded especially when becoming overwhelmed with too much movement and change in life.

Warning Flags: Constant movement can lead to constipation, weakness, arthritis, pneumonia, overall dryness can be a problem from hair to heels. Nerve disorders, twitches, confusion, palpitations, breathlessness, muscle tightness, low backache, sciatica mental restlessness and hyperactivity. Vatas become vulnerable when dealing with cold weather, sugar, caffeine and alcohol.

Vata Do's: Consistency, Stay warm, Touch and be touched, Pace yourself, Regular meal times, Light exercise for flexibility, Stay warm Suggested Foods for Vata: Oily, Warming or Heavy, Sweet, Salty and Sour, All nuts are okay, Dairy, Cooked vegetables, Heavy sweet fruits: bananas, melons

Vata Don'ts: Don't skip meals, Avoid being chilled, Don't work until you're tired...take regular breaks before you need to, Don't take on too many projects Suggested Foods food for Vata to avoid: Pungent, Bitter or Astringent. Avoid barley, corn, millet, buckwheat, and rye. Avoid uncooked, or gassy, fruits and vegetables

Vata-Kapha

Vata-Kapha: Vata is a combination of **wind** and **space**. Kapha is a combination of **water** and **earth**. Too much water makes mud. Too little water makes earth brittle.

Wind: An active element. Expansive, irregular, changeable.

Space: The container of wind.

Earth: Stability, stillness

Water: Eternally flowing, emotional, is absorbed by earth

Dosha Traits: A combination of wind and water. It's a matter of how much water is in the mix. The more water is in the air, the more humid it is. Humidity is cooling.

Characteristics: Solidly built, but not fat. More sustained stamina than Vata. The only element this dosha doesn't have is fire. This causes problems in their digestion and immune systems. They should be kind to their digestive systems.

This dosha has a difficult time with boundaries. If there is too much water in the system they absorb what others are thinking and feeling. It can be overwhelming. The water should be balanced with a warming diet. When balanced, they are peaceful, calm, creative and compassionate.

Warning Flags: All of Vata AND all of Kapha Warning Flags

Vata-Kapha Do's: Consistency, touch and be touched, explore new things, build endurance, stay warm, clear clutter

Food suggestions for Kapha-Vata: Light, dry, warm, pungent, bitter and astringent. Ginger tea with meals helps digestion. Use fresh herbs

Vata-Kapha Don'ts: Avoid dampness. Do not nap during the day unless you are ill. No dramas when upset, enjoy comedies or find something new.

Foods that Vata-Kapha should Avoid: Sweet, sour & salty. No sweets but honey (maximum of 2T a day). Avoid gassy foods, Avoid cold food and drinks on cold days

Kapha

KAPHA: A blend of **water**/emotion and **earth**/stability.

Too much water makes mud. Too little water makes earth brittle

Earth: Stability, stillness

Water: Eternally flowing, emotional, is absorbed by earth

Dosha Traits: Heavy, Slow, Steady, Solid, Cold, Soft, Oily. Responsible for the function of growth, development, stability, lubrication and storage within the body. It provides the liquid needed for the life of our cells. It lubricates our joints, moisturizes our skin, maintains immunity and helps to heal wounds. Kapha provides strength, vigor and stability.

Characteristics: Heavy set body, trouble with weight management. Kapha traits are peaceful, patient, tolerant, caring, compassionate, calm, steady mind, easy going manner and forgiving, stable, solid and faithful. Deep religious faith is common. They have excellent long-term memories, they will forgive you an insult but not forget. They take life slowly, steadily and deeply.

Warning Flags: Colds, flu, sinus congestion, bronchitis, pneumonia, sluggishness, excess weigh, diabetes, water retention and sinus headaches. Kapha is worse with the full moon. When unbalanced kapha may suffer from greed, attachment, envy, possessiveness, lust, laziness and depression.

Kapha Do's: Explore new things, Follow a routine, Stay warm, Use dry heat , to clear congestion, Clear clutter, Regular exercise

Suggested Kapha Foods: Light, dry, warm, pungent, bitter and astringent. Use small amounts of oil, Ginger tea with meals

Kapha Don'ts: Avoid naps. Avoid dampness. Avoid exposing your nose, throat and lungs to cold air. Avoid clinging to the status quo,

Foods for Kapha to avoid: Sweet, sour, and salty. Oats, rice, wheat, Avoid all sweeteners except honey, No dairy except a little ghee

The Seven Chakras

> Quoted from the Oxford English Dictionary:
> Definition of **Aura**, noun
> *The distinctive atmosphere or quality that seems to surround and be generated by a person, thing, or place.*

HAVE you ever been in a gathering of people when someone walks into the room that instantly brightens the mood of the gathering just by being there? Or someone that walks into a gathering in a very sad mood and quiets the mood of the room considerably?

Their aura (energy field) is felt by everyone in the group and everyone adjusts their moods to incorporate the newest member of the group.

The part of you that notices someone without using any of your five physical senses is your aura. It surrounds your body like a force field beginning at birth. It develops as you do.

The energy within the aura helps to keep your body, mind and spirit healthy while going through the adventures of your everyday life. How happy and healthy you are on a daily basis determines the health of your aura.

A healthy human adult aura extends out about three feet from their skin. Children and healthy older people are more than that, more like nine feet. Illness, pain, worry and stress make your field smaller. Being happy expands it. Being relaxed expands it. Being compassionate expands it.

Your very colorful aura is filled with the energy surrounding your chakras. The colors found within the aura are produced by the chakras. Each of your chakras are responsible for part of your body, mind, and spirit. All need to be healthy, or symptoms develop.

> Quoted from the Oxford English Dictionary:
> Definition of **chakra**, noun
> *(In Indian thought) each of the centers of spiritual power in the human body, usually considered to be seven in number.*
> From Sanskrit cakra (wheel or circle), from an Indo-European base meaning "turn", this base word is shared by wheel.

The doshas describe categories of traits/symptoms. The chakras are part of your energetic anatomy. They do the same thing for everyone. They have the same rules for everyone like any other part of your anatomy.

One healthy person's liver looks the same as another healthy person's liver. What your lifestyle does to it is the only reason it would look different. The same is true of a chakra.

The biggest difference between your liver and a chakra is how you fix them. If your liver isn't feeling well you can just change what you eat and stress levels for a while and it will feel better. A chakra requires a more personal effort to fix.

To make a permanent change in a chakra means you have to

make a permanent change in a part of your personality.

Chakras are about how you deal with the outside world on an emotional level. If you revert to your poorly choosing old self, your chakra will respond by being just as ill as it was before. Remarkably fast.

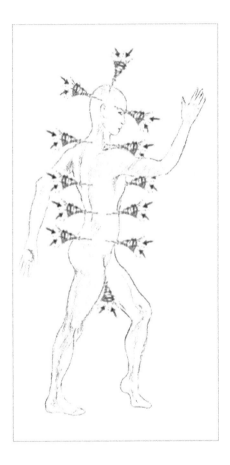

There are seven major chakras. The first is located at the bottom of your spine. Five are aligned along your spine. The seventh is on the top of your head.

A healthy adult chakra is about six inches in diameter. Five of the chakras have obvious front and back parts. The look a lot like a pair of small, peaceful, end to end tornadoes. The spinning action pulls energy into it, like the back of a fan pulls air.

The front half begins at your spine and spirals (clockwise, as if you are the clock) outward in front of you. The back half begins in the same place but spirals outward behind you.

The first chakra at the bottom of your spine has the same funnel shape, but spirals (also clockwise) downward towards the ground. The seventh chakra at the top of your head is the same funnel shape but spirals upward towards the sky (while standing). If you are lying down these two chakras spiral outward in line with your spine.

Each chakra is a different color. Some people can see them. What they are looking at are colors produced by the chakras, even the little ones. The colors of the chakras are the same as in the rainbow, in the same order.

When I was in third grade, I was taught to remember the order to the color prism by the name Roy G. Biv. The colors of the chakras begin with Red at the bottom of your spine, then Orange, Yellow, Green, Blue, Indigo and ends with Violet on the top of your head.

A wise teacher once told me that your biography becomes your biology. If your life feels like everything is working and your mind is at peace, your chakras are supplying clean energy into your body.

Your body uses that sparkling clean energy to maintain your body, clear your mind of stress and keep your spirit happy.

A healthy chakra filter out all negative aspects of your day like filters. Your energy field is like water in a fish tank. Your chakras are the filters keeping the water clean. Clear water means vibrant life inside the tank.

When a chakra is overwhelmed with something difficult, the spinning slows and the chakra decreases in size. The chakra filter is ineffective until the issue is dealt with. Since each chakra is responsible for parts of your body, mind, and spirit...symptoms will happen when a chakra is compromised.

Each dosha has at least two chakras that help keep that part of your body healthy. Each chakra also has it's own kind of remedies.

Each dosha is responsible for a different part of your physical make-up. Each chakra is responsible for a different part of how you deal with your emotions and social skills.

They are grown one at a time, in order from the first to the seventh. It is social development, not age, that determines the health of your chakra line. An adult's chakra line will not spin as fully as it should unless they are living an emotionally stable life.

If you have a lingering symptom, a chakra probably requires your assistance. It won't be easy, but the effort will be worth it

- **Root:** Red. Survival issues. Its all about you
- **Sacral:** Orange. It's about you and at least one other person. A social circle of any size.
- **Solar Plexus:** Yellow. The ability to deal with people outside your circle, but of the same culture
- **Heart:** Green. Bringing your inner truth to the culture you live in
- **Throat:** Blue. Speaking your inner thoughts in a truthful, compassionate manner to everyone you meet
- **Brow:** Indigo. Knowing that your words and actions impact people you will never meet. Able to forgive anyone. Compassionately.
- **Crown:** Violet. Compassion for all, without judgement of any kind. Nobody is better than anyone else. Ever. We are all trying to learn the same things.

The Chakras for each Dosha

The Pitta Chakras (primarily about your **BODY**, warm colors):

1. Root Chakra: Red

Muladhara: Sanskrit for Root Support. Survival issues like acquiring food, air, water, shelter, financial independence, power.

2. Sacral Chakra: Orange

Svadhishthana: Sanskrit for Dwelling place of the self. This is also where being able to have pleasure from your five senses is produced. You know what you like, and who.

3. Solar Plexus Chakra: Yellow

Manipura: Sanskrit for Jewel City. The four jewels refer to the four pearls of clarity, wisdom, self- confidence and well-being. This chakra helps you to survive in the world outside of your social circle.

THE VATA CHAKRAS (primarily about your **MIND**, mix of warm and cool colors):
3. Solar Plexus Chakra: Yellow
Manipura: Sanskrit for Jewel City. The four jewels refer to the four pearls of clarity, wisdom, self- confidence and well-being. This chakra helps you to survive in the world outside of your social circle.
4 Heart Chakra: Emerald Green
Anahata: Sanskrit for Unlimited, infinite sound. This is where your interior life is blended with the culture around.
5. Throat Chakra: Sky Blue
Vishuddha: Sanskrit for Pure Place Speaking and living your truth issues like honesty, speaking compassionately and speaking up for yourself. Also about being able to hear what is really true and being able to change an opinion.

THE KAPHA CHAKRAS (primarily about your **SPIRIT**, cool colors):
5. Throat Chakra: Sky Blue
Vishuddha: Sanskrit for Pure Place Speaking and living your truth issues like honesty, speaking compassionately and speaking up for yourself. Also about being able to hear what is really true and being able to change an opinion.
6. Brow Chakra: Indigo Blue
Ajna: Sanskrit meaning To Perceive Intuition, humor, seeing the big picture on any issue and recognizing patterns are all found here. The compassionate ability to forgive is also found here.
7. Crown Chakra: Violet and White
Sahasrara: Sanskrit meaning Thousand Petaled Deeply

thoughtful issues of spirituality, philosophy, compassion for all, imagination, completely nonjudgmental of all and living mindfully.

ROOT CHAKRA

THE ENERGY for fueling all of the chakras comes into your body from the root chakra. If your root chakra isn't functioning, less energy flows upward to the other six chakras. Its a long way to the seventh chakra.

There needs to be momentum to get it there. Without enough earth energy coming in, your root chakra can't bring in enough energy to get all the way to crown chakra on the top of your head. It needs fully charged momentum to get there.

If your root chakra ain't happy, ain't nobody gonna get happy. It is impossible to fully recharge any of the other six chakras if this one is compromised.

You open your root chakra with activity and physical movement. Exercise, dance, hiking all count. A strong root chakra turns physical activity into fuel for the whole body, mind and spirit to use.

The best thing you can do to increase your energy level is move. Every day. Start with just stretching exercises every morning or walking. Then increase it a bit every week. Every movement creates energy that ALL of your chakras need.

The root chakra is about your connection to the parts of life that you need to survive. Just you. Both feet on the ground with enough food, water, shelter and a sense of being safe. When you are confident in those things, your root chakra opens.

An open root chakra is also pretty helpful for achieving anything you work towards in the material world. It aids in having a patient strength of character that people rely on. Solidly rooted to reality. Brimming with confidence and having fun while doing it.

Basic Stats: • Sanskrit name: Muladhara. English translation: Root Support

- Located at the bottom of your spine and points downward between your legs
- This chakra is seen as **Red**

Key issues: • Survival issues like food, air, water, shelter, financial independence, power

- Basic human potential. Capable of anything.
- Libido
- Mental stability

Suggestions for Root Chakra health:

- Cooking and cleaning in your home, regularly.
- Sitting on the ground
- Walking barefoot
- Dancing
- Listening to music with percussion or drumming
- Laugh more

OVER-ACTIVE Root Chakra Traits: Selfishness, greed, materialistic, aggressive with anyone that challenges your assumed authority, overpowering, irritable, anger

OPEN Root Chakra Traits: Optimistic, graceful, feels at home, sufficient territory, daily tasks are effortless, joy of life, no doubt of your place in the world, grounded

UNDER-ACTIVE Rood Chakra Traits: Anxious, lack of confidence, feeling unloved, disorganized, easily feels unwelcome, abandonment issues, apathy, can't seem to focus, restlessness

∼

SACRAL CHAKRA

The Sacral Chakra is about relationships between yourself and at least one other person. It is also where the energy to create comes from. Not just babies, but any kind of projects or idea that you are passionate about. Creativity comes from having fun with at least one of your five senses, usually more. All five are used in cooking.

When this chakra is open, pleasure is possible in all five of your senses. This is where the sense of pleasure, and play of all kinds, starts.

Laughter of any sort, fall down giggling fun is fueled. Especially if the laughter is with at least one other person. Laughter is relaxing. The way relationships should be. This chakra is fed by the quality of relationships and level of creativity in your life.

This is the chakra that is responsible for feeling pleasure from intimacy or feeling toe-curling warm and cozy. But, those are just the sense of touch, it is also responsible for the way you feel when you see something stunningly beautiful, taste a really yummy meal, smell something from your childhood or hear music that makes you smile. This chakra fuels the fun in your life.

The root chakra provides the initial energy to get the sacral chakra moving. This chakra then absorbs and collects all of the energy of the social, creative and fun bits of your life. Making time for your relationships, creativity and fun nourish this chakra.

This chakra makes life feel more fun.

Basic Stats: • Sanskrit name: Svadhishthana. English translation: Dwelling place of the self.

- Located just below the navel
- This chakra is seen as **Orange**

Key issues:

- Relationships, pleasure
- Pleasant feelings from all five senses... **Touch:** the perfect temperature shower or bath. **Sight:** seeing anything that makes you really smile. **Taste:** a meal, or beverage that tastes so good you have to smile. **Smell:** anything that smells good to you every time. **Hearing:** enjoying any sound that makes you listen closer.

Suggestions for Sacral Chakra Health:

- Having a good time with at least one other person
- Photography, get a picture of every season of the year.
- Dance. On a dance floor, alone or while doing chores.
- Sit by water in nature. Creek, river, pond, lake or ocean.
- Laugh more

OVER-ACTIVE Sacral Chakra Traits: Over emotional, creates unnecessary drama with others, does not like others to be late or change plans, compulsive, frustration, sexual addiction, violence

OPEN Sacral Chakra Traits: Feelings flow freely, self confident, enthusiasm, enjoys intimacy, creative for fun, not pay, passion for life, optimistic, ability to bounce back from stress

UNDER-ACTIVE Sacral Chakra Traits: Self-denial, lacking creativity, always trying to fit in, loss of authentic self, poker-faced, unemotional, chronic fatigue, repressed feelings, sexually repressed

SOLAR PLEXUS CHAKRA

THE FIRST TWO chakras were about gathering and building energy from the physical world. This one turns it into usable energy. It metabolizes what happens during your day as well as everything you eat.

The first chakra (root) makes sure that you can survive on your own. The second chakra (sacral) makes sure that you can interact with another person and have fun doing it. You learn best when having fun with passions and skills you have.

Your third chakra gives you the tools to bring those skills to the world outside your door.

The Solar Plexus Chakra is about you not just surviving, but achieving your dreams in the culture you live in. This chakra is fed by how well you interact with the culture around you. In close relationships as well as groups.

This is a different set of survival skills. This chakra gives you the tools to remember that everyone is wonderfully, absurdly unique in their own ways. This gives you a strong sense of humor about your own oddities. This chakra generates that charismatic power that people can feel when you walk into the room.

Basic Stats: • Sanskrit name: Manipura. English translation: Jewel City. The jewels are the four pearls of clarity, wisdom, self-confidence, and well-being

- Just below your ribcage, center of chest
- This chakra is seen as **Yellow**

Key issues:

- Personal power
- Opinion forming
- Introversion
- Expansive nature
- All matters of growth

Suggestions For Solar Plexus Chakra Health:

- Having a good time with at least four other people
- Go to a new kind of restaurant

- Make or have a food that you have never had before.
- Do a hobby or craft that you loved as a child
- Walk in the sun. Watch a campfire. Any open flame counts as fire. Even tiny ones on candle wicks. Use several.
- Laugh more

OVER-ACTIVE Solar Plexus Chakra Traits: demanding, critical, narrow minded, abrasive, doesn't like to lose, easily finds fault with self and others, manipulative, nothing is good enough, everything always could be better in some way

OPEN Solar Plexus Chakra Traits: Accurate gut instinct, charismatic, good self-discipline, healthy self-esteem, appreciates uniqueness in others, complete control of emotions and thoughts, decisive, committed, radiate joy

UNDER-ACTIVE Solar Plexus Chakra Traits: passive and indecisive, doubt yourself and others, worry about what people think, afraid of authority, never feel good enough, dwells on the past, passive-aggressive, not ever getting what they want

HEART CHAKRA

THE FIRST THREE chakras all help you survive in the physical world around you. The physical world (body oriented) is all of the information your mind receives from your five senses, your social life and career. The world outside of your skin. All of them are stimulating to your body and life.

This fourth of seven, middle chakra is different. This one is calming. This is the first one to involve your interior life, too. The Heart Chakra combines everything about the physical world you live in and your inner life.

Your inner life is what you think, feel, dream and pray (all spirit oriented). The life under your skin, your conscience.

Keeping this chakra open means having compassion, trust, forgiveness and friendship in your life. When the heart chakra is open some amazing things happen. This is where automatic, instinctive healing energy comes from.

The heart chakra sends healing energy through your palms the moment you have compassion for someone that is hurt.

Everyone instinctively reaches for someone injured, especially a child. As soon as you touch them the energy goes from your hand to their injury. You don't even have to aim it.

We are designed to help heal each other. People that do energy work are using this natural ability. Anyone can learn how. All you need is a compassionate heart, clean chakras, and being willing to help.

Basic Stats: • Sanskrit name: Anahata. English translation: Unlimited, infinite sound

- Center of your chest
- This chakra is seen as **Emerald Green**

Key issues:

- Compassion followed by acts of Kindness
- Trust
- Unconditional Love
- Harmony
- Balancing your life between work and home

Suggestions for a healthy Heart Chakra:

- Eight hugs a day
- Surround yourself with greenery whenever possible
- Have something new for dinner
- Sit outside and feel the breeze on at least your face
- Lay in the grass

- Laugh more

OVER-ACTIVE Heart Chakra Traits: Suffocating people with love, fear of loneliness, ruled by emotions, no control, people pleaser, to a fault, possessive of others, clinging to people, afraid not to be liked, suspicious

OPEN Heart Chakra Traits: Patient, compassionate, empathy, nurturing, unconditionally loving, trust, accepting, forgiveness, okay spending time alone

UNDER-ACTIVE Heart Chakra Traits: Negative thinking, distant, emotional numbness, depression, sadness, feeling unloved and unappreciated, inability to forgive, loneliness, jealous

THROAT CHAKRA

THE FIFTH CHAKRA is about saying what you are thinking. Even if no one is there. You can do that with song, chanting, making music (not just listening to it), artwork, or conversation.

Conversation can be with anybody or anything. Singing is very therapeutic for throat chakra health. In a choir, singing along with music that makes you happy, or just busting out in song when you're inspired...all are very good for the throat chakra.

Talking to pets works pretty well, too.

Using your mouth as a weapon damages your throat chakra. Feeling guilty, making someone feel guilty, saying or doing something dishonest, speaking unkindly, taking part in gossip or creating drama ALL impact your throat chakra. Symptoms will result.

Only saying what you think people want to hear closes your throat chakra. A closed throat chakra makes your interior life unheard by others.

Even hard topics can be talked about in a calm, honest way. An open throat chakra makes your conversations more comfortable. Being comfortable expressing yourself to people gives you confidence, and makes others trust you. Speaking with confidence makes you feel heard. When someone feels heard, they feel respected.

Basic Stats: • Sanskrit name: Vishuddha. English translation: Pure place

- Located at the base of your throat in the V above your breastbone
- This chakra is seen as **Sky Blue**

Key issues:

- Living and speaking your truth
- Speaking only positive things about others
- Reducing guilt in your life
- Expressing yourself in all forms inc. singing, writing, artwork
- Lucid dreaming, the ability to be aware and active in dreams

Suggestions for a healthy Throat Chakra:

- Listening to music
- Singing
- Chanting
- Going for walks
- Look for shapes in clouds, preferably with a child
- Laugh more

OVER-ACTIVE Throat Chakra Traits: Talk too much, dominates conversation to keep others at a distance, bad listener, distraction, negativity, resentful, preoccupation with others, gullibility

OPEN Throat Chakra Traits: No problem expressing hopes and dreams, expression with art or craft, confident, honest, wise, sense of freedom, lucid dreaming, discrete, independent

UNDER-ACTIVE Throat Chakra Traits: Often misunderstood, introverted, shy, considered unreliable, doesn't keep promises, believes being honest is optional, uncomfortable with frank conversation, often answer questions with mixed messages, repressed expression

~

BROW CHAKRA

THE SIXTH CHAKRA'S center is located behind your eyes, where your optic nerves cross. This chakra is spirit oriented. Your ability to understand the big picture or long term benefits come from here.

When you can see the big picture, forgiveness is possible. You need to be able to imaging both sides of an issue before you can forgive someone.

Compassion comes *after* understanding how someone else would feel. That understanding comes from imagining it from their side. Imagination comes from this chakra.

This is also where your ability to recognize a pattern comes from. The brow chakra is the seat of intuition. You just know when something isn't quite right with what you are perceiving with one of your senses. The ability to see a pattern makes it easy to notice when something is out of place.

That explains why your sense of humor is also found here. This chakra is the first part of you to notice that something is funny because it is not expected. All humor is built on surprise.

Timing is everything.

A change in pattern surprises your mind. If it is absurdly different from normal, people laugh. Making a joke is creating an absurd surprise to a known pattern.

Laughing relaxes your body, calms your mind and refreshes your spirit. If joke is non-threatening, the happy response is healing...of everyone laughing.

Basic Stats: • Sanskrit name: Ajna. English translation: To perceive

- Located between your eyes
- This chakra is seen as **Indigo Blue**

Key issues:

- Determining your truth
- Pattern recognition in imagery, thought and life
- Compassion followed by Forgiveness
- Intuition
- Peace of Mind

Suggestions for a healthy Brow Chakra:

- Listen to relaxing music
- No sad lyrics
- Learn something new
- Go for nature walks
- Sit facing the sun on a blue sky day
- Laugh more

OVER-ACTIVE Brow Chakra Traits: Fantasize too much, spacey, hallucinations, paranoia

OPEN Brow Chakra Traits: Intuitive, focused, concentration, clairvoyance, feels in control of life, confident, no need for others to feel whole, patterns are easily seen

UNDER-ACTIVE Brow Chakra Traits: Rely on authority for opinions, rigid in thinking and beliefs, easily confused if something is different than already known ideas, lack of imagination, insensitivity, self-absorption

CROWN CHAKRA

THIS IS the only chakra with two colors. Violet and white. They swirl upward from the top of your head. The health of your crown chakra is dependent on the health of all the other six.

Remember, they are all connected. If one is blocked, everything above it is receiving less energy. The crown chakra can only open if all the chakras below are open and healthy.

Physical energy comes up from your root chakra, through all of the other chakras and leaves your body through the crown chakra.

If your crown chakra is open, healing energy can also come into your body from over your head. It travels down through your open brow and throat chakras to the heart chakra that directs it to the palms of your hands.

If you truly believe that race, religion, gender, age, culture, income level, nationality or what school you go to doesn't make a difference in anyone's real worth, your crown chakra is open. Your beliefs or lifestyle are not better than theirs, in any situation. Just different.

There is no difference in our responses to hearing a toddler giggle or belly laugh. Any child. Nobody judges if a child's innocent antics are politically correct or not.

Toddler giggles make us smile with them regardless of what background they might have. There is no difference in our automatic reactions if that same child were hurt.

We don't even think about if the child is worthy of our assistance. All children are worthy of our attention when they have just had an injury.

All people are injured in some way. Its as simple as that. If you believe you are better than someone, your crown chakra closes.

Basic Stats: • Sanskrit name: Sahasrara. English translation: Thousand Petaled

- Located at the top of your head and points upward to the sky
- This chakra is seen as **Violet**

Key issues:

- Living your truth, walking the talk
- Idealism
- Imagination
- Intuition
- Living in the now, being mindful of the present.
- Concentration

Suggestions for a healthy Crown Chakra:

- Meditation
- Prayer
- Sitting quietly in nature, without music.
- Walk to the same place every day. Every season.
- Go swimming, underwater if possible
- Laugh more

OVER-ACTIVE Crown Chakra Traits: Over-thinking an issue, addicted to spirituality or meditation, believes they are more spiritually capable than others, ignoring bodily needs, poor grasp on reality

OPEN Crown Chakra Traits: Aware, treats all people equally, selflessness, trust, inspired

UNDER-ACTIVE Crown Chakra Traits: Very rigid opinions, not aware of a need for spirituality, don't believe you are worthy, feeling isolated, doubt beliefs

16
TRADITIONAL TIBETAN-MONGOLIAN MEDICINE

It is with the deepest respect and gratitude that I present the following material. It is not my intention to teach Traditional Tibetan-Mongolian Medicine. That should only be done by those with decades of training of their art.

Their practice of this medicine was, and is, truly inspiring. It was an honor to be taught by Dr. B. Boldsaikhan of Ulan Bator, Mongolia. I was certified in Ulan Bator in 2002.

My intention is to introduce the wisdom of healthier self-care choices to my culture. I adapted what I was taught to resources, climate and a very broad spectrum of clientele here in North America.

Quoted from the Oxford English Dictionary:
Definition of **adapt**, verb
Make (something) suitable for a new use or purpose; modify.

The Classical Ayurveda era came to a close in 800 AD when Tibet began adapting that wisdom to their own resources and religion. Ayurveda is based on the resources available in India.

Most of those natural resources were unavailable in Tibet. Ayurveda is the medical science based on Hindu, the primary religion of India. Tibetans are Buddhist.

> If you don't like a thing, try to change it. If you can't change it, change the way you think about it. *Maya Angelou*

Around 800 AD a man named Asthangahrydaya is credited for beginning to think about Ayurveda differently. Tibetan kings invited physicians from India, China, Nepal, Persia and Greece to teach Tibetans their medical practices.

Over the next several hundred years they studied these medical practices as well as the practices of Assyria and Babylon. They used these studies of ancient traditions to create a new way to look at illness based on Buddhist beliefs.

Mongolians, also Buddhist, had their first translation of the finished work, The Four Tantras, in 1400. The Mongolians blended Tibetan Ayurveda into their existing medicine. They use some techniques and diagnostics from Chinese Medicine as well as Ayurveda.

> We are not human beings having a spiritual experience. We are spiritual beings having a human experience.
> *Pierre Teilhard de Chardin*

Buddhists believe that they are spiritual beings having a human experience. Each human experience comes equipped with a body that is particularly suited for the spiritual lessons that the spirit needs to learn during that body's lifetime.

Tibetans believe that you can only grow spiritually if your mind and body are not distracted by illness.

The health of your body is determined by how well you are learning your spiritual lessons. Your health is an indicator of how/what you think and how compassionately you behave towards others. All disease can be alleviated by changing the way you think and behave. Behavior includes what you eat, think, say, or do during a day.

Health is not a goal. It's a measurement of how healthy you are today. Your health changes as your life does. Your mind is responsible for making your life run smoothly, or not. It receives information from the five senses, intuition and spirit...then chooses what to do.

Your health moves your body through your life. If your mind is handling your life well, you have no mental stress or symptoms in body, mind or spirit.

After centuries of study, the Tibetans determined that if you keep your mind free of negative emotions, your health remains well balanced and your immune system handles illnesses quickly and efficiently. Illness is a distraction. The goal is to not be distracted from what is important. Compassion.

All disease is caused by your mind being distracted by one of three strong emotions...**Aggression** (or anger of any kind), emotional **Attachment** (to people, ideas or things) and **Ignorance** (closed-mindedness, not wanting to know).

Everyone experiences these emotional distractions during a regular life. The trick is learning to use them as a tool. All three can be very handy, but only when used appropriately. Then you put the tool away until you need it next time. You're not supposed to enjoy them so much that you never turn the tool off.

Your body is a barometer of how well you handle these negative emotions in your life. All other negative emotions stem from one of these three. Or a combination of them.

All three can be handled by changing what caused them to arise in the first place...or change the way you think about what caused them. Either way, the stress diminishes. Less stress, less symptoms.

All positive emotions are beneficial to your body.

Strong emotions, good or bad, have their uses. Strong negative emotions stimulate the brain into producing chemicals needed to take action. Strong positive emotions calm you down.

Your body's chemical reactions caused by the strong negative emotion are supposed fade after action has begun. If the strong emotion or thoughts lingers, they become a symptom because your body is still producing the chemical reaction to the problem. If it lingers long enough, you develop a physical symptom.

Strong positive emotions are the antidote. My mother used to tell me that the best thing to do when you are feeling down is to help someone else. There is always someone that needs help. She was right. Compassion is a powerful antidote for negative emotions

- Knowledge purifies delusion
- Emptiness (free of all attachments) purifies hatred
- Sameness purifies pride
- Discernment purifies desire
- Accomplishment purifies envy

The three emotions that are responsible for illness in the human experience are: Aggression, Attachment, and Ignorance

Aggression has its purpose. It is used best as a very quick response to something perceived as dangerous. It motivates your entire body into taking some kind of action. Once the action is taken, your body and mind should calm down to normal levels. If your body stays on high alert, or your mind just can't let something go...aggression is now a symptom.

Attachment has its natural purpose. It is the way you change and adapt to anything new. It is how new things are invented. Wanting something different, or new is natural and healthy. Once your life has created, obtained or adapted around the latest thing, the next step is supposed to be finishing the acquisition process.

Incorporate that new thing into your life and just enjoy it before acquiring or creating something else. If you are constantly acquiring new things, beginning project after project that you don't finish, or your life is changing all the time...attachment is now a symptom.

Ignorance also has a natural purpose. This is closer translated to closed-mindedness than stupidity. This strong emotion is about not wanting to know.

Not wanting to be confused by the facts because you don't want to change the way you think about something, or fighting change of any kind. It should be used as a tool for being cautious about something brand new to you.

It isn't healthy to accept everything without question. It is just as unhealthy to be closed-minded and not accept anything new. Period. If your caution is preventing you from ever changing your mind about anything...not wanting to know is now a symptom.

> A string too tight breaks, and the music dies.
> A string too slack has no sound, and the music dies.
> There is a middle way.
> Buddha

~

TIBETAN-MONGOLIAN AYURVEDA and Indian Ayurveda both use five categories of symptoms in the same order.

Indian Ayurveda calls them doshas... *Pitta, Pitta-Vata, Vata, Vata-Kapha,* and *Kapha*

Tibetan-Mongolian Medicine call them nyepas... *Circulation (Blood)* symptoms are associated with Aggression, *Bile* symptoms with Aggression and Attachment, *Wind* symptoms with Attachment, *Phlegm* symptoms with Attachment and Ignorance, and *Lymph (Yellow Water)* symptoms with Ignorance

The five categories all describe the same kind of symptoms and remedies. Differing in language, resources and religions.

There are many, many similarities in each of the five categories by both kinds of Ayurveda. Same kinds of remedies, same kinds of results, just different cultures and climate.

Symptom are used to determine what part of your human experience is giving your mind a bit of trouble. Finding the root of the problem and eliminating it from your thought process fixes the problem.

Symptoms are like dandelions. Only dealing with the symptom is like picking a dandelion flower. It will keep coming back. Dealing with the problem that is causing the symptom is like digging out the root of a dandelion.

No root, no flower. No problem, no symptom

Circulation (Blood)

HOT ACTION, Toxic emotion: Aggression

Aggression can be transformed into joyous, cautious attentiveness followed by well thought out action.

Blood

Symptoms: Stomach pains, back problems, digestive disorders, constipation, feeling tired just after eating or drinking, recurrent infections or injuries, blood disorders, sudden bouts of anger, recurrent bad dreams that cause waking in alarm, sweating, shouting or sleepwalking, red face, red eyes, gingivitis, dry nostrils, bleeding gums, high blood pressure

Healthy Characteristics: Highly active. Deep and profound thinkers who make natural leaders. They have great endurance and stamina. Sports and challenging activities are a crucial part of their lifestyle. Powerfully interested in the opposite sex. They love caffeine, sugar, meats and spicy foods. They like reading, researching and debating issues. Capable of inspiring others to be passionate about life.

TOO MUCH Circulation Traits: Red eyes and/or face, Headache, Feeling hot when it isn't, Cold sores, Mouth infections, Tooth pain

Causes of Too Much Circulation: Being angry. Too much hot, sour, salty or greasy foods. Too many saunas , too much sunbathing, too much aerobics, running, Competition

Decreasing Circulation: Wash or swim in cool water, meditation, relaxing music, avoid physical exertion. Avoid anger

TOO LITTLE Circulation Traits: Dizziness, ringing in your ears, blurred vision, heart palpitations, feeling powerless

Causes of Too Little Circulation: Becoming chilled in wet weather, washing with cold water, swimming in cool water during the winter, too much meditation, eating too much sugar

Increasing Circulation: Weight bearing exercise, sit near a fire, sunbathing, naps, walk gently, avoid feeling cold

Bile

WARMING ACTION, Toxic emotion: Aggression AND Attachment

Bile

Aggression can be transformed into joyous, cautious attentiveness followed by well thought out action. **Attachment** can be transformed into a mind that is totally clear and unimpeded.

Symptoms: Stomach pains, back problems, digestive disorders, recurrent infection or injuries, blood disorder, sudden anger, night terrors. Symptoms have slow onset, become intense and then linger. Fever, no sleep (day or night), swollen lymph nodes and fast fevers, Fast disease process, hot flashes, red eyes, red face, headache, dry nostrils, oily skin, bad smelling sweat, stool and urine, tendency towards diarrhea, mucus in stool, yellow tongue.

Healthy Characteristics Creative, impulsive, reflective, interested, excitable. Quick to sicken, quick to heal. Passionate about righting wrongs and helping the downtrodden. Deeply concerned about human rights, equality and freedom for all. They make everyone feel safe and are excellent at creating homes and communities. They are the storytellers, keepers of family history and heirlooms.

TOO MUCH Bile Traits: Jaundice, Quick to hunger, Feeling unusually hot, Fever, Hot flashes

Causes for Too Much Bile: Too much hot, sour, salty, greasy food.

Very hot, dry summer, unseasonably warm winter, keeping anger or envy hidden, recent cold, infection or virus

To Decrease Bile: Cool environments, Sitting in cool places, Swimming or washing in cool water, No physical exertion, Relax with a friend

TOO LITTLE Bile Traits: Feeling cool when it isn't, Flushed skin color, Mucus in stool

Causes for Too Little Bile: Cold summer, very cold winter, late spring, cooling off too much in the summer, not warm enough in winter, sitting on the cold ground

To Increase Bile: Weight bearing exercise, sit near high heat, sunbathing, being excited, anticipation, nap- ping on a hot day

Wind

WARMING ACTION, Toxic emotion: Attachment

Wind

Attachment can be transformed into a mind that is totally clear and unimpeded.

Symptoms: Sleep problems, yawning, sighing, Shifting pain in the hips, and joints, shifting pain in general, dislike of open spaces, anxiety, general unhappiness, joint pain, twitching, neurological problems like Parkinson's and dementia, breathing problems, pins and needle sensations, sudden fatigue or energy, cravings for food, alcohol, drugs or people. Not able to finish anything.

Healthy Characteristics Creative, impulsive, reflective, interested, excitable. Wind types are full of energy, highly intuitive and very willing to help others. They have strong bodies that they prefer to fuel with a diet of fresh fruit and vegetables, a little meat and dairy food. They love to sing and to argue, enjoy taking risks and need drama in their lives. They can be naive and sentimental. They are enchanted by music and dance and are happiest when exploring their spiritual potential.

TOO MUCH Wind Traits: Greed, constipation, talking more, dizziness, loss of strength, sighing, restlessness, obsessive thoughts

Common Causes for Too much wind: Too much bitter food, insomnia, lack of sleep or food, too active, being overwhelmed, windy days

To Decrease Wind: Cool environments, sit in cool places, swim or wash in cool water; warm, nutritious food; walk

TOO LITTLE Wind Traits: Lack of energy, talking less, feeling clogged up, unclear memory, melancholy, unvocalized pain, cold to the bone

Common Causes for Too Little Wind: Too little activity, being too cozy, very hot dry summer, windy days, sitting in a cold draft, feeling powerless

To Increase Wind: Weight bearing exercise, sit near high heat, sunbathing, dress warmly, dim lighting, candles, laugh with friends

Phlegm

Phlegm

COOLING ACTION TOXIC EMOTION: Attachment AND Ignorance (Closed mindedness)

Attachment can be transformed into a mind that is totally clear and unimpeded. **Ignorance** can be transformed into a necessary awareness of a bigger picture

Symptoms: Sleep problems, dislike of open spaces, anxiety, general unhappiness, joint pain, twitching, neurological problems like Parkinson's and dementia, breathing problems, pins and needle sensations, sudden fatigue or energy, cravings for food, alcohol, drugs or people. The difference with Cool types are that the symptoms come on slowly and linger. They become ill so slowly that they may have no idea that they have an underlying disease.

Healthy Characteristics Quiet and gentle when balanced they have a great capacity for understanding the forces of nature and communicating this to others. They understand the natural energy of the planet and are good with plants and animals. They respect tradition but have no qualms about ripping down outdated traditions and creating waves in general. They use their minds to create new ways of thinking, employing the written word as their chosen means of communication.

TOO MUCH Phlegm Traits: Greed, Congestion/cough, Detachment, Unclear sense of taste, Sluggishness, Indigestion

Common Causes for Too Much Phlegm: Over sleeping, Too much bitter, sweet, heavy and/or greasy foods. Relaxing after eating, under active, too much routine. Being in a cold, damp place.

To Decrease Phlegm: Warm, dry places. Learn something new, keep moving, dress warmly, laughter, play

TOO LITTLE Phlegm Traits: Paranoia, Over involvement, Fearful of deadline or a mistake, Writing detailed to-do lists

Common Causes for Too Little Phlegm: Eating raw grains or fruit. Not enough quality quiet time, indoors too much, being too warm in a warm room for too long, not enough sleep

To Increase Phlegm: Spend time in nature; walk, don't run; simplify, declutter, nap when tired

~

Lymph (Yellow Water)

COLD ACTION, Toxic Emotion: Ignorance (Closed mindedness)

Yellow Water

Ignorance can be transformed into a necessary awareness of a bigger picture. Learning more about new things allows you to be comfortable with the ever changing nature of life.

Symptoms: Skin outbreaks and diseases, eye problems, lung disorders, hormonal problems, lack of virility, problems conceiving and in pregnancy, eating disorders, weight problems, bone disorders, melancholy or depression and edema (water retention), stiff joints, rheumatic arthritis, coarse skin, dry skin, feeling a loss of mobility, feeling isolated.

Healthy Characteristics Traditions that help others is very important to this category. Deep thinking, an interest in philosophy and a desire for creativity of all sorts is common. They don't like sudden changes or surprise. Preferring to manage timing of any newness. If it goes against tradition, they will fight against it. They prefer simple, light foods and are happy enabling others to find fulfillment and well-being. They create new ways of thinking, choosing the written word to communicate.

TOO MUCH Lymph Traits: Greed, Excessive introspection, Water Retention, Weight management, Hair loss, Joint Pain, Inflammation, Itchiness

Common Causes for Too Much Lymph: Too long in the damp, too long in a dirty room, not dressing warmly, trauma to liver, allergies to dust/wool, strong winds; rainy, dark days

To Decrease Phlegm: Warm, dry places. Learn something new, activity after eating, physical activity, laughter

TOO LITTLE Phlegm Traits: Skin (sores) outbreaks, Eye problems, Bone disorders, Diarrhea, Muscle atrophy, Sweating, Burnout

Common Causes for Too Little Phlegm: Not sleeping, Working too hard, Sudden changes of any sort, Greed , Holding grudges, Inner anxiety, or worry

To Increase Phlegm: Spend time in nature, Walk, don't run, Simplify, Declutter, Napping when tired

17

TRADITIONAL CHINESE MEDICINE

Quoted from the Merriam-Webster Dictionary:
Definition of **Taoism,** noun
A Chinese philosophy based on the writings of Lao-Tzu (604-531 BC) that stresses living simply and honestly, and in harmony with nature.

Classic Ayurveda is a medical science of Hinduism. Traditional Tibetan-Mongolian Medicine is a medical science of Buddhism. Traditional Chinese Medicine is the medical science based on Taoism.

Tao means way of life. A thousand years before Lao-Tzu was born, ancient Taoism was a lifestyle that was legendary for people living happily to a hundred years old. Details of this ancient lifestyle was first described in the Chinese medical book called The Yellow Emperor's Canon of Medicine in 240 BC.

Yin Yang

The book reads like a dialog of questions and explanations between the Emperor and his acupuncturist. The emperor was concerned that his people were becoming and ill and dying by the age of fifty. His wise acupuncturist tells him how the ancients were able to live twice that long. Happily and without illness. The details from this book are still being used today.

>   Quoted from the Merriam-Webster Dictionary:
>   Definition of **Qi**, noun
>   *The circulating life force whose existence and properties are the basis of much of Chinese philosophy and medicine.*

ALL LIFE BEGINS with qi and ends without it. Your body comes equipped with a fixed amount of qi at birth. As qi is depleted during your every day life, it is supposed to be replenished on a regular basis by the air you breathe and what you eat. Food is considered to be a way to replenish the qi your body has used...NOT only as a fuel for the cells in your body. All your food choices have an effect on your mind as well as your body. Qi imbalance, too much or too little, is the root of all illness. Its absence is death.

Qi is your spark of life. It brings life to your body and mind. Everything you do, think, touch, see, eat, drink, or hear impacts your how well your qi flows through you. When you are happy and content with everything in your life, your qi is flowing exactly the way it's supposed to.

Stress, negative emotions and illness reduces the amount of qi available for your body and mind to use. Symptoms occur when the flow of qi isn't quite the way your body needs it to be.

The Chinese symbol for Qi is the lid of a pot being raised by steam while over a fire. Hot, cold and the movement in between the two. Hot is yang. Cold is yin. To the Chinese, everything in life is either hot, cold, or a blend of the two.

QUOTED FROM THE MERRIAM-WEBSTER DICTIONARY:
Definition of **Yang**, noun

The active male principle of the universe. Characterized as male, creative and associated with heaven/sky, heat and light. Contrasted with yin.

Yang (adds heat to your body, mind, and spirit): Hot, Light, Day, Dry, Busy, Stimulating, Extrovert, Male, Testosterone, Anger

Yang Symptoms: Hot Disease, Short term illness, Fever, High blood pressure, Migraines, Rash, Red Eyes, Hyperactive, Insomnia, Spontaneity

Quoted from the Merriam-Webster Dictionary:
Definition of **Yin,** noun
The passive female principle of the universe. Characterized as female, sustaining and associated with earth, dark and cold. Contrasted with yang.

Yin (adds coolness to your body, mind, and spirit): Cold, Dark, Night, Wet, Stillness, Calming, Introvert, Female, Estrogen, Sadness, Methodical

YIN SYMPTOMS: Cold Disease, Long term illness, Pneumonia, Low blood pressure, Stuffy head cold, Infection, Dark circles under eyes, Fatigue, Chronic oversleeping

EVERYONE IS BORN with a unique combination of yin and yang traits. When your lifestyle is replenishing and supporting this unique combination, you are healthy in mind, body and spirit. Some people have more yang by nature. Some have more yin. None of us are exactly the same. Your body was built to match your unique nature.

If you were born with more yang than yin, you are more extroverted and enjoy a busy productive day. Less seems a bit boring. If you have more yin than yang, you are more introverted, rarely bored and look forward to quiet at the end of a busy day. One is not better than the other. The only difference is their self-care. If they do their unique self- care, they are both productive, stress free and symptom free.

If you have a mostly yang nature, you need to make sure that you make calming yin choices throughout the day. Too much yang will cause yang symptoms like burnout, high blood pressure, migraines and insomnia. If you have a yin nature, you need to make stimulating yang choices throughout the day. Too much yin will cause yin symptoms like depression, pneumonia and chronic illness.

Everything you feel, think, touch, see, taste, smell or hear during your day has either a yin or yang effect on your body. It all adds up. When the amount of yin and yang in your life is balanced, your body is healthy, your spirit is happy and your mind is clear. No stress, no symptoms.

Chinese medicine divides people into five categories the same way that Indian Ayurveda and Traditional Tibetan-Mongolian Medicine (TTMM) do.

Their vocabulary is slightly different because their cultures are different. Indian Ayurveda calls the categories Doshas. Traditional Tibetan-Mongolian Medicine called the Nyepas. Traditional Chinese Medicine (TCM) calls them The Five Elements.

The Five Elements are based on nature because Taoism is based on nature. Each Element is a nature-based parable description of the traits and symptoms found within the Element.

Ayurveda Doshas: Pitta, Pitta-Vata, Vata, Vata-Kapha, and Kapha
TTMM Nyepas: Circulation, Bile, Wind, Phlegm, and Lymph
TCM Elements: Fire, Wood, Earth, Metal, and Water

Fire is the most yang (stimulating) of the elements. Wood is stimulating, but not as much. Earth moves between stimulating and calming, but is considered slightly stimulating. Metal is calming but not as calming as much as Water, the most yin (calming).

All five of the elements work together. They replenish and balance each other automatically when your lifestyle is replenishing the qi that you use up during your day. Everyone has at least a little bit of each of the elements.

How much of each determines what your unique combination is. Same as in Ayurveda. Each of the elements have foods and activities that help them balance their hot (yang) and cold (yin) traits. Just like in Ayurveda, just worded differently.

Chinese Medicine is very precise. Each of The Five Elements are responsible for a part of your body, just like Ayurveda.

Within each of the Elements this responsibility is shared by at least two meridians, one yang and one yin. Qi is delivered to very precise parts of your body through these meridians. A symptom can pinpoint exactly which meridian may need your help.

Definition of **Meridian,** noun

(In acupuncture and Chinese medicine) each of a set of pathways in the body along which vital energy is said to flow.

BLOOD (YIN) IS PUMPED by the heart through arteries and veins. Qi energy (yang) is pumped through the body with meridians. The meridians replenish energy used by your your lifestyle.

Meridians are like the wiring in your car. Each wire brings life to a different part of the car.

A complete listing of the fourteen meridians, what they do, and their particular tonic foods can be found in Chapters 18 and 19.

THE ELEMENT OF FIRE

The flame that burns twice as bright, burns half as long. *– Lao Tzu*

Fire Element Personality Traits:

Fire

- Seeking out things that spark interest.
- Bursts of enthusiasm that make you passionate about life in general.
- Cutting corners when bored or believe your way will be more efficient. Moving quickly without considering consequences or any hurt feelings.
- Optimistic
- Dislike routine
- Competitive
- Alert and aware of surroundings and situations around you.
- Charismatic
- Born leaders
- Communicates easily with others
- Love talking and socializing
- Very good at first impressions
- Intuitive
- Learns easily
- Empathic
- Gentle, warming
- Devoted
- Enthusiastic

SYMPTOMS of too much fire element in your system: Anxiety, restlessness, insomnia, talking too much or more rapidly than normal, nervous laughter, easily stimulated, profuse/frequent perspiration (your body trying to cool the body as fast as possible), flushed face, irregular or rapid heartbeat, painful urination, strong but erratic pulse, overheats easily, mouth sores, tongue sores, blistered lips, dry painful eczema.

. . .

SYMPTOMS *of not enough fire element in your system:* Weak, lackluster, bland, emotionally cold, unfeeling, slow, irregular pulse, chills or overheats easily, low blood pressure, dizzy easily, fainting, anemic, pale with flushed cheeks, tires easily.

Emotional Cause for Imbalance: Joyful overindulgence

Environmental Causes for Imbalance: Summer, drought, dry hot weather

Physical Causes for Imbalance: Too much of what they love... caffeine, hot spicy and/or sweet foods, alcohol, psychedelic drugs, stress, too little sleep, overwork, obsession

Fire Element Yin Meridians: Heart, Pericardium

Fire Element Yang Meridians: Governing, Small Intestine, Triple Warmer

Fire Element Tonics...

Symptoms of too much fire element (yang) in your body, mind, and/or spirit: Hot. Anxiety, restlessness, insomnia, talking too much or more rapidly than normal, nervous laughter, easily stimulated, profuse/frequent perspiration (your body trying to cool the body as fast as possible), flushed face, irregular or rapid heartbeat, painful urination, strong but erratic pulse, overheats easily, mouth sores, tongue sores, blistered lips, dry painful eczema.

BUILDING MOISTURE: *Sweet, bland, sour, juicy foods*

Cooling action: Almonds, apricot, black beans, pinto beans, beets, blueberries, carrots, cheese, Chinese cabbage, coconut oil, grapes, herring, honey, Jerusalem artichokes, milk, oats, olive oil, olives, oranges, oysters, peanut oil, peanuts, pineapple, plums, pork, potatoes, sardines, sesame seeds, strawberries, string beans, white sugar, tangerines

Neutral action: Almonds, apricot, black beans, pinto beans, beets, blueberries, carrots, cheese, Chinese cabbage, coconut oil, grapes, herring, honey, Jerusalem artichokes, milk, oats, olive oil, olives, oranges, oysters, peanut oil, peanuts, pineapple, plums, pork, potatoes, sardines, sesame seeds, strawberries, string beans, white sugar, tangerines

Warming action: Coconut milk, malt syrup, nectarines, peaches, pine nuts, sweet rice, rice milk, soy oil

∽

DECONGESTING QI: *Spicy, sour and bitter foods.*
Cooling action: Crab, swiss chard, watercress, wheat germ
Neutral action: Beets, eggplant, leeks, shiitake mushrooms, olives, rice bran, rose hips, saffron, sardines
Warming action: Cayenne, cherries, chives, onions, peaches, rice wine, safflower, scallions, shrimp, sweet basil, turmeric, vinegar

∽

REDUCING HEAT: *Eliminate toxic heat from the system*
Cooling action: Aloe vera, bamboo shoots, bananas, basil, aduki beans, mung beans, beet greens, cattail, clam, crab, egg whites, eggplant, endive, figs, grape leaves, grapefruit, honey, licorice, peppermint, romaine lettuce, salt, spinach beets, mung bean sprouts, summer squash, star fruit, strawberries, Swiss chard, tangerine peel, tofu

∽

BLOOD CIRCULATING TONICS: *Reduce coagulation and promote circulation*
Warming action: Basil, brown sugar, cayenne, celery, chicken, chives, clams, coriander, eggplant, ham, mustard, mustard greens, peaches, radish, sticky rice, saffron, scallion (white heads), tofu, vinegar

Heart & Stomach Tonics: Strengthens heart and stomach
Warming action: Beef, beer, cardamom seeds, chicory, clam, coffee, corn, fennel seeds, ginseng, mango, milk, shiitake mushrooms, white rice, green tea, wheat

Energy Circulation Tonics: Keeps energy moving from organ to organ
Warming action: Basil, red beans, beef, caraway, carrot, chives, clam, dill seed, eggs, fennel seed, garlic, grapefruit, kumquat, limes, malt, shiitake mushrooms, mussels, mustard greens, saffron, scallion (white part), spearmint, star anise, string bean, tangerines, turmeric, vinegar

Blood Tonics: Helps with blood loss or poor absorption of nutrients
Warming action: Beef, eggs, oxtail, oysters, spinach

Symptoms of when there isn't enough fire element (yang) in your body, mind, and/or spirit: Weak, lackluster, bland, emotionally cold, unfeeling, slow, irregular pulse, chills or overheats easily, low blood pressure, dizzy easily, fainting, anemic, pale with flushed cheeks, tires easily.
Building Blood (Essence): Sweet, sour, astringent foods.
Cooling action: Eggplant, gluten, sesame oil, spinach, spirulina
Neutral action: Aduki beans, black beans, kidney beans, beef, beef liver, beets, carrots, egg yolk, herring, milk, oysters, peanuts, pork, sardines, sesame seeds
Warming action: Anchovy, blackberries, butter, cherries, chestnuts, chicken, chicken liver, chives, currants, lamb, leeks, mussels,

nutritional yeast, pine nuts, raspberries, sticky rice, salmon, shrimp, trout, turkey, vinegar, walnuts

∾

Liver Tonics: Sour - obstruct movement. Slows abnormal discharge
Warming action: Mung beans, beef liver, black sesame seeds, chicken liver, chive seeds, peppermint, romaine lettuce, strawberries

∾

Heart Tonics: **Builds heat back into the system**
Warming action: Beer, Chicken liver, Chinese endive, Wheat

∾

Spleen Tonics: **Sweet - nourishing and invigorating, relieves spasm and pain**
Warming action: Cardamom seeds, cherries, chestnuts, cinnamon, clams, ginseng, grape leaves, mandarin oranges, shiitake mushrooms, peppermint, persimmon, pineapple, string beans, yams

∾

THE ELEMENT OF WOOD

Nature does not hurry, yet everything is accomplished. – *Lao Tzu*

Wood Element Personality Traits:

- Builds momentum, adapts, then grows.
- Deeply rooted
- Confident

- Assertive
- Bold
- Powerful
- Direct, to a fault. Often outspoken
- Strongly argue their opinions
- Forceful in disagreements
- Piercing, penetrating eyes may attract, but avoid their wrath
- Committed
- Decisive
- Powerful intellect
- Strong concentration skills
- Precise
- Sharp witted
- Strong sex drive
- Excel at planning and decision making
- Good digestion
- Needs short periods of deep sleep
- Clear vision and goals and know how to make them happen
- Physical exercise and reading restores balance.

Wood

S*ymptoms of too much wood element in your system:* Arrogant, controlling, angry disposition, workaholic, pain just below the ribs, hernias, migraines, high blood pressure, oily skin/hair, boils, cramps of long muscles, hands, feet; vertigo, ringing in ears, constipation with cramps/spasms, sciatica, heartburn, difficult swallowing, eye/ear pain, shingles, awkward and accident-prone, hard thick nails, breast pain, tendon injuries

Symptoms of not enough wood element in your system: Indecisive, without strong direction in life, stuck, repressed emotions, unable to express anger, hypoglycemia, blurry vision, sensitivity to light or sound, cystitis, urethritis, tendinitis, dry brittle nails, lax joints and tense muscles, irritable colon, chronic tension in neck and across shoulders.

Emotional Cause for Imbalance: Anger (Liver Meridian), Indecision (Gall Bladder)

Environmental Causes for Imbalance: Hot or Windy days. Wind (even watching or even listening to it) effects your neck and throat. Keep them covered on cold and/or windy days. Spring and summer both make wood imbalances worse.

Physical Causes for Imbalance: Excessive sour, greasy and/or spicy food, alcohol, opiates and amphetamines

Wood Element Yin Meridian: Liver

Wood Element Yang Meridian: Gall Bladder

Wood Element Tonics...

Symptoms of when there is too much wood element (yang) in your body, mind, and/or spirit: Arrogant, controlling, angry disposition, workaholic, pain just below the ribs, hernias, migraines, high blood pressure, oily skin/ hair, boils, cramps of long muscles, hands, feet; vertigo, ringing in ears, constipation with cramps/spasms, sciatica, heartburn, difficult swallowing, eye/ear pain, shingles, awkward and accident-prone, hard thick nails, breast pain, tendon injuries

Decongesting Essence: Spicy, sour and bitter food.
    Cooling action: Crab, Swiss chard, watercress, wheat germ
    Neutral action: Beets, eggplant, leeks, shiitake mushrooms, olives, rice bran, rose hips, saffron, sardines
    Warming action: Cayenne, cherries, chives, onions, peaches, rice wine, safflower, scallions, shrimp, sweet basil, turmeric, vinegar

Reducing Heat: Eliminating toxic heat from the system

Cooling action: Aloe vera, bamboo shoots, bananas, basil, aduki beans, mung beans, beet greens, cattail, clam, crab, egg whites, eggplant, endive, figs, grape leaves, grapefruit, honey, licorice, peppermint, romaine lettuce, salt, spinach beets, mung bean sprouts, summer squash, star fruit, strawberries, Swiss chard, tangerine peel, tofu

INTERNAL WIND TONIC: **Heat creates wind = Stress creates chaos**
Symptoms: Usually diet related. Brought on by an excess of fatty, high cholesterol animal products. Signs of wind move without pattern. Symptoms include dizziness, moving pains, convulsions, tremors, cramps, seizures, strokes, emotional turmoil, nervousness, uncertainty, spasms, itching, dizziness.
Cooling action: The cooling energy of Yin are needed to calm the wind/ chaos in your life. Look for culprit source of chaos and address it.

SPLEEN TONICS: **Sweet - nourishing/invigorating, relieves spasm and pain**
Warming action: Cardamom seeds, cherries, chestnuts, cinnamon, clams, ginseng, grape leaves, mandarin oranges, shiitake mushrooms, peppermint, persimmon, pineapple, string beans, yams

LUNG TONIC: **Increase Yin, decrease heat if grief is present**
Cooling action: (for deficient Lung yin): Seaweeds, orange, peach, pear, apple, watermelon, tomato, banana, string bean, soy milk, tofu, tempeh, flaxseed, butter, dairy products, egg, oyster, clam, pork
Warming action: (basic Lung tonic) Cheese, milk, ginseng, walnuts, yams
Warming action: (for deficient Lung qi): Rice, oats, carrot,

mustard greens, potato, ginger (fresh), garlic, molasses, barley malt, herring, licorice

∼

SYMPTOMS of not enough wood element (yang) in your body, mind, and/or spirit: Indecisive, without strong direction in life, stuck, repressed emotions, unable to express anger, hypoglycemia, blurry vision, sensitivity to light or sound, cystitis, urethritis, tendinitis, dry brittle nails, lax joints and tense muscles, irritable colon, chronic tension in neck and across shoulders.

∼

BUILDING MOISTURE: **Sweet, bland, sour, juicy foods**
   Cooling action: Almonds, apricot, black beans, pinto beans, beets, blueberries, carrots, cheese, Chinese cabbage, coconut oil, grapes, herring, honey, Jerusalem artichokes.
   Milk, oats, olive oil, olives, oranges, oysters, peanut oil, peanuts, pineapple, plums, pork, potatoes, sardines, sesame seeds, strawberries, string beans, white sugar, tangerines
   Neutral action: Almonds, apricot, black beans, pinto beans, beets, blueberries, carrots, cheese, Chinese cabbage, coconut oil, grapes, herring, honey, Jerusalem artichokes.
   Milk, oats, olive oil, olives, oranges, oysters, peanut oil, peanuts, pineapple, plums, pork, potatoes, sardines, sesame seeds, strawberries, string beans, white sugar, tangerines
   Warming action: Coconut milk, malt syrup, nectarines, peaches, pine nuts, sweet rice, rice milk, soy oil

∼

SPLEEN TONICS: **Sweet - relieves spasm and pain**
   Warming action: Cardamom seeds, cherries, chestnuts, cinnamon, clams, ginseng, grape leaves, mandarin oranges, shiitake

mushrooms, peppermint, persimmon, pineapple, string beans, yams

Spleen Tonic: Treat and prevent deficiencies for the spleen

Warming action: Beef, caraway seeds, carrot, cinnamon, dill seed, garlic, ham, perch, pineapple, sticky rice, white rice, string beans, pineapple, string beans, yams

Kidney Tonic: Salt - reduces hard masses or lumps in the body

Cooling action: Kidney beans, mung beans, brown sugar, cantaloupe, cheese, coconut milk, cow milk, crabs, dates, eggs, herring, lemons, mandarin oranges, mangoes, shiitake mushrooms, pears, rice, romaine lettuce, saffron, scallions, star anise, white sugar, thyme, tofu, walnuts, watermelon, yams

Liver Tonics: Sour - obstruct movement. Slows abnormal discharge

Warming action: Mung beans, beef liver, black sesame seeds, chicken liver, chive seeds, peppermint, purslane, romaine lettuce, strawberries

THE ELEMENT OF EARTH

The reason why heaven and earth are able to endure and continue thus long is because they do not live of or for themselves.. – *Lao Tzu*

Earth Element Personality Traits:

Earth

- Well grounded
- Always on the go
- Creative
- Enthusiastic
- Flexible in all things, to a fault
- Takes initiative
- Conversationalist
- Storyteller
- Light sleeper
- Loves excitement and new situations
- Short bursts of energy
- Likes bringing people together
- Nurturing
- Supportive
- Relaxed
- Well oriented to who and where they are
- Easily distracted
- Good mediators, natural peacemakers
- Reliable friend
- Good listener
- Poised
- Considerate
- Agreeable, sometimes to a fault
- Strong memory
- Meditation (any form) strengthens
- Enjoys preparing and eating meals

Symptoms of too much earth element in your system: Fatigue, worrying, meddling in other peoples affairs, prone to pensiveness, clouded thinking, lack of clarity, excess mucus in lungs and sinuses, soft lumps and swollen glands, weak lumbar region, weak ankles and wrists, hunger but can't decide what to eat, varicose veins, slow healing of cuts, bruises easily, spongy tender muscles, bleeding gums, tooth decay, trouble losing weight, bloats easily, poor muscle tone

Symptoms of not enough earth element in your system: Overworking- especially studying or intellectual work, canker sores, conjunctivitis, excess appetite, water retention, swollen prostate, tender gums, PMS with lethargy, aching, hunger and swelling, sores on scalp, heavy head and eyes, sticky eyelids, sticky mucus in nose and throat, sticky saliva and perspiration, swollen, sensitive spleen or liver

Emotional Cause for Imbalance: Melancholia, brooding over any issue

Environmental Causes for Imbalance: Wind (even listening or watching it). Wind causes distraction in mind, body and spirit.

Physical Causes for Imbalance: Too much dairy, sweet, sticky, cold food, raw fruits and vegetables, too much studying or mental work

Earth Element Yin Meridians: Stomach

Earth Element Yang Meridians: Spleen/Pancreas

Earth Element Tonics...

Symptoms of when there too much earth element (yin) in your body, mind, and/or spirit: Fatigue, worrying, meddling in other peoples affairs, prone to pensiveness, clouded thinking, lack of clarity, excess mucus in lungs and sinuses, soft lumps and swollen glands, weak lumbar region, weak ankles and wrists, hunger but can't decide what to eat, varicose veins, slow healing of cuts, bruises easily, spongy tender muscles, bleeding gums, tooth decay, trouble losing weight, bloats easily, poor muscle tone

Building Qi: Bland, sweet, starchy foods.

Cooling action: Moisturizing, decongesting, relaxing: Apple, avocado, banana, barely, buckwheat, corn, cottage cheese, gluten, lettuce, millet, summer squash, tofu, watercress, wheat berries, yogurt

Neutral action: Almonds, apricots, barley, black beans, kidney beans, beef, beets, carob, carrots, cashews, celery, cheese, coconut meat, currants, figs, grapes, herring, honey, Jerusalem artichoke, mackerel, maple syrup, milk, shiitake mushrooms, nutmeg, okra, papaya, peanuts, pecans, pork, potato, raisins, pearl rice, winter squash, string beans, white sugar, tapioca, tofu, turnip, vanilla, yams

Warming action: Drying, supplementing, stimulating: Artichokes, brown sugar, butter, chestnuts, coconut milk, dates, ham - fresh, lamb, malt syrup, mustard greens, sweet rice, sorghum, sweet potato

∽

BUILDING ESSENCE: *Sweet, sour, astringent foods.*

Cooling action: Eggplant, gluten, sesame oil, spinach, spirulina

Neutral action: Aduki beans, black beans, kidney beans, beef, beef liver, beets, carrots, egg yolk, herring, milk, oysters, peanuts, pork, sardines, sesame seeds

∽

WARMING ACTION: Anchovy, blackberries, butter, cherries, chestnuts, chicken, chicken liver, chives, currants, lamb, leeks, mussels, nutritional yeast, pine nuts, raspberries, sticky rice, salmon, shrimp, trout, turkey, vinegar, walnuts

∽

ENERGY TONIC: *For rebuilding strength in chronic illness or low energy. Specifically for Spleen/Pancreas/Stomach*

Warming action: Beef, beef liver, cherries, chicken, coconut meat, ginseng, grapes, honey, licorice, shiitake mushrooms, potato, sticky rice, white rice, summer squash, winter squash, sweet potato, tofu, vinegar

Damp Cold Tonics: - **Reduces phlegm**
Almonds, asparagus, tofu, black pepper, celery, clams, garlic, kohlrabi leaves, kumquats, licorice root, mushrooms, onions, oregano, peanuts, pear, peppermint, seaweed, shiitake mushrooms, thyme, walnuts

Liver Tonic: Sour - obstruct movement. Slows abnormal discharge
Warming action: Mung beans, beef liver, black sesame seeds, chicken liver, chive seeds, peppermint, purslane, romaine lettuce, strawberries

Spleen Tonic: Treat and prevent deficiencies for the spleen
Warming action: Beef, caraway seeds, carrot, cinnamon, dill seed, garlic, ham, perch, pineapple, sticky rice, white rice, string beans, yams

Kidney Tonic: Salt - reduces hard masses or lumps in the body
Cooling action: Kidney beans, mung beans, brown sugar, cantaloupe, cheese, coconut milk, cow milk, crabs, dates, eggs, herring, lemons, mandarin oranges, mangoes, shiitake mushrooms, pears, rice, romaine lettuce, saffron, scallions, star anise, white sugar, thyme, tofu, walnuts, watermelon, yams

Symptoms of too little earth element (yin) in your system: Overworking-especially studying or intellectual work, canker sores, conjunctivitis, excess appetite, water retention, swollen prostate, tender gums, PMS with lethargy, aching, hunger and swelling, sores on scalp, heavy head and eyes, sticky eyelids, sticky mucus in nose and throat, sticky saliva and perspiration, swollen, sensitive Spleen or Liver

Decongesting Qi: Spicy, sour and bitter foods.

Cooling action: Apples, bananas, endive, oat bran, radishes, rhubarb, sesame oil, wheat bran, white pepper

Neutral action: Almonds, beets, cabbage, carrots, cauliflower, figs, olive oil, peas, pineapple, plums, prunes, brown rice, rice bran, tangerines, turnip

Warming action: Anise, black pepper, blackberries, cardamom, chives, coriander, fennel, ginger root, kumquats, mustard greens, mustard seeds, peanut oil, soy oil, onions, orange peel, oranges, parsley, red cabbage, scallions, shallots, strawberries

∽

DECONGESTING MOISTURE: ***Bitter, bland, salty foods.***

Cooling action: Alfalfa sprouts, asparagus, barley, mung beans, clams, corn, endive, millet, mushrooms (button), muskmelon, pears, plantain, seaweed, black tea, green tea, watercress, watermelon

Neutral action: Almonds, amaranth, pearl barley, aduki beans, black beans, kidney beans, cabbage, celery, grapes, mackerel, papaya, pineapple, pumpkin, pumpkin seeds, rice, rice bran

Warming action: Artichoke, cinnamon, coriander, kohlrabi, mussels, parsley, shrimp, sunflower seeds, turkey

∽

DAMP HEAT TONIC: ***Eliminating heat and moisture from the system***

Cooling action: Chinese cabbage, corn silk, olives, plantains, soy oil

∽

INTERNAL WIND TONIC: **Heat creates wind = Stress creates chaos**

Symptoms: Usually diet related. Brought on by an excess of fatty, high cholesterol animal products. Signs of wind move without pattern. Symptoms include dizziness, moving pains, convulsions, tremors, cramps, seizures, strokes, emotional turmoil, nervousness, uncertainty, spasms, itching, dizziness.

Cooling action: The loss of yin adds heat and the wind at the same time. Yin is needed to calm the wind/chaos in ones life. Look for culprit source of wind.

LIVER TONIC: **Sour - obstruct movement. Slows abnormal discharge**

Warming action: Mung beans, beef liver, black sesame seeds, chicken liver, chive seeds, peppermint, romaine lettuce, strawberries

KIDNEY TONIC: **Salt. Kidneys are the root of all moisture in the body**

Cooling action: Kidney beans, mung beans, brown sugar, cantaloupe, cheese, coconut milk, cow milk, crabs, dates, eggs, herring, lemons, mandarin oranges, mangoes, shiitake mushrooms, pears, rice, romaine lettuce, saffron, scallions, star anise, white sugar, thyme, tofu, walnuts, watermelon, yams

THE ELEMENT OF METAL

In the end, the treasure of life is missed by those who hold on and gained by those who let go. – *Lao Tzu*

Metal Element Personality Traits:

Metal

- Deep inner strength
- Conscientious
- Most comfortable when they know the rules and succeed by following them.
- Need to know background, context and reason for new ideas, changes or goals
- Likes structure in life, a rhythm of daily, weekly, monthly, seasonal routines
- Self-disciplined
- Organized
- Methodical
- Trustworthy
- Tidy
- Calm
- Honorable
- Precise
- Reserved
- Dry sense of humor
- Analytical
- Can see a pattern in apparent chaos
- Love of nature
- Enjoys quiet
- Comfortable with little or no company
- Punctual

Symptoms of when there is too much Metal element in your system: Grief stricken, steeped in sadness, illness in lungs - asthma, allergies, frequent colds, chronic constipation or diarrhea, bowel disease, delicate skin, shortness of breath, congested nose, throat, sinus, moles and warts, headaches from sadness and disappointment, loss of body hair, clammy hands-feet, easy perspiration, varicose veins, cracked, dry or soft nails, enlarged lymph nodes, sneeze or cough with changes in temperature and humidity

Symptoms of when there is not enough Metal element in your system: Overly critical, trouble letting an stressful issue go, rashes, eczema and problems with sweating, dry cough with tight chest, sinus headache, nasal polyps, dry hair, dry skin, dry mucous membranes, no perspiration, stiff spine, neck and posture, constipation with tense intestine, dry, cracked nails and lips, scanty urine, dry nose-throat, tight muscles

EMOTIONAL CAUSE FOR IMBALANCE: Grief, sadness

Environmental Causes for Imbalance: Wind (watching or listening to it), extreme hot or cold. Cold effects low back and hips

Physical Causes for Imbalance: Too much dry, spicy and bitter food causes a decrease. Too much sweet, sticky and cold food causes an increase in the Metal element.

Metal Element Yin Meridian: Lung

Metal Element Yang Meridian: Large Intestine

Metal Element Tonics...

Symptoms of too much metal element (yin) in your body, mind, and/or spirit: Grief stricken, steeped in sadness, illness in lungs - asthma, allergies, frequent colds, chronic constipation or diarrhea, bowel disease, delicate skin, shortness of breath, congested nose, throat, sinus, moles and warts, headaches from sadness and disappointment, loss of body hair, clammy hands-feet, easy perspiration, varicose veins, cracked, dry or soft nails, enlarged lymph nodes, sneeze or cough with changes in temperature and humidity

BUILDING BLOOD (ESSENCE): *Sweet, sour, astringent foods.*

Cooling action: Eggplant, gluten, sesame oil, spinach, spirulina

Neutral action: Aduki beans, black beans, kidney beans, beef, beef liver, beets, carrots, egg yolk, herring, milk, oysters, peanuts, pork, sardines, sesame seeds

Warming action: Anchovy, blackberries, butter, cherries, chestnuts, chicken, chicken liver, chives, currants, lamb, leeks, mussels, nutritional yeast, pine nuts, raspberries, sticky rice,, salmon, shrimp, trout, turkey, vinegar, walnuts

∽

DECONGESTING QI: *Spicy, sour and bitter foods.*

Cooling action: Apples, bananas, endive, oat bran, radishes, rhubarb, sesame oil, wheat bran, white pepper

Neutral action: Almonds, beets, cabbage, carrots, cauliflower, figs, olive oil, peas, pineapple, plums, prunes, brown rice, rice bran, tangerines, turnip

Warming action: Black pepper, blackberries, cardamom, chives, coriander, fennel, ginger root, kumquats, mustard greens, mustard seeds, peanut oil, onions, orange peel, oranges, parsley, red cabbage, scallions, shallots, strawberries

∽

DAMP COLD TONICS: *Reduces phlegm*

Almonds, asparagus, tofu, black pepper, celery, clams, garlic, kohlrabi leaves, kumquats, licorice root, mushrooms, onions, oregano, peanuts, pear, peppermint, seaweed, shiitake mushrooms, thyme, walnuts

∽

KIDNEY TONIC: *Salt. Kidneys are the source of all moisture in the body*

Cooling action: Kidney beans, mung beans, brown sugar,

cantaloupe, cheese, coconut milk, cow milk, crabs, dates, eggs, herring, lemons, mandarin oranges, mangoes, shiitake mushrooms, pears, rice, romaine lettuce, saffron, scallions, star anise, white sugar, thyme, tofu, walnuts, watermelon, yams

Lung Tonic: Increase Yin, Decrease heat congestion in lungs (especially if grief is present)
  Cooling action: (for deficient Lung yin: Seaweeds, orange, peach, pear, apple, watermelon, tomato, banana, string bean, soy milk, tofu, tempeh, flaxseed, butter, dairy products, egg, oyster, clam, pork
  Warming action: (basic Lung tonic) Cheese, milk, ginseng, walnuts, yams
  Warming action: (for deficient Lung qi): Rice, oats, carrot, mustard greens, potato, ginger (fresh), garlic, molasses, barley malt, herring, licorice

Liver Tonic: Sour - obstruct movement. Slows abnormal discharge
  Warming action: Mung beans, beef liver, black sesame seeds, chicken liver, chive seeds, peppermint, romaine lettuce, strawberries

Heart & Stomach Tonics: Strengthens heart and stomach
  Warming action: Beef, beer, cardamom seeds, chicory, clam, coffee, corn, fennel seeds, ginseng, mango, milk, shiitake mushrooms, white rice, green tea, wheat

Symptoms of not enough metal element (yin) in your body, mind, and/or spirit: Overly critical, trouble letting an stressful issue go, rashes, eczema and problems with sweating, dry cough with tight chest, sinus headache, nasal polyps, dry hair, dry skin, dry mucous membranes, no perspiration, stiff spine, neck and posture, constipation with tense intestine, dry, cracked nails and lips, scanty urine, dry nose-throat, tight muscles

~

BUILDING MOISTURE: *Sweet, bland, sour, juicy foods*

Cooling action: Almonds, apricot, black beans, pinto beans, beets, blueberries, carrots, cheese, Chinese cabbage, coconut oil, grapes, herring, honey, Jerusalem artichokes, milk, oats, olive oil, olives, oranges, oysters, peanut oil, peanuts, pineapple, plums, pork, potatoes, sardines, sesame seeds, strawberries, string beans, white sugar, tangerines

Neutral action: Almonds, apricot, black beans, pinto beans, beets, blueberries, carrots, cheese, Chinese cabbage, coconut oil, grapes, herring, honey, Jerusalem artichokes, milk, oats, olive oil, olives, oranges, oysters, peanut oil, peanuts, pineapple, plums, pork, potatoes, sardines, sesame seeds, strawberries, string beans, white sugar, tangerines

Warming action: coconut milk, malt syrup, nectarines, peaches, pine nuts, sweet rice, rice milk, soy oil

~

REDUCING HEAT: *Eliminating toxic heat from the system*

Cooling action: Aloe vera, bamboo shoots, bananas, basil, aduki beans, mung beans, beet greens, cattail, clam, crab, egg whites, eggplant, endive, figs, grape leaves, grapefruit, honey, licorice, peppermint, romaine lettuce, salt, spinach beets, mung bean sprouts, summer squash, star fruit, strawberries, Swiss chard, tangerine peel, tofu

~

INTERNAL WIND TONIC: **Heat creates wind = Stress creates chaos**

Symptoms: Usually diet related. Brought on by an excess of fatty, high cholesterol animal products. Signs of wind move without pattern. Symptoms include dizziness, moving pains, convulsions, tremors, cramps, seizures, strokes, emotional turmoil, nervousness, uncertainty, spasms, itching, dizziness.

Cooling action: The loss of yin adds heat and wind at the same time. Yin is needed to calm the wind/chaos in your life. Look for the source of wind.

SPLEEN TONICS: **Sweet - relieves spasm and pain**

Warming action: Cardamom seeds, cherries, chestnuts, cinnamon, clams, ginseng, grape leaves, mandarin oranges, shiitake mushrooms, peppermint, persimmon, pineapple, string beans, yams

LUNG TONIC: **Increase Yin, Decrease heat if grief is present**

Cooling action: Seaweeds, orange, peach, pear, apple, watermelon, tomato, banana, string bean, soy milk, tofu, tempeh, flaxseed, butter, dairy products, egg, oyster, clam, pork

KIDNEY TONIC: **Salt. Kidneys are the root of all moisture in the body**

Cooling action: Kidney beans, brown sugar, cantaloupe, cheese, coconut milk, cow milk, crabs, dates, eggs, herring, lemons, mandarin oranges, mangoes, shiitake mushrooms, pears, rice, romaine lettuce, saffron, scallions, sugar, thyme, tofu, walnuts, watermelon, yams, peanuts, pineapple, plums, pork, potatoes, sardines, sesame seeds, strawberries, string beans, tangerines

THE ELEMENT OF WATER

Water is the softest thing, yet it can penetrate mountains and earth. This shows clearly the principle of softness overcoming hardness. – Lao Tzu

Water Element Personality Traits:

Water

- Articulates thoughts and feelings easily
- Can endure many hardships in pursuit of goals
- Perseverance by will power
- Lives with focus and direction
- Candid
- Introspective
- Watchful
- Objective
- Curious
- Resourceful
- Thrifty
- Deep thinkers
- Strong concentration
- Can look at something ordinary and see it differently
- Imaginative
- Perceptive
- Determined
- Fearless
- Observant
- Reflective
- Modest
- Innovative
- Lucid

- Deep sleepers

Symptoms of when there is too much water element in your system: Cold. Cold legs, feet, hands, cold back and belly, dark circles under the eyes, night sweats, decline in sexual vigor, incontinence, dulled vision-hearing, ringing in ears, weak and stiff spine, lower body, joints, degeneration of disks-cartilage, cold buttocks, legs, feet, frequent urination, osteoporosis, infertility, frigidity, impotence, lacks stamina, hard to wake up, loss of appetite, weak ab muscles

Symptoms of when there is not enough water element in your system: Ringing in ears, hot flashes, oversensitive vision and/or hearing, headaches above eyes, lack of sweat and urine, hardening of blood vessels and cartilage, rigidity of joints and muscles, kidney and bladder stones, Bony tumors, weak digestion, shrinking gums, needs little sleep, hypertension

Emotional Cause for Imbalance: Fear, paranoia

Environmental Causes for Imbalance: Winter and summer. Too cold causes an excess of water element, everything slows down. Too hot/dry causes a loss of water.

Physical Causes for Imbalance: Too much cold food, raw vegetables, icy, sweet, salty food and/or beverages

Metal Element Yin Meridians: Central, and Kidney

Metal Element Yang Meridian: Bladder

Water Element Tonics...

Symptoms of when there is not enough water element in your body, mind, and/or spirit: Ringing in ears, hot flashes, oversensitive vision and/or hearing, headaches above eyes, lack of sweat and urine, hardening of blood vessels and cartilage, rigidity of joints and muscles, kidney and bladder stones, Bony tumors, weak digestion, shrinking gums, needs little sleep, hypertension

BUILDING MOISTURE: *Sweet, bland, sour, juicy foods.*

Cooling action: Almonds, apricot, black beans, pinto beans, beets, blueberries, carrots, cheese, Chinese cabbage, coconut oil, grapes, herring, honey, Jerusalem artichokes, milk, oats, olive oil, olives, oranges, oysters, peanut oil, peanuts, pineapple, plums, pork, potatoes, sardines, sesame seeds, strawberries, string beans, white sugar, tangerines

Warming action: Coconut milk, malt syrup, nectarines, peaches, pine nuts, sweet rice, rice milk, soy oil

---

BUILDING BLOOD (ESSENCE): *Sweet, sour, astringent foods.*

Cooling action: Eggplant, gluten, sesame oil, spinach, spirulina

Neutral action: Aduki beans, black beans, kidney beans, beef, beef liver, beets, carrots, egg yolk, herring, milk, oysters, peanuts, pork, sardines, sesame seeds

Warming action: Anchovy, blackberries, butter, cherries, chestnuts, chicken, chicken liver, chives, currants, lamb, leeks, mussels, nutritional yeast, pine nuts, raspberries, sticky rice,, salmon, shrimp, trout, turkey, vinegar, walnuts

---

SPLEEN TONIC: *Treat and prevent deficiencies for the spleen*

Warming action: Beef, caraway seeds, carrot, cinnamon, dill seed, garlic, ham, perch, pineapple, sticky rice, white rice, string beans, pineapple, string beans, yams

---

DECONGESTING ESSENCE: *Spicy, sour and bitter foods.*

Cooling action: Crab, swiss chard, watercress, wheat germ

Neutral action: Beets, eggplant, leeks, shiitake mushrooms, olives, rice bran, rose hips, saffron, sardines

Warming action: Cayenne, cherries, chives, onions, peaches, rice wine, safflower, scallions, shrimp, sweet basil, turmeric, vinegar

REDUCING HEAT: Eliminating toxic heat from the system

Cooling action: Aloe vera, bamboo shoots, bananas, basil, aduki beans, mung beans, beet greens, cattail, clam, crab, egg whites, eggplant, endive, figs, grape leaves, grapefruit, honey, licorice, peppermint, romaine lettuce, salt, spinach beets, mung bean sprouts, summer squash, star fruit, strawberries, Swiss chard, tangerine peel, tofu

BLOOD CIRCULATING TONICS: Reduces coagulation and promotes circulation

Warming action: Basil, brown sugar, cayenne, celery, chicken, chives, clams, coriander, eggplant, ham - fresh, mustard, mustard greens, peaches, radish, sticky rice, saffron, scallion (white heads), tofu, vinegar

SPLEEN TONICS: Sweet - relieves spasm and pain

Warming action: Cardamom seeds, cherries, chestnuts, cinnamon, clams, ginseng, grape leaves, mandarin oranges, shiitake mushrooms, peppermint, persimmon, pineapple, string beans, yams

KIDNEY TONIC: Salt - reduces hard masses or lumps in the body

Cooling action: Kidney beans, mung beans, brown sugar,

cantaloupe, cheese, coconut milk, cow milk, crabs, dates, eggs, herring, lemons, mandarin oranges, mangoes, shiitake mushrooms, pears, rice, romaine lettuce, saffron, scallions, star anise, white sugar, thyme, tofu, walnuts, watermelon, yams

∽

Lung Tonic: Increase Yin, Decrease heat if grief is present

Cooling action: Seaweeds, orange, peach, pear, apple, watermelon, tomato, banana, string bean, soy milk, tofu, tempeh, flaxseed, butter, dairy products, egg, oyster, clam, pork

∽

Symptoms of when there is too much water element in your body, mind, and/or spirit: Cold. Cold legs, feet, hands, cold back and belly, dark circles under the eyes, night sweats, decline in sexual vigor, incontinence, dulled vision-hearing, ringing in ears, weak and stiff spine, lower body, joints, degeneration of disks-cartilage, cold buttocks, legs, feet, frequent urination, osteoporosis, infertility, frigidity, impotence, lacks stamina, hard to wake up, loss of appetite, weak ab muscles

∽

Decongesting Essence: Spicy, sour and bitter foods.

Cooling action: Crab, Swiss chard, watercress, wheat germ

Neutral action: Beets, eggplant, leeks, shiitake mushrooms, olives, rice bran, rose hips, saffron, sardines

Warming action: Cayenne, cherries, chives, onions, peaches, rice wine, safflower, scallions, shrimp, sweet basil, turmeric, vinegar

∽

Blood Circulating Tonics: Reduces coagulation and promotes circulation

Warming action: Basil, brown sugar, cayenne, celery, chicken, chives, clams, coriander, eggplant, ham, mustard, mustard greens, peaches, radish, sticky rice,, saffron, scallion (white heads), tofu, vinegar

Energy Circulation Tonics: Keeps energy moving from organ to organ
Warming action: Basil, red beans, beef, caraway, carrot, chives, clam, dill seed, eggs, fennel seed, garlic, grapefruit, kumquat, limes, malt, shiitake mushrooms, mussels, mustard greens, saffron, scallion, spearmint, star anise, string bean, tangerines, turmeric, vinegar

Heart & Stomach Tonics: Strengthens heart and stomach
Warming action: Beef, beer, cardamom seeds, chicory, clam, coffee, corn, fennel seeds, ginseng, mango, milk, shiitake mushrooms, white rice, green tea, wheat

Spleen Tonic: Treat and prevent deficiencies for the spleen
Warming action: Beef, caraway seeds, carrot, cinnamon, dill seed, garlic, ham, perch, pineapple, sticky rice, white rice, string beans, pineapple, string beans, yams

Kidney Tonic: Salt - reduces hard masses or lumps in the body
Cooling action: Kidney beans, mung beans, brown sugar, cantaloupe, cheese, coconut milk, cow milk, crabs, dates, eggs, herring, lemons, mandarin oranges, mangoes, shiitake mushrooms, pears, rice, romaine lettuce, saffron, scallions, star anise, white sugar, thyme, tofu, walnuts, watermelon, yams

5 Kinds Of Self-Care

18

MERIDIANS - INTRODUCTION

Each of your five Common Senses contain at least two Traditional Chinese Medicine meridians. Now measurable by western science.

There are fourteen of them. Twelve are all linked together, end to end. Where one stops, another starts. Two of the fourteen (Central and Governing) circulate around the front and back of your spine.

They carry energy through your body. Each meridian is responsible for circulating energy to very specific parts of your body. If the energy stops circulating for any reason, you develop a symptom. When a meridian isn't functioning well, the meridian that comes after it has less energy, too.

Like a traffic jam on a highway, the energy can't get through a blockage or break. Once the original problem is fixed, the traffic flow continues as it was before.

Meridians in each of the five categories are related to symptoms in that category. Fixing the meridian can be done in many ways. The most commonly known way to repair a meridian is acupuncture.

You can also fix a meridian with energy work and/or food. Not everyone knows how to do energy work, but everyone knows how to eat. Each meridian has tonic foods that alleviate all symptoms related to that meridian.

The following is a listing of what your meridians like to eat. It's a lot like eating food for vitamin deficiency. Make it fun. Eat several servings of tonic foods a day for a week.

Sometimes, this minor change of menu, for the correct meridian, is all it takes for many seemingly unrelated symptoms to disappear by themselves.

- Meridians of **Touch:** Governing, Heart, Small Intestine, Pericardium, Triple Warmer
- Meridians of **Sight:** Liver, Gallbladder
- Meridians of **Taste:** Stomach, Spleen
- Meridians of **Smell:** Lung, Large Intestine
- Meridians of **Hearing:** Central, Kidney, Bladder

19

WHAT MERIDIANS DO AND HOW TO FEED THEM

Every meridian is either stimulating (yang) or calming (yin) to your body. **Yin** energy is cooling, moisturizing, decongesting and relaxing. **Yang** energy is warming, drying, supplementing, stimulating

The most stimulating of your common senses is Touch. There are five meridians responsible for keeping that category healthy. Three of the five are stimulating.

The most calming of your common senses is Hearing. There are three meridians responsible for keeping that category healthy. Two of the three are calming.

All of the other categories have two meridians each. One stimulating, one calming, for balance. If that balance is thrown off, you develop symptoms in that category. Restoring the balance eliminates symptoms.

Each of the five Common Senses chapters includes a food list. Some of the listings say "edibility: maybe." This is why. Sometimes those foods can be too motivating or too calming if other symptoms are present.

Touch is The Element of Fire

Heart (Yin)

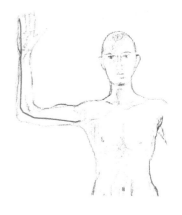

The heart propels blood through the body. The blood nurtures the body and serves as a vehicle of communication as it travels through the vessels. The tongue allows us to communicate.

Stuttering and other speech defects are said to be caused by an imbalance of the Heart. A person with a healthy heart system will be articulate, calm, loving with a healthy radiant complexion.

The heart meridian houses the spirit. If the blood is weak, the spirit has no home and the person seems spacey, forgetful, restless and probably has insomnia. Other symptoms would be poor circulation which could lead to low blood pressure, shortness of breath, cold/blue fingers or lips.

Primary Functions: Responsible for the circulation of the blood through the body and has an effect on the fluid flow of the meridians. Usual behavior and appropriate responses to the environment, governs tongue color and speech, health shows in complexion–normally ruddy in those with dominant fire traits.

Dysfunctions: Irregular blood flow, blood vessel disorders, irregular pulse. Insomnia, excessive dreaming, delirium. Pale or purple tongue, tongue ulcers, slurred speech, unusually fast talking. Poor complexion. Swollen glands, inner arm pain or weakness, weak wrists, palm pain, red eyes, thirst, throat disorders, cardiac disorders, palpitations, chest pains, and constipation.

Pericardium (Yin)

Primary Functions: Protector of the heart. It wards off negative external influences.

Dysfunctions: Pericarditis or any heart disorder due to environmental or emotional stress. Related to menstrual cramps, prostate trouble or sexual difficulties. Swollen or painful armpit, spasms of elbow and forearm, carpal tunnel syndrome, hot palms, depression, hot flashes, rapid heartbeat.

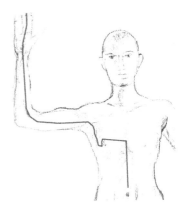

Pericardium Meridian

Governing Vessel (Yang)

Primary Functions: Involved with the integrity of the spine and nervous system.

Dysfunctions: Stiff neck, eye pain, spasms or pain in the spine, urinary incontinence, impotence or sterility, hemorrhoids, hernias.

Small Intestine (Yang)

Primary Functions: Related to indigestion, intestinal colic and other digestive issues.

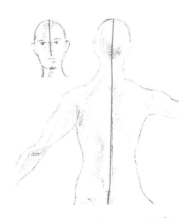

Governing Meridian

Dysfunctions: Swelling, stiffness, pain in cervical region and shoulders, ulnar neuropathy, dim eyesight, loss of hearing, TMJ, sore throat.

Triple Warmer (Yang)

Primary Functions: Thyroid conditions, digestive disturbances, infections, weight changes and crying for no reason are indicators. Fight or flight reflex.

Dysfunctions: Pain in ears, shoulder, stiffness along arm and wrist to ring finger, loss of hearing, earaches, Spontaneous sweating.

Tonics Foods for Fire Meridians...

Symptoms of too much motivation (Yang): Anxiety, restlessness, insomnia, talking too much or more rapidly than normal, nervous laughter, easily stimulated, profuse/frequent perspiration (your body trying to cool the body as fast as possible), flushed face, irregular or rapid heartbeat, painful urination, strong but erratic pulse, overheats easily, mouth sores, tongue sores, blistered lips, dry painful eczema.

Small Intestine Meridian

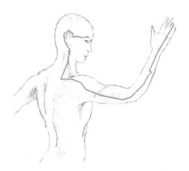

Triple Warmer Meridian

BUILDING MOISTURE: *Sweet, bland, sour, juicy foods*

Calming: Almonds, apricot, black beans, pinto beans, beets, blueberries, carrots, cheese, Chinese cabbage, coconut oil, grapes, herring, honey, Jerusalem artichokes, milk, oats, olive oil, olives, oranges, oysters, peanut oil, peanuts, pineapple, plums, pork, potatoes, sardines, sesame seeds, strawberries, string beans, white sugar, tangerines

Neutral/Nourishing: Almonds, apricot, black beans, pinto beans, beets, blueberries, carrots, cheese, Chinese cabbage, coconut oil, grapes, herring, honey, Jerusalem artichokes, milk, oats, olive oil, olives, oranges, oysters, peanut oil, peanuts, pineapple, plums, pork, potatoes, sardines, sesame seeds, strawberries, string beans, white sugar, tangerines

Stimulating: Coconut milk, Malt syrup, Nectarines, Peaches, Pine nuts, sweet rice, Rice milk, Soy oil

DECONGESTING QI: *Spicy, sour and bitter foods.*
Calming: Crab, Swiss chard, watercress, wheat germ
Neutral/Nourishing: Beets, eggplant, leeks, shiitake mushrooms, olives, rice bran, rose hips, saffron, sardines
Motivating: Cayenne, cherries, chives, onions, peaches, rice wine, safflower, scallions, shrimp, sweet basil, turmeric, vinegar

REDUCING HEAT: *Eliminating toxic heat from the system*
Calming: Aloe vera, bamboo shoots, bananas, basil, aduki beans, mung beans, beet greens, cattail, clam, crab, egg whites, eggplant, endive, figs, grape leaves, grapefruit, honey, licorice, peppermint, romaine lettuce, salt, spinach beets, mung bean sprouts, summer squash, star fruit, strawberries, Swiss chard, tangerine peel, tofu

BLOOD CIRCULATING TONICS: *Reduces coagulation and promotes circulation*
Motivating: Basil, brown sugar, cayenne, celery, chicken, chives, clams, coriander, eggplant, ham-fresh, mustard, mustard greens, peaches, radish, sticky rice,, saffron, scallion (white heads), tofu, vinegar

Heart & Stomach Tonics: Strengthen heart and stomach
Motivating: Beef, beer, cardamom seeds, chicory, clam, coffee, corn, fennel seeds, ginseng, mango, milk, shiitake mushrooms, white rice, green tea, wheat

Energy Circulation Tonics: Keeps energy moving from organ to organ
Motivating: Basil, red beans, beef, caraway, carrot, chives, clam, dill seed, eggs, fennel seed, garlic, grapefruit, kumquat, limes, malt, shiitake mushrooms, mussels, mustard greens, saffron, scallion, spearmint, star anise, string bean, tangerines, turmeric, vinegar

Blood Tonics: Helps with blood loss or poor absorption of nutrients
Motivating: Beef, eggs, oxtail, oysters, spinach

Symptoms of not enough motivation (Yin): Weak, lackluster, bland, emotionally cold, unfeeling, slow, irregular pulse, chills or overheats easily, low blood pressure, dizzy easily, fainting, anemic, pale with flushed cheeks, tires easily.

Building Blood (Essence): Sweet, sour, astringent foods.
Calming: Eggplant, gluten, sesame oil, spinach, spirulina
Neutral/Nourishing: Aduki beans, black beans, kidney beans, beef, beef liver, beets, carrots, egg yolk, herring, milk, oysters, peanuts, pork, sardines, sesame seeds
Motivating: Anchovy, blackberries, butter, cherries, chestnuts, chicken, chicken liver, chives, currants, lamb, leeks, mussels, nutri-

tional yeast, pine nuts, raspberries, sticky rice, salmon, shrimp, trout, turkey, vinegar, walnuts

Liver Tonics: Sour–obstruct movement. Useful for slowing abnormal discharge
 Motivating: Mung beans, beef liver, black sesame seeds, chicken liver, chive seeds, peppermint, purslane, romaine lettuce, strawberries

Heart Tonics: Builds heat back into the system
 Motivating: Beer, Chicken liver, Chinese endive, Wheat

Spleen Tonics: Sweet–nourishing and invigorating, relieves spasm/pain
 Motivating: Cardamom seeds, cherries, chestnuts, cinnamon, clams, ginseng, grape leaves, mandarin oranges, shiitake mushrooms, peppermint, persimmon, pineapple, string beans, yams

Sight is The Element of Wood

Gall Bladder Meridian (Yang):

Primary Functions: Related to headache cases that are related to dietary indiscretions or eating many fats. When the liver is consistently stagnant the gall bladder cannot flush toxic sediments. The sediments become stones that clog the bile duct.
 Dysfunctions: Headaches, stiffness in trapezium, tightness in ribs, pain or arthritis in hips, generalized joint pains, bitter taste in mouth,

throat pain, tightness in thorax. When there is sediment present the symptoms are indigestion, flatulence, pain below the right rib cage, tension in the back of the shoulders near the neck, and a bitter taste in the mouth.

Liver Meridian (Yin):

Primary Functions: The liver rules the tendons, eyes and most importantly smooth flow of energy throughout the body and mind.

Dysfunctions: Physical problems related to glaucoma and spots in front of the eyes. Pain or tightness in ribs, pelvic complaints, hernias, eye pain, "Plum–pit" obstruction in throat, tightness in diaphragm area of abdomen. Symptoms are often emotional difficulties related to anger such as impatience, frustration, arrogance, stubbornness and aggression.

Gall Bladder Meridian

Tonics Foods for Wood Meridians...

Symptoms of too much enthusiasm (Yang): Arrogant, controlling, angry disposition, workaholic, pain just below the ribs, hernias, migraines, high blood pressure, oily skin/hair, boils, cramps of long muscles, hands, feet; vertigo, ringing in ears, constipation with cramps/spasms, sciatica, heartburn, difficult swallowing, eye/ear pain, shingles, awkward and accident–prone, hard thick nails, breast pain, tendon injuries

Liver Meridian

DECONGESTING ESSENCE: *Spicy, sour and bitter food.*

Calming: Crab, Swiss chard, watercress, wheat germ

Neutral/Nourishing: Beets, eggplant, leeks, shiitake mushrooms, olives, rice bran, rose hips, saffron, sardines

Motivating: Cayenne, cherries, chives, onions, peaches, rice wine, safflower, scallions, shrimp, sweet basil, turmeric, vinegar

REDUCING HEAT: *Eliminating toxic heat from the system*

Calming: Aloe vera, bamboo shoots, bananas, basil, aduki beans, mung beans, beet greens, cattail, clam, crab, egg whites, eggplant, endive, figs, grape leaves, grapefruit, honey, licorice, peppermint, romaine lettuce, salt, spinach beets, mung bean sprouts, summer squash, star fruit, strawberries, Swiss chard, tangerine peel, tofu

INTERNAL WIND TONIC: *Heat creates wind = Stress creates chaos*

Symptoms: Usually diet related. Brought on by an excess of fatty, high cholesterol animal products. Signs of wind move without pattern. Symptoms include dizziness, moving pains, convulsions, tremors, cramps, seizures, strokes, emotional turmoil, nervousness, uncertainty, spasms, itching, dizziness.

Calming: The cooling aspects of Yin are needed to calm the wind/chaos in your life. Look for culprit source of chaos and address it.

SPLEEN TONICS: *Sweet–nourishing and invigorating, relieves spasm pain*

Motivating: Cardamom seeds, cherries, chestnuts, cinnamon, clams, ginseng, grape leaves, mandarin oranges, shiitake mushrooms, peppermint, persimmon, pineapple, string beans, yams

LUNG TONIC: Increase Yin, Decrease heat congestion in lungs (especially if grief is present)
Calming: (for deficient Lung yin): Seaweeds, orange, peach, pear, apple, watermelon, tomato, banana, string bean, soy milk, tofu, tempeh, flaxseed, butter, dairy products, egg, oyster, clam, pork
Motivating: (Lung tonic) Cheese, milk, ginseng, walnuts, yams
Motivating: (for deficient Lung qi): Rice, oats, carrot, mustard greens, potato, ginger (fresh), garlic, molasses, barley malt, herring, licorice

SYMPTOMS of not enough enthusiasm (Yin): Indecisive, without strong direction in life, stuck, repressed emotions, unable to express anger, hypoglycemia, blurry vision, sensitivity to light or sound, cystitis, urethritis, tendinitis, dry brittle nails, lax joints and tense muscles, irritable colon, chronic tension in neck and across shoulders.

BUILDING MOISTURE: Sweet, bland, sour, juicy foods
Calming: Almonds, apricot, black beans, pinto beans, beets, blueberries, carrots, cheese, Chinese cabbage, coconut oil, grapes, herring, honey, Jerusalem artichokes, milk, oats, olive oil, olives, oranges, oysters, peanut oil, peanuts, pineapple, plums, pork, potatoes, sardines, sesame seeds, strawberries, string beans, white sugar, tangerines
Neutral/Nourishing: Almonds, apricot, black beans, pinto beans, beets, blueberries, carrots, cheese, Chinese cabbage, coconut oil, grapes, herring, honey, Jerusalem artichokes, milk, oats, olive oil, olives, oranges, oysters, peanut oil, peanuts, pineapple, plums, pork, potatoes, sardines, sesame seeds, strawberries, string beans, white sugar, tangerines

Motivating: Coconut milk, Malt syrup, Nectarines, Peaches, Pine nuts, sweet rice, Rice milk, Soy oil

SPLEEN TONICS: *Sweet–nourishing and invigorating, relieves spasm and pain*
Motivating: Cardamom seeds, cherries, chestnuts, cinnamon, clams, ginseng, grape leaves, mandarin oranges, shiitake mushrooms, peppermint, pineapple, string beans, yams

SPLEEN TONIC: *Treat and prevent deficiencies for the spleen*
Motivating: Beef, caraway seeds, carrot, cinnamon, dill seed, garlic, ham-fresh, perch, pineapple, sticky rice, white rice, string beans, pineapple, string beans, yams
Kidney Tonic: Salt–reduces hard masses or lumps in the body
Cooling action: Kidney beans, mung beans, brown sugar, cantaloupe, cheese, coconut milk, cow milk, crabs, dates, eggs, herring, lemons, mandarin oranges, mangoes, shiitake mushrooms, pears, rice, romaine lettuce, saffron, scallions, star anise, white sugar, thyme, tofu, walnuts, watermelon, yams

LIVER TONICS: *Sour–obstruct movement. Useful for slowing abnormal discharge*
Motivating: Mung beans, beef liver, black sesame seeds, chicken liver, chive seeds, peppermint, purslane, romaine lettuce, strawberries

Taste is The Element of Earth

Stomach Meridian (Yang)

Primary Functions: Registers pain and stress. It includes allergy problems and dietary intakes.

Dysfunctions: Headache on side of head, sinus pain, stiff neck, swollen throat, chest tightness, digestive pain and complaints, rumbling, pelvic pain and congestion, thigh pain, stomach complaints, frequent hunger, gastritis

Stomach Meridian

Spleen Meridian (Yin)

Primary Functions: Used in all forceful arm movements and is often an indicator for allergies and intolerance for sugar, caffeine or tobacco.

Dysfunctions: Abdominal pain and distention, pelvic complaints, general fatigue in limbs, stiffness at the base of tongue, loss of appetite, nausea, stomach complaints, bunions

Tonics Foods for the Common Sense of Taste...

Spleen Meridian

Symptoms of not enough adapting (Yin):
Fatigue, worrying, meddling in other peoples affairs, prone to pensiveness, clouded thinking, lack of clarity, excess mucus in lungs and sinuses, soft lumps and swollen glands, weak lumbar region, weak ankles and wrists, hunger but can't decide what to eat, varicose

veins, slow healing of cuts, bruises easily, spongy tender muscles, bleeding gums, tooth decay, trouble losing weight, bloats easily, poor muscle tone

BUILDING QI: *Bland, sweet, starchy foods.*

Calming: Moisturizing, decongesting, relaxing: Apple, avocado, banana, barley, buckwheat, corn, cottage cheese, gluten, lettuce, summer squash, tofu, watercress, wheat berries, yogurt

Neutral action: Almonds, apricots, barley, black beans, kidney beans, beef, beets, carob, carrots, cashews, celery, cheese, coconut meat, currants, figs, grapes, herring, honey, Jerusalem artichoke, mackerel, maple syrup, milk, shiitake mushrooms, nutmeg, okra, papaya, peanuts, pecans, pork, potato, raisins, pearl rice, winter squash, string beans, white sugar, tapioca, tofu, turnip, vanilla, yams

Motivating: Drying, supplementing, stimulating: Artichokes, brown sugar, butter, chestnuts, coconut milk, dates, ham–fresh, lamb, mustard greens, sweet rice, sorghum, sweet potato

BUILDING ESSENCE: *Sweet, sour, astringent foods.*

Cooling action: Eggplant, gluten, sesame oil, spinach, spirulina

Neutral/Nourishing: Aduki beans, black beans, kidney beans, beef, beef liver, beets, carrots, egg yolk, herring, milk, oysters, peanuts, pork, sardines, sesame seeds

Motivating: Anchovy, blackberries, butter, cherries, chestnuts, chicken, chicken liver, chives, currants, lamb, leeks, mussels, nutritional yeast, pine nuts, raspberries, sticky rice, salmon, shrimp, trout, turkey, vinegar, walnuts

ENERGY TONIC: *For rebuilding strength in chronic illness or low energy. Specifically for Spleen/Pancreas/Stomach*
Motivating: Beef, beef liver, cherries, chicken, coconut meat, ginseng, grapes, honey, licorice, shiitake mushrooms, potato, white rice, summer squash, winter squash, sweet potato, tofu, vinegar

DAMP COLD TONICS: *–Reduces phlegm*
Almonds, asparagus, tofu, black pepper, celery, clams, garlic, kohlrabi leaves, kumquats, licorice root, mushrooms, onions, oregano, peanuts, pear, peppermint, seaweed, shiitake mushrooms, thyme, walnuts

LIVER TONIC: *Sour–obstruct movement. Useful for slowing abnormal discharge*
Motivating: Mung beans, beef liver, black sesame seeds, chicken liver, chive seeds, peppermint, purslane, romaine lettuce, strawberries

SPLEEN TONIC: *Treat and prevent deficiencies for the spleen*
Motivating: Beef, caraway seeds, carrot, cinnamon, dill seed, garlic, ham-fresh, perch, pineapple, sticky rice, white rice, string beans, yams

KIDNEY TONIC: *Salt–reduces hard masses or lumps in the body*
Calming: Kidney beans, mung beans, brown sugar, cantaloupe, cheese, coconut milk, cow milk, crabs, dates, eggs, herring, lemons, mandarin oranges, mangoes, shiitake mushrooms, pears, rice,

romaine lettuce, saffron, scallions, star anise, white sugar, thyme, tofu, walnuts, watermelon, yams

SYMPTOMS *of too much adapting (Yang):* Overworking– especially intellectual work, canker sores, pink eye, excess appetite, water retention, swollen prostate, tender gums, PMS, sores on scalp, heavy head and eyes, sticky eyelids, sticky mucus in nose and throat, sticky saliva and perspiration, swollen, sensitive spleen or liver

DECONGESTING QI: *Spicy, sour and bitter foods.*
   Calming: Apples, bananas, endive, oat bran, radishes, rhubarb, sesame oil, wheat bran, white pepper
   Neutral/Nourishing: Almonds, beets, cabbage, carrots, cauliflower, figs, olive oil, peas, pineapple, plums, prunes, brown rice, rice bran, tangerines, turnip
   Motivating: Anise, black pepper, blackberries, cardamom, chives, coriander, fennel, ginger root, kumquats, mustard greens, mustard seeds, peanut oil, soy oil, onions, orange peel, oranges, parsley, red cabbage, scallions, shallots, strawberries

DECONGESTING MOISTURE: *Bitter, bland, salty foods.*
   Calming: Alfalfa sprouts, asparagus, barley, mung beans, clams, corn, endive, millet, mushrooms (button), muskmelon, pears, plantain, seaweed, black tea, green tea, watercress, watermelon
   Neutral/Nourishing: Almonds, amaranth, pearl barley, aduki beans, black beans, kidney beans, cabbage, celery, grapes, mackerel, papaya, pineapple, pumpkin, pumpkin seeds, rice
   Motivating: Artichoke, cinnamon, coriander, kohlrabi, mussels, parsley, shrimp, sunflower seeds, turkey

Damp Heat Tonic: Eliminating heat and moisture from the system
Calming: Chinese cabbage, corn silk, olives, plantains, soy oil, star fruit

∽

Internal Wind Tonic: Heat creates wind = Stress creates chaos
Symptoms: Usually diet related. Brought on by an excess of fatty, high cholesterol animal products. Signs of wind move without pattern. Symptoms include dizziness, moving pains, convulsions, tremors, cramps, seizures, strokes, emotional turmoil, nervousness, uncertainty, spasms, itching, dizziness.
Calming: The loss of yin contributes both the heat and the wind at the same time. Yin is needed to calm the wind/chaos in ones life. Look for culprit source of wind.

∽

Liver Tonic: Sour–obstructs movement. Useful for slowing abnormal discharge
Motivating: Mung beans, beef liver, black sesame seeds, chicken liver, chive seeds, peppermint, purslane, romaine lettuce, strawberries

∽

Kidney Tonic: Salt. Kidneys are the root of all moisture in the body
Calming: Kidney beans, mung beans, brown sugar, cantaloupe, cheese, coconut milk, cow milk, crabs, dates, eggs, herring, lemons, mandarin oranges, mangoes, shiitake mushrooms, pears, rice, romaine lettuce, saffron, scallions, star anise, white sugar, thyme, tofu, walnuts, watermelon, yams

∽

Smell is The Element of Metal

Lung Meridian (Yin)

PRIMARY FUNCTIONS: Relates to the ability to regulate breathing, the diaphragm and lung difficulties.

Dysfunctions: Pain in shoulder, tennis elbow, stiff forearm, wrist disorders, carpal tunnel syndrome, disorders of throat, trachea, vocal cords, "voice", coughing, spontaneous sweating, shortness of breath, disorders of breathing, chest tightness, bronchitis, asthma, emphysema

Lung Meridian

Large Intestine Meridian (Yang)

Primary Functions: Relates to intestinal problems of constipation, spastic colon, colitis and diarrhea, also chest soreness and breast pain with menstruation.

Dysfunctions: Neck stiffness, pain in trapezium, bursitis, shoulder pain, forearm pain, tennis elbow, index finger stiffness, hand pain and weakness, disorders of teeth, nose, sinusitis, associated lung complaints, intestinal disorders, rumbling, abdominal pain and swelling.

Large Intestine Meridian

Tonics Foods for the Common Sense of Smell...

Symptoms of too little structure (Yin): Grief stricken, steeped in sadness, illness in lungs–asthma, allergies, frequent colds, chronic constipation or diarrhea, bowel disease, delicate skin, shortness of breath, congested nose, throat, sinus, moles and warts, headaches from sadness and disappointment, loss of body hair, clammy hands-feet, easy perspiration, varicose veins, cracked, dry or soft nails, enlarged lymph nodes, sneeze or cough with changes in temperature and humidity

∽

BUILDING BLOOD (ESSENCE): *Sweet, sour, astringent foods.*
   Calming: Eggplant, gluten, sesame oil, spinach, spirulina
   Neutral/Nourishing: Aduki beans, black beans, kidney beans, beef, beef liver, beets, carrots, egg yolk, herring, milk, oysters, peanuts, pork, sardines, sesame seeds
   Motivating: Anchovy, blackberries, butter, cherries, chestnuts, chicken, chicken liver, chives, currants, lamb, leeks, mussels, nutritional yeast, pine nuts, raspberries, sticky rice,, salmon, shrimp, trout, turkey, vinegar, walnuts

∽

DECONGESTING QI: *Spicy, sour and bitter foods.*
   Calming: Apples, bananas, endive, oat bran, radishes, rhubarb, sesame oil, wheat bran, white pepper
   Neutral/Nourishing: Almonds, beets, cabbage, carrots, cauliflower, figs, olive oil, peas, pineapple, plums, prunes, brown rice, rice bran, tangerines, turnip
   Motivating: Black pepper, blackberries, cardamom, chives, coriander, fennel, ginger root, kumquats, mustard greens, mustard seeds, peanut oil, onions, orange peel, oranges, parsley, red cabbage, scallions, shallots, strawberries

Damp Cold Tonics: –*Reduces phlegm*

Almonds, asparagus, tofu, black pepper, celery, clams, garlic, kohlrabi leaves, kumquats, licorice root, mushrooms, onions, oregano, peanuts, pear, peppermint, seaweed, shiitake mushrooms, thyme, walnuts

Kidney Tonic: Salt. Kidneys are the root of all moisture in the body.

Calming: Kidney beans, mung beans, brown sugar, cantaloupe, cheese, coconut milk, cow milk, crabs, dates, eggs, herring, lemons, mandarin oranges, mangoes, shiitake mushrooms, pears, rice, romaine lettuce, saffron, scallions, star anise, white sugar, thyme, tofu, walnuts, watermelon, yams

Lung Tonic: Increase Yin, Decrease heat congestion in lungs (especially if grief is present)

Calming: (for deficient Lung yin: Seaweeds, orange, peach, pear, apple, watermelon, tomato, banana, string bean, soy milk, tofu, tempeh, flaxseed, butter, dairy products, egg, oyster, clam, pork

Motivating: (basic Lung tonic) Cheese, milk, ginseng, walnuts, yams

Motivating: (for deficient Lung qi): Rice, oats, carrot, mustard greens, potato, ginger (fresh), garlic, molasses, barley malt, herring, licorice

Liver Tonic: Sour–obstruct movement.

Motivating: Mung beans, beef liver, black sesame seeds, chicken liver, chive seeds, peppermint, purslane, romaine lettuce, strawberries

HEART & Stomach Tonics: Strengthens the heart and stomach
Motivating: Beef, beer, cardamom seeds, chicory, clam, coffee, corn, fennel seeds, ginseng, mango, milk, shiitake mushrooms, white rice, green tea, wheat

Symptoms too much structure (Yang):

Overly critical, trouble letting an stressful issue go, rashes, eczema and problems with sweating, dry cough with tight chest, sinus headache, nasal polyps, dry hair, dry skin, dry mucous membranes, no perspiration, stiff spine, neck and posture, constipation with tense intestine, dry, cracked nails and lips, scanty urine, dry nose–throat, tight muscles

BUILDING MOISTURE: Sweet, bland, sour, juicy foods
Calming: Almonds, apricot, black beans, pinto beans, beets, blueberries, carrots, cheese, Chinese cabbage, coconut oil, grapes, herring, honey, Jerusalem artichokes, milk, oats, olive oil, olives, oranges, oysters, peanut oil, peanuts, pineapple, plums, pork, potatoes, sardines, sesame seeds, strawberries, string beans, white sugar, tangerines

Neutral/Nourishing: Almonds, apricot, black beans, pinto beans, beets, blueberries, carrots, cheese, Chinese cabbage, coconut oil, grapes, herring, honey, Jerusalem artichokes.

Milk, oats, olive oil, olives, oranges, oysters, peanut oil, peanuts, pineapple, plums, pork, potatoes, sardines, sesame seeds, strawberries, string beans, white sugar, tangerines

Motivating: Coconut milk, Malt syrup, Nectarines, Peaches, Pine nuts, sweet rice, Rice milk, Soy oil

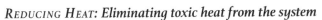

Reducing Heat: Eliminating toxic heat from the system

Calming: Aloe vera, bamboo shoots, bananas, basil, aduki beans, mung beans, beet greens, cattail, clam, crab, egg whites, eggplant, endive, figs, grape leaves, grapefruit, honey, licorice, peppermint, romaine lettuce, salt, spinach beets, mung bean sprouts, summer squash, star fruit, strawberries, Swiss chard, tangerine peel, tofu

Internal Wind Tonic: Heat creates wind = Stress creates chaos

Symptoms: Usually diet related. Brought on by an excess of fatty, high cholesterol animal products. Signs of wind move without pattern. Symptoms include dizziness, moving pains, convulsions, tremors, cramps, seizures, strokes, emotional turmoil, nervousness, uncertainty, spasms, itching, dizziness.

Calming: The loss of yin contributes to both the Heat and the wind at the same time. Yin is needed to calm the wind/chaos in ones life. Look for culprit source of stress.

Spleen Tonics: Sweet–nourishing and invigorating, relieves spasm/pain

Motivating: Cardamom seeds, cherries, chestnuts, cinnamon, clams, ginseng, grape leaves, mandarin oranges, shiitake mushrooms, peppermint, persimmon, pineapple, string beans, yams

Lung Tonic: Increase Yin, Decrease heat congestion in lungs (especially if grief is present)

Calming: Seaweeds, orange, peach, pear, apple, watermelon, tomato (fresh), banana, string bean, soy milk, tofu, tempeh, flaxseed, butter, dairy products, egg, oyster, clam, pork

KIDNEY TONIC: **Salt. Kidneys are the root of all moisture in the body.**
Salt slows the flow of water. Use sparingly.

Calming: Kidney beans, mung beans, brown sugar, cantaloupe, cheese, coconut milk, cow milk, crabs, dates, eggs, herring, lemons, mandarin oranges, mangoes, shiitake mushrooms, pears, rice, romaine lettuce, saffron, scallions, star anise, white sugar, thyme, tofu, walnuts, watermelon, yams, peanuts, pineapple, plums, pork, potatoes, sardines, sesame seeds, strawberries, string beans, white sugar, tangerines

Hearing is The Element of Water

Central Meridian (Yin)

PRIMARY FUNCTIONS: Important in thinking. It is affected by stress, anxiety and pain–any activity connected to the brain.

Dysfunctions: Eczema, throat obstruction, hot flashes, pain in pit of stomach, abdominal pain, pain and swelling in genitals and pelvis, menstrual disorders

Kidney Meridian (Yin)

Primary Function: Related to low back pain, kidney disturbances, improper blood filtration system therefore affecting skin conditions.

Dysfunctions: Hot, dry tongue, cough, lung congestion, pains in spine, aching kidneys, painful soles of the feet

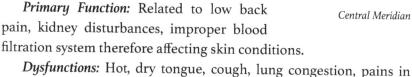

Central Meridian

Bladder Meridian (Yang)

Primary Function: Related to stiff back, foot and ankle problems.

Dysfunctions: Pain and stiffness along spine, weak lower back, stiffness in hip and knees, head cold, clogged sinuses, nosebleed, kidney pain, soreness in kidney and bladder, hemorrhoids

Tonics Foods for the Common Sense of Hearing...

Symptoms of too much calm in your life (Yin): Cold legs, feet, hands, cold back and belly, dark circles under the eyes, night sweats, decline in sexual vigor, incontinence, dulled vision–hearing, ringing in ears, weak and stiff spine, lower body, joints, degeneration of disks–cartilage, cold buttocks, legs, feet, frequent urination, osteoporosis, infertility, frigidity, impotence, lacks stamina, hard to wake up, loss of appetite, weak ab muscles

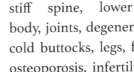

Kidney Meridian

Bladder Meridian

∼

DECONGESTING ESSENCE: *Spicy, sour and bitter foods.*
Calming: Crab, Swiss chard, watercress, wheat germ

Neutral/Nourishing: Beets, eggplant, leeks, shiitake mushrooms, olives, rice bran, rose hips, saffron, sardines

Motivating: Cayenne, cherries, chives, onions, peaches, rice wine, safflower, scallions, shrimp, sweet basil, turmeric, vinegar

∼

Blood Circulating Tonics: **Reduces coagulation and promotes circulation**

Motivating: Basil, brown sugar, cayenne, celery, chicken, chives, clams, coriander, eggplant, ham–fresh, mustard, mustard greens, peaches, radish, sticky rice,, saffron, scallion (white heads), tofu, vinegar

∼

Energy Circulation Tonics: **Keeps energy moving from organ to organ**

Motivating: Basil, red beans, beef, caraway, carrot, chives, clam, dill seed, eggs, fennel seed, garlic, grapefruit, kumquat, limes, malt, shiitake mushrooms, mussels, mustard greens, saffron, scallion (white heads), spearmint, star anise, string bean, tangerines, turmeric, vinegar

∼

Heart & Stomach Tonics: **Strengthens the heart and stomach**

Motivating: Beef, beer, cardamom seeds, chicory, clam, coffee, corn, fennel seeds, ginseng, mango, milk, shiitake mushrooms, white rice, green tea, wheat

∼

Spleen Tonic: **Treat and prevent deficiencies for the spleen**

Motivating: Beef, caraway seeds, carrot, cinnamon, dill seed, garlic, ham-fresh, perch, pineapple, sticky rice, white rice, string beans, pineapple, string beans, yams

Kidney Tonic: Salt—reduces hard masses or lumps in the body
Cooling action: Kidney beans, mung beans, brown sugar, cantaloupe, cheese, coconut milk, cow milk, crabs, dates, eggs, herring, lemons, mandarin oranges, mangoes, shiitake mushrooms, pears, rice, romaine lettuce, saffron, scallions, star anise, white sugar, thyme, tofu, walnuts, watermelon, yams

Symptoms of too little calm in your life (Yang) Ringing in ears, hot flashes, oversensitive vision and/or hearing, headaches above eyes, lack of sweat and urine, hardening of blood vessels and cartilage, rigidity of joints and muscles, kidney and bladder stones, Bony tumors, weak digestion, shrinking gums, needs little sleep, hypertension

Building Moisture: Sweet, bland, sour, juicy foods.
Calming: Almonds, apricot, black beans, pinto beans, beets, blueberries, carrots, cheese, Chinese cabbage, coconut oil, grapes, herring, honey, Jerusalem artichokes, milk, oats, olive oil, olives, oranges, oysters, peanut oil, peanuts, pineapple, plums, pork, potatoes, sardines, sesame seeds, strawberries, string beans, white sugar, tangerines
Motivating: Coconut milk, Malt syrup, Nectarines, Peaches, Pine nuts, sweet rice, Rice milk, Soy oil

BUILDING BLOOD (ESSENCE): *Sweet, sour, astringent foods.*
   Calming: Eggplant, gluten, sesame oil, spinach, spirulina
   Neutral/Nourishing: Aduki beans, black beans, kidney beans, beef, beef liver, beets, carrots, egg yolk, herring, milk, oysters, peanuts, pork, sardines, sesame seeds
   Motivating: Anchovy, blackberries, butter, cherries, chestnuts, chicken, chicken liver, chives, currants, lamb, leeks, mussels, nutritional yeast, pine nuts, raspberries, sticky rice,, salmon, shrimp, trout, turkey, vinegar, walnuts

SPLEEN TONIC: *Treat and prevent deficiencies for the spleen*
   Motivating: Beef, caraway seeds, carrot, cinnamon, dill seed, garlic, ham-fresh, perch, pineapple, sticky rice, white rice, string beans, pineapple, string beans, yams

DECONGESTING ESSENCE: *Spicy, sour and bitter foods.*
   Calming: Crab, swiss chard, watercress, wheat germ
   Neutral/Nourishing: Beets, eggplant, leeks, shiitake mushrooms, olives, rice bran, rose hips, saffron, sardines
   Motivating: Cayenne, cherries, chives, onions, peaches, rice wine, safflower, scallions, shrimp, sweet basil, turmeric, vinegar

REDUCING HEAT: *Eliminating toxic heat from the system*
   Calming: Aloe vera, bamboo shoots, bananas, basil, aduki beans, mung beans, beet greens, cattail, clam, crab, egg whites, eggplant, endive, figs, grape leaves, grapefruit, honey, licorice, peppermint, romaine lettuce, salt, spinach beets, mung bean sprouts, summer squash, star fruit, strawberries, Swiss chard, tangerine peel, tofu

Blood Circulating Tonics: Reduces coagulation and promotes circulation

Motivating: Basil, brown sugar, cayenne, celery, chicken, chives, clams, coriander, eggplant, ham-fresh, mustard, mustard greens, peaches, radish, sticky rice,, saffron, scallion (white heads), tofu, vinegar

Spleen Tonics: Sweet-nourishing and invigorating, relieves spasm and pain

Motivating: Cardamom seeds, cherries, chestnuts, cinnamon, clams, ginseng, grape leaves, mandarin oranges, shiitake mushrooms, peppermint, persimmon, pineapple, string beans, yams

Kidney Tonic: Salt-reduces hard masses or lumps in the body

Calming: Kidney beans, mung beans, brown sugar, cantaloupe, cheese, coconut milk, cow milk, crabs, dates, eggs, herring, lemons, mandarin oranges, mangoes, shiitake mushrooms, pears, rice, romaine lettuce, saffron, scallions, star anise, white sugar, thyme, tofu, walnuts, watermelon, yams

Lung Tonic: Increase Yin, Decrease heat congestion in lungs (especially if grief is present)

Calming: Seaweeds, orange, peach, pear, apple, watermelon, tomato, banana, string bean, soy milk, tofu, tempeh, flaxseed, butter, dairy products, egg, oyster, clam, pork

20

DEDICATIONS & LAST WORDS

I owe all I am to my parents, Charles and Aldron Wolff. Their joyful dedication to service, love of family, patience and faith have been the cornerstones of my life. I hope to teach all I learned from them to my beloved granddaughter, Zoey.

But, finishing this work is dedicated to Dan, my son. He taught me that every nanosecond of life is a gift in some way, never take it for granted.

∽

Last words are for my sister, Claire. The End.

21
ABOUT THE AUTHOR

After four years of study, Catherine Durand was certified in Traditional Tibetan-Mongolian Medicine and as a Healing Touch Practitioner in 2002. Her fifteen year private practice in Vermont taught her clients how to effectively use ancient medicine in every day life.

When she retired her clients, and their doctors, asked her to write down her methods. This book is the result of that request.

Catherine lives and plays in both Newport, Oregon and Bristol, Vermont. She maintains a small private practice in Oregon and teaches her passion for this material in classes whenever asked.

Contact her with any questions at cathywolffd@gmail.com Visit her website usingcommonsenses.com for more information about the material here or the latest class schedule.

As Dan said, be better than just healthy. Thrive!

22
BIBLIOGRAPHY & TEACHERS

- *Dr. Aparna Bapat, BAMS*, Ayurveda - The Vata Dosha, online article
- *Harriet Beinfield, LAc and Efrem Korngold, LAc, OMD* Between Heaven and Earth (Ballentine Publishing Group, New York, 1991)
- Dr. B. Boldsaikhan, Ulan Bator, Mongolia. My teacher of Traditional Tibetan-Mongolian Medicine.
- Dr. Mary Jo Bulbrook, RN, CHTPI, Co-founder of Healing Touch, Founder...and my teacher of many levels...of Energy Medicine Partnerships.
- *Deepak Chopra*, Understanding the two dosha type, by (online article, India Times - Spirituality)
- Dr. Effie Chow, East West Academy of Healing Arts, my teacher of Traditional Chinese Medicine
- Myrna Dennison, RN, CHTPI, my teacher of Healing Touch
- Sister Rita Jean Dubrey, RN, CHTPI, my teacher of Healing Touch
- *Dr. Duo Gao* (consultant editor) and *Barbara Bernie* (special

consultant), Chinese Medicine (Thunder's Mouth Press, New York, NY, 1997)
- *Dr. Duo Gao* (consultant editor), The Encyclopedia of Chinese Medicine (Carton Books Limited, 2000)
- Rosemary Gladstar, my teacher and mentor of Sage Mountain Herbology
- *Gary Gran, RYT, DAy*, Wind and Water, online article
- *Garn Gran, RYT, DAy*, Running Hot and Cold, online article
- *Christopher Hansard*, The Tibetan Art of Living by (2001 Atria Books)
- Alexandra Johnson, RN, CHTPI, my Healing Touch teacher
- *Ted J. Kaptchuk, OMD*, The Web That Has No Weaver (Contemporary Books - Division of McGraw-Hill Companies, 2000)
- *Sabah Karimi*, What is Your Dosha Type?, online article
- *Vasant Lad, BAMS, MASc*, The Complete Book of Ayurvedic Home Remedies, (1998 Three Rivers Press, New York, NY, 1998)
- *Henry C. Lu*, Chinese Natural Cures (Black Dog & Leventhal Publishers, Inc., New York, NY, 1994
- Janet Mention, RN, BSN, CHTPI, Founder of Healing Touch and my teacher of several levels of HT.
- *Paul Pitchford*, Healing with Whole Foods by (North Atlantic Books, Berkeley, California, 2002)
- *Robert Sachs*, Health for Life by (Heartsfire Books, Sante Fe, NM, 1995)
- Judy Turner, RN, CHTPI, and my teacher of Healing Touch